"This is a most important book introducing students to the profound depth of Jewish Family Ethics found in classic Jewish literature."
> —RABBI MEL GOTTLIEB, president, Academy for Jewish Religion, California

"A richly rendered, sensitive, and nuanced volume. As a beloved teacher of Jewish studies in a pluralistic Jewish high school, Scheindlin presents cutting-edge issues that loom large for today's youth with warmth and empathy toward his audience and a reverence for Jewish tradition."
> —ELLIOTT RABIN, director of thought leadership at Prizmah: Center for Jewish Day Schools, New York City

"This is the book we have been waiting for! For inquisitive high school students and adults of all ages and streams of Jewish life who are eager to wrestle with questions of ethics, this creative book by an esteemed teacher grounds the most urgent moral issues of our time in eye-opening texts. *The Jewish Family Ethics Textbook* is sure to generate lively conversations from the classroom to the dinner table."
> —RABBI JUDD KRUGER LEVINGSTON, director of Jewish studies, Jack M. Barrack Hebrew Academy, Bryn Mawr, Pennsylvania, and author of *Sowing the Seeds of Character: The Moral Education of Adolescents in Public and Private Schools*

"Neal Scheindlin's book is a gold mine for educators. Distilling decades of wisdom from a master teacher, this rich trove of important Jewish texts bears on challenges that teenagers, families, and schools grapple with every day."
> —RABBI JOSHUA CAHAN, educator, Leffell School, Westchester, New York

"This is an essential study guide for parents, educators, young adults, and teens seeking to clarify and deepen their understanding of and relationship to Jewish ethics. Educators will appreciate this well-curated collection of cases and texts as a valuable compass to navigate explorations with teens about challenging essential questions of our day. In an era when opinions are so often shaped by influencers and sound bites, this book provides substantive Judaic source material to ground student learning about ethical dilemmas in our tradition in our times."

> —MIRIAM HELLER STERN, national director, Rhea Hirsch School of Education, Los Angeles

"In this thoughtful and thorough work, Rabbi Scheindlin brings traditional Jewish texts directly into conversation with contemporary Jewish voices, managing to both honor the tradition and the values of our day. Rabbi Scheindlin does not shy away either from the aspects of the tradition that seem most remote from—or offensive to—our own social mores or from the thorny real-life dilemmas of our experience in twenty-first-century America. This guide speaks directly to our most difficult questions. It is an extraordinarily useful resource for all those who seek to teach the tradition—whether in a synagogue, school, or home—and all those who seek to live an ethical life rooted in Jewish tradition and responsive to contemporary life."

> —RABBI RACHEL TIMONER, senior rabbi, Congregation Beth Elohim, Brooklyn, New York

The Jewish Family Ethics Textbook

The Jewish Publication Society expresses its gratitude for the generosity of the sponsors of this book.

Molly Senor and Mel Cohen, in honor and memory of Rabbi Lou Silberman ז״ל

University of Nebraska Press
Lincoln

The Jewish Family Ethics Textbook

Rabbi Neal Scheindlin

The Jewish Publication Society
Philadelphia

Ilana Kushan's "The Danger of Being Seen" first appeared
on her blog at https://ilanakurshan
.com/2009/09/06/the-danger-of-being-seen-bava
-batra-2a-b/ and is used with permission. Arnold
Samlan's "The Ten Commandments of Social Media" first
appeared on Jewish Techs at https://jewishtechs.com
/rabbi-arnold-samlans-10-commandments
-social-media/ and is used with permission.
Michael Panitz's "Must a Jew Have Children?: A
Conservative Answer" first appeared on Jewish
Values Online at http://www.jewishvaluesonline
.org/question.php?id=970&cprg=%2Fsearch
.php%3Fsearchtxt%3Dchildless%26what%3DA and
is used with permission.

Library of Congress Cataloging-in-Publication Data
Names: Scheindlin, Neal S., author.
Title: The Jewish family ethics textbook / Rabbi Neal
Scheindlin.
Description: Lincoln: University of Nebraska Press, 2021. |
Series: JPS Essential Judaism | Includes bibliographical
references.
Identifiers: LCCN 2021008005
ISBN 9780827613232 (paperback)
ISBN 9780827618800 (epub)
ISBN 9780827618817 (pdf)
Subjects: LCSH: Jewish ethics—Textbooks. | Families—
Moral and ethical aspects—Textbooks.
Classification: LCC BJ1285.2 .S33 2021 |
DDC 296.3/6—dc23
LC record available at https://lccn.loc.gov/2021008005

Set in Merope by Mikala R. Kolander.

In memory of my parents

Contents

Preface

My interest in Jewish ethics accompanied my love of studying Rabbinic texts from my first encounters with them as a teenager. As I trained for and entered the rabbinate, it struck me that the ideals of Jewish tradition have much to contribute to solving real-life problems. One of my teachers memorably advocated steeping oneself so deeply in Judaism that one would never have to ask, "What is the Jewish response to this issue?" Instead, one's instinctive response would be an authentically Jewish one.

I do not claim I ever reached that level of immersion, and as the material collected here will show, there is rarely a single "Jewish response" to a difficult question. Nevertheless, I continued exploring ethical problems through traditional Jewish sources and their modern interpreters. Members of the congregations I served expressed interest in learning what Judaism might contribute to thinking about challenges they faced: raising children, helping aging parents, making difficult medical decisions, and more.

It was with great excitement, then, when I joined the faculty of Milken Community Schools, a pluralistic Jewish high school in Los Angeles, that I prepared to teach a course entitled Jewish Law and Ethics. Here was a chance to shape the minds of high school students by introducing them to the kind of Jewish text study I loved. Together we would discover how Judaism might help us with the most difficult problems of our time.

As I began to teach, I noticed that the American environment that shaped my students created barriers that hindered their engagement with Jewish ethical ideas. Where Judaism traditionally privileges the community, they preferred the individual. Where Jewish tradition honors the authority of certain books and people, they recognized only what each person thinks. Though they did not know the terminology, their ethical approach verged on subjectivism: they regularly told me that what is right depends on what a given person thinks. No one else may criticize the individual's choices.

Their repeated assertion that they would make decisions based on "morals and values" made me wonder: How did they identify morals to live by? How did they know which values mattered in a given situation? What happens when values conflict? Those are basic questions in the field of ethics. I tried to convince my students that studying Jewish ethics would teach them better ways to think ethically. It would also help clarify what they truly believed about how to make important decisions by offering a menu of values for making hard choices.

While accepting the authority of tradition is difficult for modern, Western Jews—even more so for those aged sixteen and seventeen—I believe that Judaism has much to offer us when we confront the challenges of family ethics. Fortunately, as the material in this book demonstrates, classical Judaism welcomes dissent and includes multiple points of view. We need not accept any of our forebears' ideas uncritically. The texts provide opportunities to discover ideas that help us think through ethical dilemmas, while leaving space for new values and interpretations. That aspect of studying Jewish texts helped many of my students see value in considering problems on the basis of an ethical tradition. They welcomed the chance to evaluate ideas from Jewish tradition, while adding their own thoughts to the conversation.

Studying family ethics in a Jewish framework also brings new perspectives to familiar controversies. Judaism, for example, analyzes the problems of abortion in a manner outside the rigid categories of "pro-life" and "pro-choice." As Jews, we can make a unique contribution to important contemporary debates.

This textbook covers subject matter that all of us encounter. From the moment we recognize ourselves as members of a family, we confront choices about how to treat our relatives. Moving out into the world, we face challenges to our integrity in dealing with others, ranging from when to tell or hide the truth to how we treat sexual partners. Social media and other technologies present ethical dilemmas unknown before the present century. Most of us face medical concerns, our own or our loved ones', whether at the beginning of life or near its end. Jewish tradition offers

xxii *Preface*

insight into all of these, in ways that help us think about our situations and reach the best decisions we can.

As we studied texts and debated important problems, many of my students grew in their appreciation of Jewish tradition as a source of ethical guidance. Teaching the ideas in the sources over two decades fed my desire to present them to a larger audience. I hope you too enjoy the intellectual and spiritual challenges of reading and interpreting classical Jewish texts. More than that, I hope you will discover ways of meeting the ethical problems life presents that both draw on and enhance Jewish tradition.

Acknowledgments

This textbook began when I opened an email from my friend and Milken Community Schools colleague Rabbi Shawn Fields-Meyer with the mysterious subject line, "What about you?" She forwarded an inquiry, posted on a Rabbinical Assembly listserv, from Rabbi Barry Schwartz, director of The Jewish Publication Society (JPS), seeking someone to write a textbook on Jewish ethics for teenagers. Since I had spent eighteen years developing an ethics curriculum for eleventh graders, the request piqued my interest. In time Barry and I broadened the scope of the project to subjects beyond that curriculum, and the audience beyond teens to adults at all levels of knowledge. I remain grateful to Shawn for bringing the opportunity to my attention.

My deep appreciation goes to all the Milken colleagues who, beginning in 2002, collaborated with me in thinking through many of the text interpretations presented here. Not least, I am thankful for the many Milken students whose sharp minds raised questions that spurred me to refine my understanding of Jewish ethics.

I am grateful to Rabbi Barry Schwartz, who enthusiastically believed in this project and in my ability as a first-time author. His thoughtful suggestions improved my work. Joy Weinberg, the JPS managing editor, served as a kind of ideal reader, helping improve my explanations of the material in countless instances. She worked tirelessly to polish my writing and ready the book manuscript for submission to the University of Nebraska Press for publication. I am grateful to the University of Nebraska Press for copublishing this volume and supporting the study of Jewish texts. I would also like to thank Elliot Rabin and Joshua Cahan for helpful feedback on early versions of chapters 1 and 6. Their comments improved my work. Sheryl Stahl and her staff at the Frances-Henry Library of the Hebrew

Union College–Jewish Institute of Religion Skirball Campus graciously helped me locate materials as I researched the subjects discussed here.

Completing a work on family ethics requires me to acknowledge all the blessings I have received from my own family. My parents of blessed memory, Phyllis and Stanley Scheindlin, modeled both devotion to Judaism and ethical living. This textbook is dedicated to them. I appreciate the encouragement my children, Micah and Noah, and my daughter-in-law Elana provided throughout the years I worked on this textbook. The loving companionship of my wife, Dvora Weisberg, has brought me joy for more than three decades. Dvora, herself an experienced author, was my primary support and cheerleader, and sometimes my writing partner. To express my feelings to her, I would paraphrase the words of Rabbi Akiva and say: my Torah is also hers.

How to Use This Book

This book presents an introductory course in aspects of Jewish ethics. The topics it covers fit under the general rubric of "family ethics," meaning matters that affect almost everyone in the course of family life. Every chapter takes up an ethical challenge area: parents and children living together and separating as the children reach adulthood (chapter 1), personal and academic integrity (chapter 2), social media technologies (chapter 3), sexual intimacy (chapter 4), medical issues in conception (chapter 5), abortion (chapter 6), and medical problems near the end of life (chapter 7). Over the course of each chapter, through a process of ever-deepening text study and analysis, readers will encounter Jewish teachings and values from antiquity to modernity that can inform our decision-making in those many times where the right thing to do is far from clear.

Each chapter begins with a general introduction to the issues at stake, followed by several case studies—some created, others drawn from real life—that concretize how ethical dilemmas play out in people's lives and ask: What does Judaism say about how to handle this situation? The heart of the chapter is a series of texts drawn from Jewish legal and ethical literature. Moving chronologically from the earliest sources to the most recent, these texts from both the Written and Oral Torah teach Jewish values and ideals that shed light on the case studies. Preceding each text is a brief introduction to that text and its author(s). Explanations of terms like Written Torah and Oral Torah appear in the introduction (see the subsection "Works and History of Classical Jewish Literature").

Originally, students needed to master Rabbinic Hebrew and Aramaic in order to study the Oral Torah and fully participate in conversations about Jewish values. Fortunately, from the last quarter of the twentieth century on, increasingly more Oral Torah works have appeared in English. For this volume, I have done my own translations of the original texts, in order to both present what the texts say and allow readers to analyze them with the depth and attention to detail that lends richness to study. Those who can understand the Hebrew and Aramaic (the reading of which adds nuance) can find the original of every text in this book on the JPS website, jps.org/study-guides/. You can also find them at my website, rabbinealscheindlin.com.

Several "Questions for Inquiry" following each text will help the reader zero in on the most relevant aspects of the text to the problems at hand. Readers have the option to weigh the questions and develop their own textual interpretations before continuing to read my subsequent comments and analysis. I proceed to explain the ideas expressed in the biblical, Rabbinic, and contemporary sources; offer one or more interpretations; and, when most useful, delve into the implications for the case studies.

After all the texts and comments, a conclusion summarizes the chapter's findings, identifying how each text contributes to addressing the ethical questions posed in each of the case studies. The conclusion also points ahead to related ethical challenges likely to confront us in the not-so-distant future.

Using the Book in a Classroom Setting

Sophisticated and accessible, this book will work well in a variety of classroom settings for both teens and adults, among them pluralistic community day schools (like the one in which I taught), supplemental high schools, youth groups, confirmation classes, undergraduate classes in Jewish ethics, and adult education programs. You will get even more out of it by using the book's online Study and Discussion Guide (more on that below).

As you plan your approach to this material, consider the background your students bring to text study. Have they studied Ḥumash with commentaries? Have they learned any Mishnah or other Rabbinic literature? Are they trained in structured methods for analyzing and interpreting unfamiliar texts? Groups less familiar with the Jewish textual tradition might benefit from learning the background and history first, reading the material in "A Brief Jewish Lexicon" below. Some instructors may choose to assign the entire introduction, using the two texts included in it to teach the methodology they want their students to employ in text study. Informal classes like adult education groups, or families learning together, might choose to start directly with the chapter about a topic that interests them, referring back to the introduction when they want more background information.

Think about how you will scaffold your students' text study and how much independence you expect from them. In some settings, having students pair up to work in *havruta* part of the time can be productive, though in my experience, instructing high school students to pair up, read a text, and answer the Questions for Inquiry can also yield cursory readings of the text, the first answer to each question that occurs to them, and a declaration that their work is finished. Serious engagement with these texts requires developing a number of skills that students of all ages and backgrounds may need to practice, among them asking open questions that lead to careful analysis of the text and an expectation to find values and ideas there that were not noticed on the first reading. If students study in *havruta*, they may also need to practice listening to their partners' ideas, challenging them when necessary, and supporting their own interpretations using specific textual evidence. As students grow in these skills, they will uncover more layers of meaning in the texts, which will lead to more sophisticated conversations about ethical dilemmas.

I suggest beginning each unit by discussing the case studies. In my experience they serve as "hooks" to attract interest in the topic. You may prefer one case study over another, or choose to have groups within the class focus on different case studies in the same chapter. I've found it worthwhile to ask my students to respond to the cases before learning any of the material. What does intuition tell them about the rights and wrongs of each case? Usually that question provokes spirited discussion. Later in the unit, students will be able to compare their initial thoughts with the insights of Jewish tradition—an exercise that also teaches how ethical thinking tests our intuitions, forcing us to develop more careful, defensible responses. And more than that: Ethical thinking, offering reasoning and evidence in place of assertions and emotional reactions, makes it possible to listen to those with whom we disagree.

One challenge of using this book is working out how to enable students to engage the texts on their own without being unduly influenced by the author's commentary. If you want your students to discover for themselves what the texts mean, you'll want to plan accordingly. Some instructors may have students use the comments to help when something in the text stumps them. Others may want the class to read the comments only after discussion of the students' independent interpretations. It is entirely possible to treat the comments section as a text in its own right—to ask students to read and analyze the strengths and weaknesses of the author's approach to the sources. Alternatively, you might choose to use the comments for review and reinforcement after engaging in text study.

To get even more out of the volume, download this book's Study and Discussion Guide on the Study Guide to JPS Books website, https://jps .org/study-guides/. There you'll find class activities for each chapter, with different sections for teens and adults. For formal classes, you will find suggestions for projects and other assignments. For teenage groups, the guide includes activities that teachers can adapt for class sessions. The guide includes more Questions for Inquiry, suggestions for how to organize units of study around each chapter, and suggestions for further reading both for instructors and for students or readers who want to go deeper into a specific topic. The author's website, rabbinealscheindlin .com, also includes a section where you can post ideas that worked with your students to share with other teachers.

Teachers can adapt this textbook to specific settings and the amount of time available for study. A day school class or confirmation class might study all of the chapters as a year's curriculum; similarly, an undergraduate course in Jewish ethics could be built around all the subjects and the relevant text studies. Meanwhile, teachers interested in exploring a specific topic—say, euthanasia, but not assisted dying—could take advantage of each chapter's division into several text studies covering distinct aspects of the problem: in this case teaching, from chapter 7,

Text Studies #1 and #2 ("Basic Principles of Jewish Medical Ethics" and "When Death Is Inevitable") but not Text Study #3 ("Suicide"). When even less time is available for study—let's say a synagogue board or school committee wants to develop a policy around social media use (chapter 3)—staff could facilitate study of the relevant texts solely within Text Study #1 ("Permitted and Forbidden Speech") to help the group understand Jewish values that can inform their decisions. The detailed table of contents will help you easily find the texts most relevant to the ideas you want to teach and the questions you wish to resolve.

Some final thoughts: This textbook covers aspects of family ethics. Our society's understanding of "family" has changed radically in recent years, and continues to evolve. By contrast, ancient and medieval Jewish sources assume that families exist in a specific configuration: a male parent, a female parent (either of whom may be living or dead), and children. Your students may well live in families that look nothing like this model. When teaching any text about family relationships, take care to acknowledge these differences. I suggest using inclusive language and pointing out the biases implicit in the texts—as well as, where appropriate, the biases inherent in our assumptions about social norms.

Other topics discussed in this book may raise personal issues for individual students, among them assisted reproduction, adoption, and surrogacy (topics considered in chapter 5). Discussing the always emotional topic of abortion (chapter 6) necessitates care in creating a safe classroom environment that fosters respectful disagreement. Model civility in your own speech. It may be worth spending the time to write a "covenant" with the class about how they will engage in debate and respond to disagreement. Consider teaching your students the introduction's Text 2 about how the school of Shammai and the school of Hillel debated. You may also want to point out that the Talmud encourages us to understand all sides of an issue: "Develop an understanding heart to grasp the words of those who declare impure and the words of those who declare pure; the words of those who forbid and the words of those who permit" (Ḥagigah 3b). When we train students to develop their own views while understanding the reasoning of those who disagree, we enable them to truly participate in the work of Jewish ethics.

Using the Book without a Teacher

This work suits a family audience. A family might read it together. Studying texts around the Shabbat table, during a yearly family retreat, or at other fixed times will foster interesting conversations between the generations. Family members could take turns leading discussion of an individual text or an entire text study within a chapter.

If you bought this book on your own, consider finding a partner to study it with you. Traditionally, Jews always studied texts with a partner — the Hebrew term is *ḥavruta*, from *ḥaver*, friend or companion. Two minds working together can uncover more meaning in the texts than either one could alone. As you and your partner learn each other's styles and develop trust, you can challenge each other to refine your ideas and emerge with a stronger understanding of the material.

Next, I recommend downloading this book's study guide at rabbinealscheindlin.com or https://jps.org/study-guides/. There you'll discover aids like "How to Study in Havruta," additional Questions for Inquiry, and Suggestions for Further Reading on different areas of Jewish family ethics.

Whether working alone or with a partner, start with the chapter that most interests you. Read its introduction and the case studies. Stop and think about the case studies before continuing. What do you think the issues are? What values would you bring to respond to them? How might your personal experiences shed light on the issues? Jot down some notes. Later, you can compare the author's comments with those of others (if applicable) as well as your own, and find anything you (all) may have overlooked.

Now you are ready to begin studying texts. Each text deserves in-depth consideration before moving on to the next one. Read a new text carefully and see what you think it means.

Next, contemplate the Questions for Inquiry (in the book and the online study guide), designed to both help you find ideas in the texts and focus your thinking on how the specific text relates to the issues educed by the case studies. What are your takeaways from the text at this moment?

With all this information in hand, proceed to read my comments. Do you agree with my summation and interpretations? Why or why not? If not, what evidence from the texts under discussion or other Jewish texts supports your point of view?

If you're reading this book with a partner or in a small group, stop at any point in the process to discuss what you're learning. The exchange of ideas will help each of you derive as much meaning as possible from the material.

Introduction

Every one of us, I imagine, considers him- or herself a good person. We try to do what is right, and we tell ourselves that we know or can figure out the right option in any situation. From time to time, however, we confront situations where we cannot readily decide the best approach. Good reasons exist to support more than one option; put differently, we need to select between two conflicting "goods." On what basis can we choose?

A straightforward example: Doctors inform a woman that she is likely to die if she continues her pregnancy. The woman, her family, and doctors must decide if she should abort. The woman's life is a positive moral value. The fetus's opportunity to develop and eventually live is also a positive moral value. Which should she prefer? For what reasons? How can she know if she chose the right option?

The field of ethics exists to help in such situations. It provides tools to analyze the available options and discover reasons for choosing among them. It helps us to fulfill our intention to be good people as it leads us to evaluate what is good and how to accomplish it.

Within this rubric it's important to distinguish between two terms often used as synonyms: morals and ethics. *Morals* are standards of good behavior. They are ideals we recognize as virtues, the principles we accept to guide our lives and choices. *Ethics* is the study of how to apply these principles in actual situations. It is an area of knowledge that tries to work out how to identify relevant moral principles and how to use them.

This textbook begins from the premise that instead of making ad hoc decisions when situations arise, it is better to know what moral standards we believe in and how to apply them. Studying ethics teaches us to articulate good reasons for the principles we claim to uphold and, if good reasons are wanting, to find better principles. It also provides us with a set of tools for making the principles work in the actual situations we confront as we go through life.

Theories of Ethical Decision-Making

That said, ethicists themselves do not always agree—not even about which tools would best be used to make ethical decisions.

One way of thinking about ethics centers on *virtue*. It links ethics to individual character, and starts by identifying desirable qualities a person should cultivate in order to be morally good. Different thinkers propose various lists of virtues. Many agree on such qualities as wisdom, honesty, sincerity, and generosity. Each of us, they claim, should develop these virtues in ourselves and guide our actions by them. Doing so constitutes ethical living.

Another theory begins with *consequences*. It judges actions by their results. An action that leads to good results must be right; one that leads to bad results must be wrong. One version of consequentialism in ethics is *utilitarianism*. It judges an action by its utility or usefulness. Acts that produce more good are right; those that lead to less good, or cause harm, are wrong. Thinkers often disagree about how to calculate the amount of good or ill a given choice will cause, but they agree that people should choose the path that leads to the greatest good for the greatest number of people.

A different approach argues for a *duty* theory of ethics that identifies basic principles obligating all people in all times and places. Some ethicists holding this view argue that rational thought can work out these principles. For example, reason tells us not to treat others in ways we would not like them to treat us. Other forms of duty-based ethics, especially religious forms, assert that the basic principles are revealed by divine or other authority. All duty theories hold that we must follow these obligatory principles regardless of the consequences. The ethical person does what is right even if that means suffering losses as a result.

Another group of ethical theories centers on *contracts*. These argue that good decisions fulfill implicit agreements that bind members of a society. This agreement, usually called the "social contract," elaborates the rules members of a given group agree to live by. The rules may be explicit, recorded as laws, or implicit, as when people wait their turn in a checkout line.

Some recent thinkers place the idea of *care* at the center of ethics. Stressing relationships over following rules, the care approach proposes that the right action is the one that displays care for others and maintains relationships. Many care-based ethical theories originate in feminist thought. Some thinkers offer care-based ethics as a replacement for rule- and contract-based systems; others propose that it can supplement them. Care-based ethical theories do not necessarily propose general principles.

To better understand how these theories work in practice, let's look briefly at how each one might tackle the dilemma of the pregnant woman mentioned above.

Adopting a virtue theory would require us to identify which qualities of character matter most for this decision. Perhaps the quality of generosity offers a useful insight: the prospective mother could decide that since she has already lived a number of years, she will sacrifice the rest of her time so that the future baby can live. Or, one could suggest that giving up one's life exceeds the requirements of generosity.

Consequentialist ethics proposes a different analysis. It asks which choice would produce more good: carrying the pregnancy and risking the mother's life, or aborting the fetus? Again we can construct arguments for both sides. On the one hand, saving the pregnant woman increases her well-being and that of her partner (if she has one), as well as that of others who love her. From that good, of course, we have to deduct the negative consequences of ending the fetus's development. On the other hand, we might argue for the good that would result from allowing the pregnancy to continue, even at the cost of her life. Those who love the woman will also love her child, whose birth will increase their well-being; beyond this, the good to the future child is immeasurable. Yet we must deduct from these welcome outcomes the child's growing up without its mother.

A duty-based approach requires us to decide what moral obligations come into play. One relevant duty here might be a responsibility to preserve life. Clearly, the pregnant woman is a living human being: isn't it our duty to preserve her life? Is the fetus too a human life? Do we have the same responsibility to preserve the fetus's life as we have the mother's?

Contract-based ethics would lead us to consider the effects of our choice on society. We might first look at law. In a society that outlaws abortion, our hypothetical woman would not be justified in disobeying the law. If, on the other hand, the laws in her society are less straightforward, and so the ethical problem remains, she might choose to pursue a social contract approach to her situation by soliciting feedback from smaller groups she is part of, such as extended family or religious groups.

An ethics of caring, focused on relationships, might prioritize how the woman's decision will affect her partner, others who care about her, and her relationship with her recently conceived child. She might conclude that bringing this child into the world to grow up without knowing her is unfair to the child; alternatively, she might decide that the child would grow up to appreciate the mother who sacrificed her own life in giving birth.

In each approach to ethics we find a number of possibilities to ponder, none of which necessarily guides us to a specific conclusion.

This brief outline of how ethical theories work in practice illustrates a reality we will confront countless times throughout this textbook: ethical dilemmas rarely lend themselves to easy solutions. Many times the most we can do is to make the best argument we can for the decision that seems, on balance, more right than wrong. This reality can frustrate those who seek direct, clear answers. But it is part of what makes the study of ethics fascinating and stimulating. Ethics helps us understand some of the most important challenges we face. It requires us to clarify our values, to articulate what matters most to us and why. This subject teaches us to argue effectively for our point of view. It gives us opportunities to change our minds when we confront more convincing reasoning. Ethics is a subject we can return to many times and learn something new from each encounter.

How Jews Approach Ethical Problems

We now turn our attention to understanding a specifically Jewish approach to this area of philosophy. Judaism offers ethical ideas unique to the tradition in addition to ones it shares with the general theories of ethics outlined above.

Jewish ethical thought does not align with consequentialist theories. Whether through identifying virtues or enumerating duties, it distinguishes right from wrong in absolute terms. Tradition does not encourage weighing the relative harm or benefit of doing the right and the good.

Judaism does present a form of virtue ethics. It proposes a set of virtues every Jew should cultivate in order to be a virtuous individual and to build a virtuous society. Those who live by them build a moral society, what the Torah calls holiness. Above all, Jewish tradition emphasizes the importance of human life. It avers that humans carry within them the image of the Divine (Gen. 1:26) and instructs us always to choose life (Deut. 30:19). It urges us to develop the virtuous habit of choosing truth over falsehood (Exod. 23:7). It repeatedly urges kindness toward the stranger (Deut. 10:19) and others like the widow and orphan who lack social standing (Exod. 22:20). Some thinkers use these virtues, among others, as the foundation of arguments about how to respond authentically as Jews to the ethical dilemmas we face.

Some traditional sources express ideas similar to those found in care-based ethical systems. The Talmud (Shevuot 39a) expresses the thought that each Jew should take responsibility to care for every fellow Jew this way: "All Israel are responsible for one another." It uses a Hebrew word, *areivin*, whose meaning includes the sense of "collateral," implying that each Jew should be available to settle a debt or solve a problem for every other Jew. Some contemporary Jewish writers we will encounter in this book, aware of modern philosophers' insights into care-based ethics, adapt these theories to Jewish contexts.

At first glance, Jewish tradition looks like a contract-based system, since it begins with the covenant between God and Israel that imposes ethical duties, among others, on members of the covenant. However, contract theories rely on agreements among equal parties—certainly not how Jews characterize the relationship between human beings and the Divine.

We can more logically describe Judaism as a duty-based tradition. The Jewish people's unique covenant with God spells out responsibilities both God and Israel must uphold: God promises protection and other blessings in return for obedience to God's instructions, the commandments (in

Hebrew, *mitzvot*). In this regard, Judaism also falls into the category of ethical systems in which humans know the right way to behave because a higher authority has revealed it to them. Within this construct, obedience to God's law as detailed in the Torah and other Jewish literature enables us to live moral lives. Divine revelation contains all the guidance we need. As with any duty-based system of ethics, arguments may still arise about what specific duty matters most in a given situation, or how to interpret a given commandment.

To the extent that Judaism proffers a duty ethics rooted in the Torah's commandments, its morality emerges through law. That characteristic distinguishes it from many other moral traditions, including religious ones. Through law, Jewish values find concrete expression. Through the give and take of legal debate, moral ideals find practical application in the complex realities of human life. For this reason, many of the texts in this book are legal texts.

The Jewish ethics presented in this textbook emerge from close reading of the texts that articulate the values of Jewish tradition. For centuries, Jewish thinkers analyzed ethical dilemmas by searching sacred texts for relevant material. Legal texts suggested precedents that served as analogies for new problems; other sources taught values and ideals that ethicists needed to bear in mind to make choices in line with Jewish tradition. For the most part, this book shares the assumption that the work of Jewish ethics begins in the sources that contain the thoughts and decisions of millennia of Jewish thinkers.

Works and History of Classical Jewish Literature

The starting point of Jewish law and tradition, roughly equivalent to its constitution, is the Torah. *Torah*, from a Hebrew root meaning "instruction," has two senses, one narrow and one broad. Narrowly, it refers to the first five books of the Hebrew Bible, sometimes called the Five Books of Moses or the Pentateuch, from the Greek for "five books." In its broad sense, Torah refers to all the teachings of Judaism.

For two millennia, Jews have recognized not one, but two Torahs. We distinguish between the Written Torah and the Oral Torah (some refer to the combination as the Dual Torah). The Written Torah, consisting of the twenty-four books of the Hebrew Bible, is divided into three parts: Torah, the five books associated with Moses; Prophets (Hebrew: *Nevi'im*), including books that describe the history of Israel after Moses's death until the fall of the First Temple and books of the ancient prophets; and Writings (Hebrew: *Ketuvim*), a diverse anthology of prose and poetry. The traditional term for the Hebrew Bible is an acronym of the first letters of all three parts: TaNaKh.

The Written Torah's contents were set down in writing at an early stage in history. While copies were rare in ancient times, the custom spread that every synagogue needed at least a copy of the Five Books of Moses handwritten on a scroll. Other books of the TANAKH could be written individually on scrolls, or a few books together in one scroll. At first, however, tradition forbade writing down those teachings that grew up around the Written Torah. That gives us the term Oral Torah—Torah transmitted only orally from teacher to student and in conversation among those who studied it. Early in the third century CE, however (for reasons still debated by scholars), Rabbinic leaders felt the need to collate and write down at least some of the profusion of oral material.

Notably, no literature after the Hebrew Bible claims to originate with God. At a certain point in history, working out what God wants became a human responsibility. The Torah itself seems to anticipate that development, as the following text elucidates:

Text 1—Deut. 17:8–11

IF A CASE IS too baffling for you to decide, be it a controversy over homicide, civil law, or assault—matters of dispute in your courts—you shall promptly repair to the place that the LORD your God will have chosen, and appear before the levitical priests, or the magistrate in charge at the time, and present your problem. When they have announced to you the verdict in the case, you shall carry out the verdict that is announced to you from that place that the LORD chose, observing scrupulously all their instructions to you. You shall act in accordance with the instructions given you and the ruling handed down to you; you must not deviate from the verdict that they announce to you either to the right or to the left.

NOTE: Here is the first opportunity to engage in the kind of text study to which this textbook invites the student. After reading the text, you may wish to answer the Questions for Inquiry, which suggest possibilities for thinking about what the text means and what ideas might derive from it. Following the questions you will find the author's comments on the text.

QUESTIONS FOR INQUIRY

1. What problem does the Torah anticipate here?
2. What instructions does it give if the problem arises?
3. Based on these verses, who has authority to decide what the Torah means in a novel situation?

COMMENTS

This passage in Deuteronomy forms part of Moses's farewell address to the People Israel. It recognizes that later generations will not always understand how exactly to follow the Torah's commands. When they encounter new situations the Torah does not explicitly mention, they will feel "baffled." How can they figure out what God requires?

The Torah's answer: turn to the appropriate human authorities. Verse 9 mentions two groups that hold authority. First are the "levitical priests" — that is, priests descended from the tribe of Levi, who the TANAKH reports wielded both legal and ritual authority in ancient Israel. The second type of official is a magistrate, or judge. The Torah imbues both the priests and judges with the authority to enforce and interpret its laws. In verses 10–11, we read strict warnings to follow their rulings and not to deviate from them in the slightest.

Rabbinic tradition derives significant meaning from a phrase in verse 9 that at first glance appears innocuous. The Torah orders us to go to the authorities "in charge at that time." Of course, we can hardly appeal to leaders who live before or after our time. But Rabbinic tradition understood "at that time" to imply that whoever is in charge at a given time has the same authority to determine the law as the original lawgiver. Since we no longer have prophets like Moses to bring us God's word directly, we must follow the rulings made by the leaders of our own era. Their binding decisions clarify God's will for each succeeding generation.

In a sense, then, the entire Oral Torah developed out of the need to understand "baffling" matters in the Written Torah. Each generation's legal and religious leaders have interpreted Torah in ways that made sense for their times.

A Brief Jewish Lexicon

The process of interpreting the Written Torah described above led to the development of a rich and complex literature. The following brief history of the Oral Torah and its major works will help readers understand the terms used in studying both classical and modern rabbinic literature and something of the historical context from which each work emerged.

Over the centuries, new authority figures emerged to take the place of the levitical priests and judges. Late in the biblical period—roughly the last four or five centuries before the Common Era—experts called scribes emerged. *Scribe* derives from a Latin word meaning "to write"; the equivalent word in Hebrew, *sofer*, describes someone who writes or copies scrolls or books. This etymology tells us that the scribe's first responsibility was to copy and preserve the accurate text of the Torah. That work later extended to teaching the Torah and expounding its meaning. Ezra the Scribe—a book of *Ketuvim* or Writings is named for him—played this role for the Jews who returned to the Land of Israel from Babylonian exile in the mid-fifth century BCE. Traditions in the Talmud credit Ezra with establishing the official Torah text transmitted down the generations.

After the scribes, other interpreters emerged who eventually coalesced into the group we now know as "the Rabbis." The title *rabbi* came into use early in the Common Era. Deriving from a Hebrew word meaning "great," it literally means "master." The term may indicate mastery of a corpus of knowledge, or it may reflect the sense in which *master* is a synonym of *teacher*.

We do not know exactly when and how Rabbis emerged to constitute a self-conscious movement. We know that a group calling themselves

Pharisees, "those who separate themselves," challenged the priests' authority in the last decades of the Second Temple (which the Romans burned down when they defeated the Great Revolt in 70 CE). The Pharisees subscribed to a distinctive interpretation of Jewish law. They practiced ritual purity associated with eating sacrificial foods in the Temple outside of that ritual context. After the Temple's destruction, the rabbinic leadership class appears to have emerged out of Pharisaic circles.

Much of the earliest Rabbis' work responded to the crisis the people Israel faced after the destruction of the Temple. Up to that time, Jewish practice had revolved around the sacrificial rituals performed in the Temple. The priests and Levites (who assisted the priests and provided music during Temple service) wielded the power to determine correct practice in the Israelite religion. After the priestly caste lost its center of authority in the first century CE, oral traditions created in rabbinic circles grew over several centuries into what became Judaism—the religious practice of the Jews.

The earliest Rabbis—some whose names are recorded in their literature, others whose names are lost—studied the Written Torah on the assumption that every word and letter in it taught lessons. They read the text as closely as possible in order to derive as much meaning from it as they could. They applied this approach both to matters of law and to recommendations for living a good life. Traditional Jewish law in these sources is called *halakhah*, derived from a Hebrew root meaning "to go, to walk." Metaphorically, halakhah is the path a Jew follows through life.

Everything in the Oral Torah other than legal discussions is called *aggadah*. The word comes from the Hebrew root meaning "to tell a story." It includes narratives, including tales of the Rabbis' lives, but also the Rabbis' teachings on morality, food and medicine, history, and more.

Close reading of the Written Torah begins with investigation of its meaning on its own terms: what the texts' authors originally meant, without any consideration as to how we might view it today. Traditional sources call this level of interpretation *pshat*. Since the term is closely related to words that in later Hebrew mean "simple, straightforward," we often hear the claim that *pshat* represents the simple or literal meaning of a TANAKH verse. A closer look reveals that in Rabbinic literature, the word denotes explanations of the text that go well beyond simple and literal understandings. At times, a literal reading misleads, such as in Leviticus 19:16, "Do not stand on your neighbor's blood." A glance at the context of the verse shows that it cannot mean simply that we must avoid standing in a pool of someone else's blood. The verse actually means "Do not stand by while your neighbor comes to harm." That is its *pshat*.

Of course, later generations cannot always understand precisely what earlier writers meant. *Pshat* understanding represents the best available hypothesis about the text's intention.

In this book, *pshat* generally refers to the likely meaning of a verse, in its context, before it underwent the process of interpretation known as *midrash*. *Midrash* refers to methods the early Rabbis developed for study and interpretation of the Written Torah that eventually gave rise to the earliest literature of Oral Torah. This term, too, can cause confusion, because midrash is both a *method* of study and a *genre* of literature resulting from that method. *Midrash* derives from the Hebrew root *d-r-sh*, which in Rabbinic Hebrew (the language of the Rabbinic literature of the early centuries of the Common Era) means "to ask, investigate" and also "to interpret." Midrash is a set of tools by which early scholars closely examined and interpreted the Written Torah, and established what that Torah could mean for successive generations, including ways of living by the Torah's words. Midrash is also the name given to the literature recording the application of midrashic techniques to the biblical text.

The literature of midrash divides into legal and non-legal categories: *midrash halakhah* and *midrash aggadah*. While some *midrashim* (plural of midrash) developed much later in the Common Era, the work of the classical Rabbis began as early as the last century BCE and continued into the first few centuries CE. Jews now have collections of halakhic midrashim on the books of the Torah that contain the majority of laws—Mekhilta on Exodus, Sifra on Leviticus, Sifrei on Numbers and Deuteronomy—works referred to as tannaitic midrashim. *Tanna* is the general term for the Rabbis who flourished up to about 220 CE.

Perhaps the best-known collection of aggadic midrashim, Midrash *Rabbah*, is the work of a later group. It includes a volume on each of the books of the Pentateuch—*Genesis Rabbah, Exodus Rabbah,* etc.—as well as a volume on each of the Five Scrolls (Hebrew: *ḥamesh megillot*). Midrash

Rabbah is not a single work. Each volume within it has its own history and its own style. All of them appear to be the work of the *amoraim*, the rabbis from 220 CE until the close of the Babylonian Talmud (600–650 CE).

Several important scholars among the *tannaim* like Rabbi Akiva and Rabbi Meir produced collections of oral traditions based on what they learned from their teachers. Building on the work of his teacher R. Meir, Rabbi Yehuda HaNasi, leader of the sixth generation of the *tannaim*, selected and compiled halakhic traditions passed down orally into a work known as the Mishnah, completed around 220 CE. The Mishnah eliminates almost all of the underlying discussion and interpretations of the Written Torah and presents only the legal decision. While generally teaching what Rabbi Yehuda HaNasi understood to be the halakhah, the Mishnah also regularly records the opinions of multiple rabbis on a subject and preserves minority points of view. While the Mishnah primarily discusses law, it does contain a few sections of *aggadah*. One entire volume, *Avot* (sometimes called *Pirkei Avot*), records sayings of the *tannaim* about how to live the best possible life.

Jewish tradition preserves other works of the *tannaim* as well. One collection of traditions similar in style and organization to the Mishnah is known as the Tosefta. *Tosefta* is an Aramaic word meaning "addition, supplement." (Aramaic, a language cognate to Hebrew, was the daily spoken language of the Land of Israel and much of the Middle East at the time.) The Tosefta, dating from the early third century (probably slightly later than the Mishnah) and associated with a student of Yehuda HaNasi named Rabbi Ḥiyya and his colleague Rabbi Oshaya, was seen as supplementing the Mishnah, preserving other traditions contemporary with it.

Still other oral traditions that Yehudah HaNasi excluded from the Mishnah came down to us through the work of scholars of his time and later. The Talmud (introduced below) records many of these traditions. They are called *baraitot* (singular: *baraita*), from an Aramaic word meaning "outside" — these are *tannaitic* teachings left out of the Mishnah.

The Mishnah's terse style put scholars in a position similar to where earlier generations stood in relation to the Written Torah. Students wanted to understand why one rabbi held one opinion and another the opposite. Teachers needed to explain how the authorities named in the Mishnah decided the law. They tried to connect the opinions of the *tannaim* back to the Written Torah and to show how these Rabbis might have interpreted the verses to arrive at their conclusions. Thus, the habit of close study and investigation persisted in the generations that followed the publication of the Mishnah.

Over time, that close examination of the Mishnah expanded to include new legal issues that arose. New oral traditions developed. Meanwhile, beginning in the third century CE, the center of learning—along with much of the Jewish population—shifted from the Land of Israel to Babylonia (east of Israel, roughly equivalent to today's Iraq). The scholars of this time period are known as *amoraim* (singular *amora*), an Aramaic word meaning "teacher."

The *amoraim* carried out a process similar to the one that produced the Mishnah. Later generations felt the need to collect, sift, and finally write down the multitude of oral traditions. This process first came to completion in the Land of Israel. The work of the *amoraim* is called the Gemara, from an Aramaic root meaning "to study." Together the Mishnah and Gemara comprise the Talmud. The Talmud produced in the Land of Israel is called in Hebrew *Talmud Yerushalmi*, the Jerusalem Talmud—misleadingly, since the centers of Rabbinic work in those centuries were in the Galilee, far from Jerusalem. In English it is usually called the Palestinian Talmud. It was completed around 400 CE.

Another group of *amoraim* worked in Babylonia. Eventually, they produced a Gemara and another Talmud, its latest sections completed about 600–650 CE. This is the *Talmud Bavli*, the Babylonian Talmud. For complicated reasons relating to the decline of the Jewish community in the Land of Israel, the Babylonian Talmud became authoritative for Jews worldwide. When we refer just to "the Talmud," we mean the Talmud of Babylonia.

The Talmud follows the structure established by the Mishnah. The Mishnah is divided into six sections called orders (*seder*), each representing a major area of halakhah. These are: Seeds (*Zera'im*)—agriculture and laws of prayer; Seasons (*Mo'ed*)—Shabbat and holidays; Women (*Nashim*)—marriage, divorce, and related topics; Damages (*Nezikin*)—property and torts; Holy Things (*Kodashim*)—laws of the Temple; and

Purities (*Tohorot*)—ritual purity and impurity. Each order is divided into volumes called *massekhtot* (singular: *massekhet*) or tractates. Each of the 63 tractates is further divided into chapters. Each chapter contains a varying number of paragraphs, each of which is designated a mishnah.

The Gemara follows this pattern of organization by order, tractate, and chapter. Neither Talmud discusses all 63 tractates. For example, Babylonians apparently did not study the agricultural laws that applied only in the Land of Israel; the Palestinian Gemara discusses those tractates. On the other hand, the Bavli discusses a number of tractates in *Seder Kodashim* that the Yerushalmi omits.

Once the Talmud became a finished work, the Oral Torah continued to develop. Some midrashim, especially aggadic midrashim, continued to be written. Rabbis also developed ways to respond to new legal (halakhic) questions. Beginning around the eighth century, Jews from around the world wrote letters to the leading rabbis in Baghdad, the center of Jewish learning in Babylonia, posing their questions about halakhah, to which the heads of the academies (*yeshivot*) responded with answers based on passages in the Talmud. This correspondence became known as "questions and answers"—the Hebrew phrase is *she'elot u-teshuvot*. Jews usually refer to the resulting literature as *teshuvot*, or by the English word responsa. In later times, a rabbi's responsa, even if begun as correspondence, were sometimes collected in a book. Responsa continue to be written today. As we will see, American and Israeli rabbis of all denominations produce them. In Orthodox communities, responsa are usually the work of individual rabbis. Liberal denominations like the Reform and Conservative movements in North America appoint committees to research issues and publish official responsa.

In the medieval period, some Rabbinic authorities felt the need to summarize all of halakhah up to their time and present it in a single reference work. Such a reference work claiming to contain the entire law is called a code. In this textbook, we will frequently study excerpts from two of the most important codes of halakhah.

First of these chronologically—and according to many, first and foremost among all halakhic codes—is the *Mishneh Torah*. The work of the great Sephardic (that is, Spanish origin) scholar Moshe ben Maimon, known as

Rambam or Maimonides, the *Mishneh Torah* appeared in 1180. Unlike many codes, which include only areas of law necessary for everyday practice, the *Mishneh Torah* covers the halakhah in its entirety. It surveys obsolete matters like the sacrificial rituals of the ancient Temple and the agricultural laws practiced only in the Land of Israel when the Temple stood, as well as halakhah intended for a theoretical future when (according to traditional belief) a king of the line of David will return to the throne of Israel. Each of its fourteen books subdivides into sections named for the area of law they cover, for example, "Laws of Buying and Selling."

The second code we will frequently study is the Shulḥan Arukh. Many Jewish communities consider it the most authoritative statement of the halakhah. Understanding its title requires a bit of background. In the first half of the fourteenth century, a scholar named Jacob ben Asher compiled many halakhic rulings in a work called the *Arba'ah Turim* ("Four Rows," a phrase derived from the four rows of precious stones on the breastpiece of the High Priest described in Exod. 28:17), the Tur for short. The Tur details legal disputes and many Ashkenazic (French-German) authorities' rulings and rationales. About two centuries later, a Sephardic scholar then living in the Land of Israel, Joseph Karo, used the Tur as a template for his code, the Shulḥan Arukh, a Hebrew phrase meaning "set table." While Karo organized his work into the same four sections as the Tur, unlike the Tur, with its extensive surveys of the halakhic landscape, he set out his Shulḥan Arukh to be a reference work for judges, students, and indeed any reader who needed to know how to apply the law. Further, he codified only laws in practical use. That explains the metaphor in the code's title. One who reads Karo's work will find the halakhah laid out like a table already set for a meal. The student need only sit down and consume it.

A historical accident led the Shulḥan Arukh to become the most significant halakhic code. At the same time Karo set to work, a Polish (Ashkenazic) scholar named Moshe Isserles was writing his own summary of the laws in the Tur. He titled his work *Darkhei Moshe*, "Moshe's Ways." Before Isserles finished, Karo published the Shulḥan Arukh in 1550. In response, Isserles wrote notes to the Shulḥan Arukh describing ways in which Ashkenazic practice differed from Karo's presentation of Sephardic tradition. These notes are called the *Mappah*, "tablecloth."

When the Shulḥan Arukh and the Mappah were published together, they represented a complete summary of how Jews around the world at that time practiced halakhah. Its reputation for covering the totality of Jewish law gave the Shulḥan Arukh unmatched prestige. Even today, some communities consider it the ultimate source of halakhic rulings.

One other common genre of Oral Torah is relevant to our study of Jewish ethics. Each of the central works of this literature surveyed here, and many others, gave rise to works that explain and interpret it for new generations. Such works fall into the category of commentary. Often, commentaries are printed in one volume alongside the works they elucidate. Some volumes of TANAKH include one or more commentaries from the medieval period. Modern synagogues provide commentaries written in English to help North American worshipers follow the weekly Torah reading. Major codes also generate centuries' worth of commentary, some of which appear in the standard editions of each code.

Traditional study of Oral Torah includes attention to commentaries. For example, in many settings, students first learn the Talmud as interpreted by Rashi, Rabbi Solomon ben Isaac (1040–1105), whose commentary helps them to follow the arguments in the Gemara. Standard editions print Rashi's commentary on one side of the Talmud text in a specific font ("Rashi Script") associated with that commentary. Note that a commentary is not the final word on the meaning of the text it discusses. If we read Rashi's explanation of a passage of Talmud, or Abraham ibn Ezra's comments on a verse in the Torah, we may find their explanations convincing or not. Further, not everything in Oral Torah literature counts as a commentary. Only if the book has no independent existence—if it came into being only because the author wanted to explain his understanding of an earlier work—is it considered a commentary.

Oral Torah is far from a static genre. It continues to develop organically throughout Jewish history. As society changes and new issues emerge, rabbis expand halakhic discourse to address them. Later codes, some of which we will encounter in the following chapters, have supplemented the material in the Shulḥan Arukh to describe practice in later centuries. Rabbis continue to write and publish responsa. Authors produce a variety of books on Jewish law and ethics.

Ultimately, all this work over multiple generations can be understood as supporting an essential Jewish principle of text study: rarely does a text have a single meaning. Our texts are subject to multiple interpretations, and furthermore, one explanation does not cancel another. Surprising as it may seem, two divergent explanations may be simultaneously true to the text. The Talmud itself suggests this possibility in a famous story about two schools of learning in the era of the *tannaim*, one founded by Hillel and the other by Shammai:

Text 2 — *Eiruvin* 13b

RABBI ABBA SAID THAT Shmuel said: For three years, the school of Shammai and the school of Hillel disputed. These said: "The halakhah is as we say"; and these said: "The halakhah is as we say."

A heavenly voice went out and said: "These and these are the words of the living God, and the halakhah is as the school of Hillel says."

But since these and these are the words of the living God, on what basis did the school of Hillel deserve to have the halakhah established according to their words?

Because they were kind and humble, and they taught their words and the words of the school of Shammai. And not only that, but they put the words of the school of Shammai before their own.

QUESTIONS FOR INQUIRY

1. What does "these and these are the words of the living God" mean?
2. How can "these and these" be true at the same time?
3. Why does the halakhah follow the opinion of the school of Hillel?
4. What is the significance of the school of Hillel's attitude toward the school of Shammai's ideas?
5. What overall lesson does the text teach about the nature of the halakhic tradition?
6. Where outside of halakhic tradition can opposites simultaneously be true?

Shammai and Hillel were leading scholars among the early *tannaim*. The Mishnah and Gemara record many of their disputes. On almost every halakhic issue, they and the schools of thought they founded reached different conclusions. These disagreements had practical consequences: one group, for example, might consider something kosher to eat, while the other school forbade it. For our purposes, it is important to recognize that each side defended its views with cogent reasons. The Written Torah they shared gave rise to these equal but opposite opinions.

In this story, the schools of Shammai and Hillel spend three years locked in argument, each insisting that the halakhah follows their opinion in every area. Nothing resolves the dispute until a heavenly voice renders a fascinating verdict: both schools' views are the "words of the living God," but halakhic practice follows the opinion of the school of Hillel. This verdict validates both points of view as reflecting the word of God revealed in the Written Torah. Both schools have discovered aspects of the full reality of God's will. In daily life, when Jews need to know how to act, we follow the law according to the school of Hillel.

This clear statement in the Talmud that Torah can have multiple meanings should hopefully reassure us that the manifold, even contradictory meanings we find within the Torah all have legitimacy.

But if both sides find truth, why privilege the views of the school of Hillel over those of the school of Shammai? Significantly, the Talmud does not praise the school of Hillel's superior intellect or understanding of Torah, but rather their conduct: their kindness, modesty, and serious consideration of their opponents' ideas — even to the point that they learn and describe the views of the other side before explaining their own! Here the Talmud appears to teach that the school of Hillel exemplified intellectual humility, the ability to acknowledge that the other side has a point and that one's own side might be wrong.

The story teaches us that we are entitled to hold strongly to our positions (unless we find ourselves convinced by our opponents' arguments); after all, the school of Hillel persisted in dispute with the school of Shammai for three years. But we have an equal obligation to listen and give serious thought to the ideas of those with whom we disagree.

This story provides important insight into the nature of the text study before you. When studying both ancient and modern Jewish texts that bear on contemporary ethical issues, you need not feel constrained to agree with the ideas they propound. You are invited to argue with the authorities whose words appear in the book, and with this author as well.

The same applies to the way you relate to those you may be studying alongside (see "How to Use This Book"). An important concept in Rabbinic literature is the honoring of disagreements during Torah study—what the *tannaim* and *amoraim* called *maḥloket*, from a root meaning "to split, divide," implying respectful differences of opinion. Typically each side offers reasons or interpretations of specific verses in the Written Torah to support its opinion. The Talmud (*Ḥagigah* 3b) encourages each student to "acquire an understanding mind" that can grasp the ideas of those on opposite sides of each argument. In other words, the Torah's guidance emerges precisely from the clash of views among sincere students of the tradition both in their own time and as part of an ever-continuing dialogue over the centuries.

Classical Literature as Understood by Modern Jews

Beginning in the eighteenth century, and to an increasing extent from the late nineteenth century to the present, the majority of Jews discarded the traditional understanding of the Torah's origins and authority. Most accepted the theory that the Pentateuch is a composite document edited by many hands over many centuries, rather than a single work revealed all at once by God to Moses. Those who deny divine authorship of the Torah logically do not accord it the same authority as those who consider it God's word.

That change in attitude led to changes in the way modern Jews (generally speaking, those other than Orthodox Jews) approach the literature of the Dual Torah. While seeing themselves as heirs to the tradition, and believing that their ideas continue the Oral Torah's development, most Jews today grant the authors of earlier texts less authority than premodern Jews did. As the thinking goes, we understand the specific circumstances we live in, the needs of our day; our ancestors' wisdom cannot prevent us from exercising our best judgment.

Nonetheless, many Conservative movement thinkers maintain a commitment to halakhic authority. Such thinkers also search for ethical precedents in the texts. More often than the Orthodox, they reject or modify earlier ideas if they believe they have sufficient reason: Conservative ideology asserts that new moral insights require us to reject our ancestors' ways of thinking. The movement's Committee on Jewish Law and Standards (CJLS) debates halakhic issues and writes responsa for its rabbis. In keeping with the tradition of *maḥloket* (the clash of opposing ideas), the CJLS often approves more than one responsum on a given question. When that happens, individual rabbis decide which point of view best suits their community.

Reform Judaism rests on the principle that each Jew makes autonomous decisions. In theory, Jews should educate themselves about the teachings of Jewish tradition and use what they learn to inform their choices. Unlike Orthodox rabbis or the Conservative rabbis' CJLS, who write responsa to tell questioners what to do, the Reform movement's Responsa Committee writes to persuade. As the Central Conference of American Rabbis Responsa Committee chair Rabbi Mark Washofsky explains: "Whatever authority any responsum possesses lies in its ability to persuade its readers that *this* answer, as opposed to other plausible answers, is the best interpretation of Jewish tradition on this particular subject."[1] The ideology of informed, autonomous choice means that if readers are not convinced, they may follow their conscience.

Many contemporary Jews subscribe to none of these denominational outlooks. For them, the Dual Torah tradition represents just one voice among many that may inform their ethical thinking. Generally speaking, such Jews prefer autonomy to authority and give pride of place to individual conscience.

At times, ethicists committed to Judaism resort to arguing that traditional values lead us so far astray from modern understandings of morality that we must reject them altogether. For example, consider LGBTQ sexuality (chapter 4). The Torah, at least as traditionally understood, categorically rejects sexual relations between men. Some thinkers in the last twenty years or so have reinterpreted the Written and Oral Torah to find ways for LGBTQ Jews to live full Jewish lives. Others argue that if the

Torah rejects the humanity of gay Jews, Judaism must change to affirm that they, too, reflect God's image. That adjustment requires us to reject those passages in the Torah.

Readers of this book will encounter both ways of thinking. The premodern texts may present a certain approach toward an issue. The modern sources may then divide into those that accept the tradition's judgment and those that reinterpret or reject it. Readers will need to evaluate the arguments for overriding the judgment of tradition. Do advocates make a convincing case that values embedded in Jewish life should overrule the existing halakhah, or does the traditional side have stronger arguments? Since Rabbinic Judaism values *maḥloket* (the clash of opposing ideas), truth—or at least a better approximation of it—should emerge from a thorough airing of all sides of each question.

Ultimately, I hope every reader of this book will imagine they are in conversation with the texts in it, with earlier readers of those texts, with their teachers and fellow students, and with me. Out of those conversations, real or imaginary, more truth and a more complete truth will emerge.

The Jewish
Family Ethics
Textbook

1

Parents and Children

The relationship between parents and children, the foundation of family, is the central relationship to study when considering family ethics. Common wisdom holds that the strength of the Jewish family lies at the center of Jewish practice, and even explains the Jewish people's survival. If so, we need to understand the ethical underpinnings of parent-child interactions in order to create the firmest possible ground for building the Jewish family.

As we will see, Jewish tradition asks us to treat our parents with a degree of respect that can prove challenging at any stage of life. Each of us wants to assert the ways we differ from our parents. When asserted, that independence can interfere with living the way tradition dictates. As we study texts from the tradition, we will explore how their implied lessons play out in the world in which we actually live.

Difficulties also arise from changing social norms. Biblical and Rabbinic expectations of how parents should treat children and how children should treat parents are very different from our own, creating tensions between the ideals the tradition expresses and our own preferences and the expectations of the society surrounding us.

In this chapter, we will explore the ethical challenges of living with, honoring, and revering our parents. We will ask how to find the appropriate balance between parental responsibility and children's responsibility. Conflicts familiar in our times, and further identified by means of three case studies, appear throughout the traditional texts, enabling us to develop a Jewish lens for examining these issues.

Case Study #1: Who Chooses Where to Go to College?
Daniel worked hard all four years of high school in California in hopes of being admitted to a top college. Now he has achieved his dream: a

top-ranked East Coast university has offered him admission. While he also has other good offers, the East Coast school is his first choice.

To his dismay, Daniel's parents have other ideas. They value family closeness above all else. While proud of their son's accomplishment, they don't want him to leave their extended family on the West Coast. They expect him to enroll in one of the nearby schools that accepted him. They expect him to enroll in one of the nearby schools that accepted him.

Daniel explains his belief that the East Coast school offers him both the best education in his area of interest and the strongest possibilities when he is ready to look for a job in his chosen field. He reminds his parents that he can always return to the West Coast after college. But his parents remain firm. They expect their children to remain physically close to the family, even to come home from college sometimes for their customary Shabbat dinners.

Daniel believes his parents should accept his point of view. He, after all, is the one who did all the work to win this opportunity. Aren't they responsible for his education? Don't they owe it to him to help him pursue his dreams? His parents, in contrast, focus on family loyalty. They believe firmly that a son owes his parents obedience. In their view, Daniel should accept their decision as final.

This scenario raises challenging questions about what parents and children owe each other. Few would argue with the idea that parents should support their children and pay for their education. But how far does that obligation extend? Does the fact that the parents fund the education give them the right to decide how and where that education will take place? Is a decision about college, or graduate or professional school, different from the choices parents make about which schools their younger children will attend?

We might also wonder about the child's responsibilities. How far does the duty of obedience extend? In this case, Daniel believes he understands better than his parents what decision will best suit his interests. Does he have the moral right to push back against his parents' preferences and try to convince them of his point of view?

Case Study #2: Caring for a Parent with Dementia

Bill and Susan have been caring for Susan's widowed father, Victor, as he ages. A couple of years ago, Victor accepted their invitation to move into a room in their house. He enjoyed seeing his teenage grandchildren regularly, and Bill and Susan felt pleased that they could help with Victor's medical appointments, make sure he ate properly, and otherwise insure he remained safe.

But after a year or so, Victor showed signs of dementia. He forgot common words, had trouble getting dressed, and could not focus on a task. Like many others in the so-called sandwich generation, both Bill and Susan work full-time and need both incomes, with one child in college and two children still at home. But how can they manage Victor's care on top of all this? Should they move Victor into a home where he will receive professional care for persons with dementia? Would doing so fulfill their obligation to show Susan's father the honor Jewish tradition requires?

This scenario is becoming increasingly common in our day. As the average life span grows longer, many adults find themselves responsible for the care of their aging, infirm parents. Especially in the United States, they may face financial problems when the elder generation's funds run out. Given the paucity of public assistance, many people try to care for their elders in their own homes, but as the parents' physical and mental condition worsens, they find themselves incapable of doing everything themselves.

As the text study in this chapter will show, Judaism requires us to show our parents honor throughout their lives. Halakhah defines that responsibility to include caring for parents' physical needs when they can no longer care for themselves. Situations like this one test the boundaries of this requirement, asking us to weigh how far adult children must go for their parents. Must children deliver care personally? Does hiring professional caregivers, or moving elders to a setting where they can receive necessary care, fulfill the responsibility tradition imposes?

Case Study #3: Distancing from an Abusive Parent

Sarah had a difficult childhood. Her mother regularly insulted her looks and intelligence. Her mother inflicted corporal punishments, beating her at times in physically abusive ways. Once she left home for college, she decided it would be best to avoid her mother. She never visited and only rarely spoke to her mother on the phone.

Despite her mother's mistreatment, Sarah never stopped feeling guilty about cutting her off. As a Jew, she wonders, doesn't she owe certain duties to her parent, regardless of how her mother treated her?

Here, as we will see, the Torah seems unequivocal in commanding every child to honor and revere both mother and father. As the text study will show, Rabbinic tradition delineates specific actions children must take and behaviors they must avoid to fulfill these commandments. Yet this legal approach makes it hard to discern what exceptions exist. Do some parents forfeit their title to their children's honor and reverence?

As we prepare for text study, we should keep in mind that honoring parents is the fifth of the Ten Commandments. As one of the "words" that the Torah depicts all Israel hearing directly from God as they stood at the foot of Mt. Sinai, this commandment stands out as one of the most important in Judaism. A related commandment appears in the passage (from Lev. 19) known today as the "Holiness Code," which lays out the ways in which the community of Israel must live a life of holiness. Our text study begins with these two Torah verses and a passage from the Talmud that tries to explain one of the differences between them.

Note that the first of the two aforementioned Torah verses, the commandment to honor one's parents, actually appears twice in the Torah, as part of the Torah's two different tellings of the giving of the Ten Commandments. In Exodus, Israel stands at the foot of Mt. Sinai, Moses ascends the mountain, God appears in clouds and thunder, and the people hear a voice issuing the Commandments. In Deuteronomy, Moses reviews events from the departure from Egyptian slavery until the end of the forty years of wandering in the wilderness.

Text Study #1: Children's Twin Obligations to Parents — Honor and Reverence

Text 1a — Exod. 20:12

HONOR YOUR FATHER AND YOUR MOTHER, that you may long endure on the land that the Lord your God is assigning to you.

HONOR YOUR FATHER AND YOUR MOTHER, as the Lord your God has commanded you, that you may long endure, and that you may fare well, in the land that the Lord your God is assigning to you.

QUESTIONS FOR INQUIRY

1. What does the Torah command us to do in these verses?
2. What is the connection between performing the commandment and the rewards the verses promise?

COMMENTS

At first glance, the verses appear straightforward. The commandment instructs us to honor our father and mother (and, notably, does not limit itself, as the Torah often does, to the masculine). To a point, the meaning seems clear. Children owe their parents a duty of honor.

Looking a bit deeper, though, the meaning of the commandment is not so obvious. What is the exact signification of the word *honor*? How will we recognize it? How will we know when children honor their parents, or fail to honor them?

Also puzzling is the fact that this is one of few commandments in the Torah that promises a specific reward for keeping it. If you honor your father and mother, you will "endure" a long time on the land that God promises the people Israel. The Hebrew literally says "so that your days will be long" on the land. Many readers take this to mean that the Torah promises long life in return for honoring parents. Why would this mitzvah earn such a significant reward?

In Leviticus, the Torah introduces a second obligation of children to their parents.

Text 2 — Lev. 19:3

YOU SHALL EACH REVERE his mother and his father, and keep My sabbaths; I the Lord am your God.

1. What in this verse is similar to Exodus 20:12? What is different?
2. What does reverence for parents have to do with keeping the Sabbath?
3. What does the phrase "I the Lord am your God" add to our understanding of the verse?

COMMENTS

Here the Torah presents a second commandment concerning children's treatment of their parents. Exodus told us to "honor" them; Leviticus instructs us to "revere" them. What are the differences, if any, between honor and reverence? If this verse represents a completely separate commandment from the one found in Exodus 20:12, what exactly does it involve? What might fulfilling this mitzvah look like?

Also, how are we to recognize the difference between revering mother and father and failing to revere them?

Another question arises with regard to the order of giving parents honor or reverence. Close readers will notice that in Exodus, the father comes before the mother; here in Leviticus, the verse lists the mother before the father. Does the word order make any difference? The early Rabbis took note of the change and developed ideas about its meaning. Text 5 explores that question.

The Talmud also investigates the reference to keeping Shabbat in this verse. In the Exodus passage, Shabbat and honoring parents are two separate commandments which appear consecutively, with Shabbat coming first. Here, the command to revere mother and father precedes a reminder to "keep My sabbaths." Text 7b suggests a way of connecting these two seemingly disparate subjects.

Working in a similar manner, the Talmud finds significance in the addition of the phrase "I the Lord am your God" at the end of this commandment. The phrase does not appear in Exodus 20:12. Sometimes the Torah reminds us that God gives the commandments and sometimes it does not. For the early Rabbis, who believed every word in the Torah added layers of meaning, the decision to include God's identity here became significant. We will explore their response to this issue, too.

The ancient Rabbis developed techniques for interpreting the TANAKH called *midrash*. (For more information on midrashic literature, see the introduction.) Using this form of close reading, a midrash on the legal sections of Exodus offers a way to understand the connection between honoring parents and long life.

Text 3 — *Mekhilta, Massekhta de-BaḤodesh 8*

"HONOR YOUR FATHER AND YOUR MOTHER."

If you honor them, [the result is] "that your days will be long"; and if not, that your days will be short.

For the Torah's words can be understood as abbreviated. The Torah is interpreted using the logic: from the affirmative, derive the negative, and from the negative, derive the affirmative.

QUESTIONS FOR INQUIRY

1. What does the midrash add to our understanding of Exodus 20:12?
2. How do you understand the logical principle the midrash offers to support the conclusion it draws?
3. Does it make sense to honor our parents in hopes of a divine reward?

COMMENTS

This midrash illustrates the Rabbis' understanding of the second half of Exodus 20:12. The Torah promises a specific reward for honoring parents. Anyone who honors them will live a long life; anyone who fails to honor them will not. Honoring parents becomes a unique mitzvah, one that determines an individual's life span.

The text demonstrates something interesting about the early Rabbis' method of reading the Torah. They use the logical principle that the affirmative implies the negative, and the negative implies the affirmative. In this case, that reasoning leads to this conclusion: If honoring parents lengthens a person's life, *not* honoring parents must shorten a person's life. In a sense, then, the verse tells us both the reward and the punishment involved in the mitzvah of honoring parents.

If this reading of the verse is correct, Daniel's choices in our first case study carry especially high stakes. For those who believe our actions earn divine rewards and punishments, Daniel's interactions with his parents over his college choice may determine his life span. It's hard to imagine a more serious choice than that. The implications for Susan and her father in Case Study #2, and for Sarah in Case Study #3, may be equally far reaching.

Next, we consider a short *baraita*, a source contemporary to the Mishnah that appears in the Gemara of the Babylonian Talmud. The tractate *Kiddushin* discusses the mitzvot between parents and children at length. Since both the commandment and its reward come from God, the Sages in this selection consider the relationship between the duties we owe our parents and the duties we owe God.

Text 4a — *Kiddushin* 30b

OUR RABBIS TAUGHT IN a baraita:
    It is said, "Honor your father and your mother,"
    And it is said, "Honor the Lord with your wealth." [Proverbs 3:9] —
    Scripture compares honor for father and mother to honor for God.
    It is said, "You shall each revere his mother and his father,"
    And it is said, "Revere only the Lord your God and worship Him alone." [Deut. 6:13] —
    Scripture compares reverence for father and mother to reverence for God.

QUESTIONS FOR INQUIRY
1. What is the main idea of the passage?
2. How does the author arrive at that idea?
3. What implications does this idea have for understanding children's duties to their parents?

The *baraita* addresses the question of why the Torah reminds us that the Lord is God while giving commandments relating to children's treatment of their parents. It uses a *midrashic* technique called *gezeira shavah*, meaning something like "equal or identical category." The *darshan* (author of the interpretation) points out that two verses on different subjects use the same word. That implies that the two seemingly disparate subjects have something in common. The commonality is the lesson of the *drash* (interpretation).

Here, the author of the *baraita* points out that the TANAKH uses the same language in regard to parents and God. We are commanded to honor parents; we are commanded to honor God. We are commanded to revere parents; we are commanded to revere God. It follows (so the argument goes) that honor and reverence for parents is comparable to honor and reverence for God. When we fulfill our duties to our parents, we fulfill our duties to God.

It's also interesting to notice that the verse in Proverbs specifies honoring God with one's wealth. Does this phrase hint that we should also use our material resources to honor father and mother? We will return to this question below, as we analyze more passages from the Talmud about this mitzvah.

This passage also expresses a typical view within Rabbinic theology. The Rabbis often compare God to a parent, specifically a father, as we see in such phrases in the prayer book as *avinu malkeinu*, "Our Father, our King." For ancient Jews, the metaphor of God as father reflected their experience of God's closeness. Like a father with his children, God watches what we do and cares about our welfare.

The same metaphor expresses an idea about God that may be less familiar and less comfortable for us. Just as a father punishes his children when they do wrong, we can expect punishment from God when we fail to live up to the Torah's requirements. Here, the Rabbis' view of fatherhood was more distant and punitive than ours typically is today.

Even if we do not believe in a God who directly rewards and punishes, we might find a valuable lesson in this text. Showing the proper respect to parents might add a spiritual dimension to our family relationships.

Honor and reverence might be means of bringing the Divine—however we understand it—into our homes. Such comportment may create an atmosphere that leads children and parents alike to appreciate the highest human aspirations.

The next *baraita* we will study, from the same discussion in Tractate *Kiddushin*, relates honor for parents and for God to other ideals of Jewish tradition. It deepens the talmudic Rabbis' theological understanding of the mitzvah to honor parents.

Text 4b—*Kiddushin* 30b (continued)

OUR RABBIS TAUGHT IN a *baraita*:
> There are three partners in a human being:
> the Holy One of Blessing, and his father and his mother.
> When a person honors his father and his mother,
> the Holy One of Blessing says,
> I credit it to them as if I dwelt among them, and they honored Me.

QUESTIONS FOR INQUIRY

1. According to the text, in what sense is God a partner with the father and mother of each human being?
2. According to this text, what kind of credit do we earn for honoring our parents?
3. What does this text add to the ideas of the previous text, 4a?

COMMENTS

This *baraita* reminds us of a basic idea in Judaism. Because God created us, and because of God's omnipresence, everything people do, in a sense, involves God. The mysterious biology of reproduction makes us especially aware of God's role. While two of the partners physically create the new life, safe fetal development and birth lie outside their control. In religious terms, that part depends on God. It follows, then, that God acts as the "third partner" in creating each person.

If God serves as a partner alongside parents, it follows that when we honor our parents, we also honor God. This conclusion supports the lesson found in Text 4a as well. Tradition considers honor of parents and honor of God closely linked. Each supports the other.

Thinking through how this valuation of our parents plays out in our lives requires us to think about what we believe about the "third partner." Those who believe God—however defined—plays a role will work out ways to let this Rabbinic notion guide them. Those who do not believe may find it hard to integrate any version of this approach. Either way of looking at it affects our thinking about the case studies and view of child-parent relationships.

Later in the discussion excerpted in Texts 4a and 4b, the Rabbis consider the reality that children may relate to their fathers and mothers in different ways. In our next text, Rabbi Yehuda HaNasi, who compiled the Mishnah, uses that difference to explain a feature of the Torah's language in Exodus 20:12 and Leviticus 19:3 that we noticed earlier. From that linguistic point, we may derive a larger lesson about parent-child relationships.

Text 5 — Kiddushin 30b–31a

IT WAS TAUGHT:

Rabbi [Yehuda HaNasi] says, It is revealed and known before the One who spoke and created the world that a son honors his mother more than his father, because she teaches him right from wrong with loving words. Therefore, the Holy One of Blessing placed the father's honor before the mother's.

And it is revealed and known before the One who spoke and created the world that a son reveres his father more than his mother, because the father teaches him Torah (and speaks harshly to him). Therefore, the Holy One of Blessing placed the mother's reverence before the father's.

QUESTIONS FOR INQUIRY

1. What problem in the text of the Torah does this passage attempt to solve?

2. What difference does the text identify between the way mother and father relate to their child?
3. How does Rabbi Yehudah HaNasi resolve the problem?
4. How true is this passage to your experience of children's relationships with their mothers and their fathers?

COMMENTS

This Talmud passage contains one of the classic Rabbinic responses to the presence of two closely related mitzvot telling children how to treat their parents. We already noticed that understanding "honor" and "reverence," and the differences between them, requires more detailed explanation than the Torah provides. Here the Talmud interprets a detail that may have escaped our notice. In commanding honor for parents, the Torah mentions the father first; in commanding reverence, it mentions the mother first. Attentive to meaning hidden in even the smallest differences, the Talmud wonders what we are to learn from that change in order.

Rabbi Yehuda HaNasi's answer derives from gender roles common in his time (and still seen, in some circles, as appropriate roles for men and women). The father's job includes teaching his son Torah (we will learn more about this responsibility in Text 12a). Teaching, in Rabbi Yehuda's view, involves harsh treatment. Presumably, the father speaks harshly to the son when he fails to concentrate on his lesson, or fails to put in the effort necessary to master it. The mother, on the other hand, has the role of developing her son's character. R. Yehuda HaNasi assumes that she teaches her child by kindly and lovingly correcting his behavior.

Based on those assumptions, it follows that a child will more readily honor his mother. Therefore, the Torah places the father's honor first, to emphasize that children owe him honor, too. On the other side of the coin, a son will more readily revere his father, out of fear of the father's harsh rebuke. Therefore, the Torah puts the mother's reverence first, to emphasize that children owe her reverence, too.

We might feel that this passage does not adequately reflect the actual behavior of mothers and fathers in our time. Our society no longer delineates strictly separate roles for each parent. Some mothers take the stricter role in the family, while some fathers take the more nurturing role. Some parents trade off, each playing different roles at different times.

Adding an additional layer of complexity to this discussion, family structures today are not necessarily the same as those assumed by this source. There may not be one parent of each sex. Children of same-sex parents might wonder what duties they owe to their two fathers or two mothers; children in a household led by a single parent, man or woman, may have similar questions.

The Talmud, of course, could not have imagined such family structures. Yet we need not reject Rabbi Yehuda HaNasi's teaching as irrelevant. The lesson that all parents deserve both honor and reverence from children remains. It can still serve as a pillar of Jewish ethics in the area of parent-child relations.

If so, then we need clear definitions of both honor and reverence. Only if we understand exactly what each word means can we consider how to practice both in response to the Torah's commands.

In the next text study, we look at the definitions the Talmud offers to distinguish between the two mitzvot and to describe how a child carries each of them out.

Text Study #2: The Mitzvot Children Owe to Parents

Text 6 — *Kiddushin* 31b

OUR RABBIS TAUGHT IN a *baraita*:
What is reverence and what is honor?
Reverence: [The child] does not stand in his place,
Nor sit in his place,
Nor contradict his words,
Nor tip the balance in his favor.
Honor: Give him to eat and drink;
Clothe him and cover him;
Help him go in and out.

---

1. What do the actions listed under *reverence* have in common?
2. What do the actions listed under *honor* have in common?
3. Based on these lists, what are the Rabbis' definitions of honor for parents and reverence for parents?
4. What qualities or character traits do the Rabbis who composed this *baraita* want us to develop through honoring and revering our parents?

COMMENTS

Typically for Rabbinic literature, this passage in the Talmud defines the abstract terms *honor* and *reverence* through lists of concrete actions. Reading the lists, we begin to see how the halakhic tradition understands the Torah's commandments concerning children's treatment of their parents.

The Talmud first describes reverence. Interestingly, it phrases all of the examples illustrating reverence in the negative: reverence becomes a matter of what the child does *not* do. The prohibited activities remind us of the implication of fear contained in the word *reverence*: the son may not stand or sit in a place where the father usually stands or sits, may not contradict his father, and may not attempt to resolve his father's halakhic dispute with another person, even if he "tips the balance" in his father's favor.

In explaining honor, the Talmud names affirmative acts the son must perform. Notably, all of them seem to refer to a time when the father (or parent) can no longer care for himself: helping the parent eat and drink, or providing food and drink for him; helping him dress, or making sure he has adequate clothing; and helping the parent move around. (In further discussion, the Talmud considers whose money pays for the food and clothing; we will take up this subject in Text 8a.)

In the discussion of honor, we see a reversal of roles. The Rabbis ask children to do for parents those things that (it is assumed) the parents did for the children when they were small. That reinforces the idea that the family is the place where we begin to learn about ethics. First parents, then children, live according to the basic ethical ideal of helping others in their time of need.

The actions that comprise the mitzvot of honor and reverence are meant to develop positive qualities in the person who performs them. They foster helpfulness. They promote thinking of the needs of others rather than one's own. It may be that these actions also teach the younger generation gratitude. Many of these actions are means to show appreciation for what our parents did for us in our early years. The Talmud depicts a kind of measure-for-measure responsibility: just as our parents made sure we ate and drank in our infancy, we assist them in these activities in their dotage. Just as they carried us when we were born, we help them go from place to place when they grow old.

We can also deduce that the Rabbis want these mitzvot to impress us with respect for our elders. The actions that show reverence for a parent exemplify this. So great should our respect be that we do not even sit in a chair our father prefers. It's easy to understand that we should not embarrass our parent by contradicting him or her in front of other people. But the Talmud seems to go beyond that: it says simply that the son "does not contradict" the father. That implies, even in private conversation. (Text 7c suggests a way that a child can point out his or her parent's error without violating this rule.)

It may appear that the Talmud holds the child to a very high standard. Trying to reach this level of honor and reverence helps move a person that much closer to possessing the good character traits described in these comments.

Our next text comes from the Shulḥan Arukh, the most widely recognized code of halakhah, which summarizes and explains the laws derived from the Talmud and other sources. Published in 1550 by R. Yosef Karo, a prominent Sephardic authority, the Shulḥan Arukh also includes notes—indicated by the use of *Note*—by R. Moshe Isserles, a leading Polish rabbi who was Karo's younger contemporary. Isserles' notes describe how Ashkenazic practice differs from the Sephardic tradition Karo explicates.

WHAT IS MEANT BY reverence?

[The son] must not sit in the place designated for [his father] in the councils of elders among his colleagues, or in a place designated for [his father] to pray. And he must not sit in [father's] designated place to recline at home. And he must not contradict his words, nor support his words in his presence, even to say, "Father's words make sense."

And he must not call him by name, neither in his lifetime nor after his death. Instead he says, "My father, my master."

If his father's name was common, he changes their names [when addressing them]. This applies to an unusual name, that people do not usually call him. But a name that people usually call others, the son is allowed to use outside his father's presence.

1. What does the Shulḥan Arukh add to the passage from *Kiddushin* 31b (Text 6)?
2. How does this text provide information missing from the Talmud in *Kiddushin* 31b (Text 6)?

COMMENTS

Drawing directly from *Kiddushin* 31b (Text 6), the Shulḥan Arukh codifies the laws of reverence, while filling in details missing from the Talmud. Now we see that "do not stand in father's place" refers to the father's place among the elders, or among those who debate legal issues for the community. Karo also explains (which seems to be the plain meaning of the *baraita*) that "the son does not sit in the father's place" refers to a chair the father uses at home. In practice, this might be the father's seat at the dining table, or we might imagine a lounger the father favors for watching TV.

From the words of the Shulḥan Arukh, we learn the tradition's understanding of the Talmud's phrase, "tip the balance in his favor." If the son hears the father arguing with others, the son must not intervene, not even to offer support for his father's view. The Shulḥan Arukh goes so far as to instruct the child not even to say just "Father's words make sense."

Once again, it appears that the halakhah holds us to a very high standard of behavior toward our parents. How hard it can be to stand by silently when we feel we have something to add to the conversation! If we think of a new point that would support our parent's side, why must we keep silent? The tradition asks us to hold our parents so high in reverence that in their presence, we act as if we only learn from them. We conduct ourselves as if we have nothing to add to their wisdom.

This rule presents an interesting problem, because Jewish tradition otherwise values open debate and full participation by those who study Torah. Halakhah allows students to challenge their teachers' ideas, as long as they speak respectfully. Further, modern child-rearing and education both encourage independence of thought. Many parents today enjoy matching wits with their children—as long as the children know how to disagree respectfully.

Nevertheless, it's one thing for children to debate with their parents in private and another to do the same in front of other people. Others might misinterpret the child's intention as wanting to subtly put down the parent. Even offering support could make the wrong impression if it appears that the child believes the parent cannot hold his or her own in debate.

An additional halakhah we learn here is the way a child addresses the parent directly. It would violate standards of reverence to call the parent by his or her name. One must always use a title—the Shulḥan Arukh prefers "my father, my teacher," again emphasizing the father's role as the child's most important Torah teacher. The halakhah carries this idea even further. A child must not use the father's name even to address other people of that name. However, the code limits this requirement. If the father's name is so common that the child encounters many people of the same name, the child need not avoid using it.

Here, too, we experience changing attitudes. Today, most—though not all—would probably agree that children should not call their parents by the parents' given names, but never calling anyone by a name that a parent happens to carry seems excessive. Here, a broader and perhaps more applicable lesson might be to offer appropriate deference to those who are not our peers, including our elders and people with authority over us. We might not show our respect in the expected ways of the sixteenth century when the Shulḥan Arukh was composed, but we can find ways of doing so appropriate to the norms of our time and place.

Even the premodern texts acknowledge that the requirement to show honor to parents cannot exist without any limits. Next, we will briefly explore one limit they set. This teaching from the Talmud is summarized by Rashi (1040–1105), a leading Ashkenazic scholar whose influential commentary explains the Torah as understood by the classical rabbinic tradition.

Text 7b — Rashi on Lev. 19:3

AND KEEP MY SABBATHS.

[The verse] juxtaposed keeping Shabbat with reverence for parents, to teach that even though I [God] warned you about reverence for parents, if your parent tells you to desecrate Shabbat, you must not listen to him. The same is true of all the other mitzvot. (Derived from *Bava Metzia 32*)

QUESTIONS FOR INQUIRY

1. What anomaly in the wording of the verse leads Rashi to make this comment? Hint: Look at Leviticus 19:3 (Text 2). What looks like it does not belong in the verse?
2. How does Rashi's comment resolve that problem?
3. What limit does this comment (drawn from the Talmud) set on parental authority?
4. In Texts 4a and 4b, the Talmud compares parents to God. How does this interpretation alter our understanding of that idea?

COMMENTS

With its penchant for close analysis of the Torah's words, the Talmud (followed by Rashi here) wonders why Leviticus brings up the need to keep Shabbat in a verse primarily commanding reverence for mother and father. In response, it uses a standard technique in midrash called *semikhut*, "juxtaposition": deriving meaning from noticing what subjects the Torah discusses next to each other.

In this instance, Rashi suggests that Shabbat appears in the verse to teach us about a limit on the commandment of revering our parents. That requirement extends only to the point at which the mother or father instructs the child to do something in violation of Shabbat. If that happens, the child should remember that the Torah says to revere parents "*and* keep My sabbaths." God's command to observe Shabbat overrides the need to obey one's parents.

The fact that the duties children owe their parents must yield to duties owed to God adds to our understanding that while our responsibilities to our parents are extensive, they are not unlimited.

The next selection comes from the *Mishneh Torah*. Maimonides (also known by the Hebrew acronym Rambam, for **R**abbi **M**oshe **b**en **M**aimon), the great Sephardic scholar, composed this code of halakhah in the twelfth century. Organized by topic, the *Mishneh Torah* summarizes all of Jewish law up to its time. In this discussion of the halakhah, Maimonides offers further insight into the interplay of the commandment of honor with the Torah's other commandments.

Text 7c — *Mishneh Torah*, Laws of Rebellion 6:11

EVEN IF ONE'S FATHER is wicked and sins all the time, one still must show him honor and reverence. If the child saw the father violating something from the Torah, one must not say, "Father, you violated the Torah." Instead, one should say: "Father, isn't this and that what's written in the Torah?"—as if he's asking him, not as if he's scolding him.

QUESTIONS FOR INQUIRY

1. What potential difficulty in carrying out the mitzvah of reverence does the *Mishneh Torah* address here?
2. What solution to the problem does the author propose?

3. What do we learn from this about the nature and extent of reverence owed to parents?

The *Mishneh Torah* raises the ironic problem of a child trying to fulfill Torah's commandments while the Torah requires revering a person who violates those same commandments. If the parent is a sinner, do the commandments to honor and revere still apply?

Maimonides holds that even a wicked, sinful parent is still to receive the honor and reverence due all parents. Thus he offers a clever work-around to the problem of a child seeing the parent do something that clearly violates the Torah. Strictly speaking, the child cannot say to the parent, "That is wrong," because doing so would violate the Talmud text in *Kiddushin* (Text 6), a law codified in the Shulḥan Arukh (Text 7a). So to avoid contradicting one's parent, a child should ask a "naive" question, "Doesn't the Torah say this?," as if needing the parent's help in recalling. The idea, of course, is to remind parents indirectly of the sin they are about to commit. That may be enough to get parents to change their ways.

Modern children may find it useful to adopt Rambam's suggestion more generally when they find aspects of a parent's behavior distasteful. Confronting them directly might not accord with the respect we owe them, and might harm our relationships. But pretending to ask an innocent question, presenting the matter as if we are seeking guidance from our parent, may enable us to have a calm, dispassionate conversation about the matter at hand. Perhaps, then, we can show our parents reverence while still engaging in honest discussion of our disagreements.

Next we return to the Shulḥan Arukh for details on how to uphold the mitzvah to honor our parents. (Reminder: Any appearance of *Note* in a Shulḥan Arukh excerpt introduces a comment by the Ashkenazic authority R. Moshe Isserles.)

Text 8a—Shulḥan Arukh, *Yoreh De'ah* 240:4–5

WHAT IS MEANT BY honor?

[The son] provides the parent with food and drink; clothes and covers him, and helps him move in and out. He must give him with a good grace. Even if he feeds him expensive food every day, but shows him an angry face, the son will be punished for that. . . .

The food and drink he provides his parent comes from the father and mother's money, if they have it. And if the father does not have money, but the son does, [a court] can force him to provide food for his father, as much as he can afford.

But if the son does not have, he is not required to go begging door to door in order to feed his father.

Note: There are those who say [the son] is only required to give [the father] as much as he is required to give to tzedakah. But in any case, if he can afford it, may a curse come on one who supports his father from his tzedakah funds.

But if the father has many sons, they calculate their financial situations. If some of them are rich and some poor, they obligate the rich ones alone [to support the father].

But [the son] is required to honor his father in person, even though it causes him to abandon his work, and he winds up begging from door to door.

That means, specifically if the son has enough food to eat that day. But if he does not have enough, he is not required to abandon his work and beg from door to door.

QUESTIONS FOR INQUIRY

1. What parts of this excerpt are recognizable from the passage from *Kiddushin* 31b (Text 6)?
2. What questions raised by that text does this work try to answer?
3. Which of these requirements seem reasonable today? Which seem unreasonable?

COMMENTS

Now with the mitzvah of honor, the Shulḥan Arukh builds on the primary Talmud passage defining these responsibilities, adding details and filling in some important blanks.

We saw in the Talmud that adult children must make sure their parents have enough to eat and drink. An obvious question is: Who pays? Does that mean that part of the children's income goes to feeding the parents (as the parents' income did when the children were minors)? Or could it mean that the children use the parents' funds to support their elders?

The halakhah rules that the child uses the parents' money, but the Shulḥan Arukh adds that if the parents do not in fact have enough money but the child does, the child must pay for the parents' food and drink. The parents may even take the child to court, which will enforce the obligation to pay, within the limits of what the child can reasonably afford.

If, on the other hand, the child does not have enough money, the halakhah does not force the child to descend into poverty to support the father. One need not become a beggar to help one's parents.

In the note describing differences in Ashkenazic practice, R. Moshe Isserles draws our attention to an opinion holding that the son need only provide his father the amount the son would give to *tzedakah*. That amount would not impoverish the child, while providing the father with at least a subsistence level of support. Perhaps that is why Isserles hastens to add that anyone who can afford to must support his father to a higher standard. He calls down a curse on anyone who can, but avoids giving his parents more than the minimum of support. Some understand the word for "curse," *me'erah*, as meaning that the cursed individual will himself become impoverished.

Notice, though, that unlike Karo, Isserles does not claim that the courts can force the son to do more. Apparently, the courts cannot enforce more than the minimum legal obligation. Isserles therefore resorts to moral language. Even if the law cannot touch him, anyone who fails to do more than the absolute minimum for parents deserves to come to harm.

In effect, the support children provide their parents must deserve the description of "honor." It must allow the parents to live comfortably, in a way that will not cause others to pity them. While the authors go on to balance that law with the statement that all depends on what the son can afford, their preference for children doing as much as possible for the parents is evident.

Next comes a practical discussion about how to divide the responsibility for supporting elderly parents among several children. The Shulḥan Arukh proposes that the local court assess the children's ability to pay. Some may be wealthier than others. In the interest of fairness, and because no one should become a pauper to fulfill this mitzvah, the court requires the better-off children to do more than their poorer siblings.

At the end of his fifth paragraph, R. Karo notes that a child should honor parents in person. One drops what one is doing in order to respond to the parents' needs. More realistically than the stories in the Talmud (see Text 9a), however, he rules that only the child who can afford to leave his place of work to serve the parents should do so. If leaving work might cause both him and his parents not to eat that day, the child must not leave work for his parents' sake.

Adult children today face the same challenges the Shulḥan Arukh describes here. Susan of Case Study #2 can be viewed as falling into this category. While she may in fact earn more than the bare minimum needed to provide for each day's needs, she and Bill will only be able to support themselves, pay college tuition, and save for their younger children's educations if they both work. That seems a good modern analogy for the "son who is not required to abandon his work and beg from door to door."

From a Jewish perspective, it appears that the goal would be to honor one's parents by supporting them to the best of one's ability. Children must be willing to make financial sacrifices to support their parents. Presumably these mirror the sacrifices the parents made in raising the child. If so, we may conclude that the halakhah asks nothing more of us than what is fair.

None of this, of course, tells us exactly how much children must give up to help their parents. What if the parent's condition deteriorates to the point that the child simply cannot handle caring personally for the parent? Rabbinic law considered this issue long before modern medicine, as the next source shows.

Text 8b — *Mishneh Torah*, Laws of Rebellion 6:10

WHEN SOMEONE'S FATHER OR MOTHER loses mental capacity, the child tries to treat them according to their remaining understanding until God has mercy on them. But if the child cannot handle the degree of their derangement, the child leaves and departs from them, and charges others to provide them with appropriate care.

QUESTIONS FOR INQUIRY

1. According to the text, how should children take care of their parents if it is impossible for them to handle the situation personally?
2. How do you understand the phrase, "until God has mercy upon them" in this paragraph?

COMMENTS

It's interesting to realize that people in the twelfth century experienced the same challenges we do. Here we see the halakhah responding in a practical and compassionate manner to the sad situation of parents who become too severely demented for their children to care for on their own. While maintaining the standard that children should do all they can for their parents, it recognizes that not everyone can handle every situation. It provides a way for children to provide what their parents need without having to attend to them personally.

Specifically, Maimonides asks that children do their best, according to the parent's mental condition, but says that when it becomes too hard for the children to continue, they may leave their parents. Yet, of course, they must "charge others with caring for [the parent] in an appropriate manner." In our terms, the children must arrange for professional care. While it can become very expensive, we fortunately live in a time when (in principle) specialized nursing facilities can provide for the specific needs of severely demented elderly patients.

This important halakhah also demonstrates that the tradition recognizes limits to the commandments of honor and reverence. In the case the *Mishneh Torah* describes, all children must make an individual decision about when the situation exceeds their capacity. Some will be able to bear their parent's "derangement" longer than others. Whenever that time comes for that individual, the child has permission to hand the parent over to professional caregivers.

The *Mishneh Torah* thus offers guidance to Susan and Bill (Case Study #2). While Victor has not yet reached the advanced state of dementia the text describes, he has started down that road. The halakhah recorded here implies that when Susan judges she can no longer bear the challenges of her father's worsening condition, she may leave him with professional caregivers experienced in treating patients with dementia. Certainly, she is to visit him regularly and try to keep him aware of her and her family as much as possible. But this law releases Susan from the sense that she must take full, personal responsibility for her father's daily care. She may instead pay for professional care and continue her own daily routines.

Sarah (Case Study #3) might use this halakhah as the basis to argue that she can end contact with her mother. The reasoning might go along these lines: Both the memories of how her mother treated her when she was young and the way her mother continues to insult her today make her company intolerable to Sarah. It is "impossible for her to remain" with her mother. Therefore, she may refuse to see her mother until "God has mercy" in the form of her mother apologizing and repenting for her sins against her daughter.

Such an argument does not settle the issue, however. Given the extent of the tradition's requirements for the honor and reverence children must show their parents, Jews always struggle to set appropriate boundaries. Next, a contemporary rabbi, David Golinkin, uses the problem of a parent living with dementia to explore the limits of what parents may expect and what children must do.

Rabbi Golinkin's discussion takes the form of a responsum, a rabbinic response to a halakhic question. Among the responsa he has written for the Masorti movement (the branch of the Conservative movement active in the State of Israel) is his answer to this question: "As life expectancy grows, many people are faced with the difficulties of caring for a parent with Alzheimer's disease. According to Jewish law, is it permissible to institutionalize such a parent?" We will study excerpts from his conclusion, which has legal authority for members of the Israeli Masorti movement.

Text 8c—Golinkin, "Institutionalizing Parents with Alzheimer's Disease"

IT APPEARS . . . THAT THERE are three legitimate halakhic options:

1. A child with stamina and emotional fortitude can follow the line of thought expressed by [some ancient and medieval authorities]. They view "honor thy father and thy mother" as an absolute value which cannot be absolved by the erratic behavior of the parent. Regardless of how the son feels, he must *personally* take care of his parents as commanded by the Torah and must not "leave [them] all the days of his life."

2. Others may place their parent in a nursing home, . . . as interpreted by Maimonides and his followers. According to this view, a child is not *personally* obligated to care for the parent, if he must sacrifice his own emotional health in the process. They further state that in cases of mental deterioration, the honor of the parent can be better served by an outsider who can do things the child cannot do and that the parent would not want him to do.

3. Yet I believe the preferred halakhic solution is . . . to keep the parent *at home* but pay an outsider to attend to the functions which are painful or inappropriate for the child to perform. . . . On the one hand, the parent *feels* wanted and loved by his or her child, a feeling frequently lacking in an institutional setting. . . . By keeping the parent at home, the child fulfills the commandment to "honor your father and your mother" in a direct and personal fashion. . . . On the other hand, . . . the child protects the parent's honor and the child's own emotional health by ensuring that a professional is on hand who can perform functions not in keeping with the honor owed a parent by a child.[1]

QUESTIONS FOR INQUIRY

1. What three options does the responsum offer?
2. How is each one justified?
3. What advantages and disadvantages does each option have?

This contemporary responsum takes a realistic attitude toward the interaction between the halakhah and real-life challenges. While most *teshuvot* (plural of *teshuvah*, the Hebrew word for responsum) instruct the questioner in exactly what halakhah requires, this one offers choices. Each option draws on a part of the tradition.

The first option follows the strictest understanding of how we perform honor and reverence for our parents. It holds that each child must personally attend to every parental need, no matter how hard it gets or how embarrassing it becomes. In this view, it does not matter how the child feels about it; tending to elderly parents is the Torah's command.

The second option, drawing directly from the previous text, acknowledges that not all children can perform every act of caregiving. It also points out something the *Mishneh Torah* does not say: even the parent may prefer that the child not perform intimate acts of personal care. It would be better to hire qualified people to provide the care with minimal embarrassment to all parties.

The third option, which does not appear directly in the earlier sources, but represents Golinkin's attempt to find a middle path, combines the strand of the tradition that emphasizes the children's personal responsibility and the other strand that allows children to pay others to do what they cannot. By hiring professionals to care for a declining parent in their own home, children show a degree of honor and willingness to sacrifice. This demonstrates the children's continuing love and respect for the parent. At the same time, it prevents children from having to take on more than they can handle.

We see, then, that the halakhic tradition provides a degree of flexibility. One rule need not cover every ethical dilemma. Instead, decision-making can take into account differences among individuals trying their best to do what is right.

Susan, the daughter in Case Study #2, might consider the options presented here. If her family can afford to provide for her elderly father's needs in their home, both she and her father might feel more comfortable than if she chooses to move him into a care facility. If keeping him at home proves impractical, she might then follow the lead of Maimonides and others (see Text 8b, the *Mishneh Torah*) and find a place where her father can receive the necessary care.

Before making that decision, Susan would also best consider other trends in Jewish ethics that require children to go even further to honor and revere their parents. As we will see, stories in the Talmud (Text 9a) and laws codified by Maimonides in the *Mishneh Torah* (Texts 9b, 9c, and 9d) present an idealistic view of children's responsibilities.

Text 9a — *Kiddushin* 31a–b

RABBI TARFON HAD A mother. When she wanted to climb into bed, he would bend down to let her ascend [by stepping on him]. And whenever she wanted to get down, she would step down on him.

He went to the *beit midrash* and boasted.

They said to him: You have not even reached half the honor [due her]. Has she thrown your wallet into the sea in front of you without you protesting? . . .

Rav Yehuda quoted Shmuel:

They asked Rabbi Eliezer, "How far does honoring father and mother go?"

He replied: Go see what a certain gentile in Ashkelon by the name of Dama ben Netina did for his father.

The sages wanted to buy from him precious stones for the High Priest's garments for 600,000 *denarii*. (Rav Kahana taught, 800,000 *denarii*.) But the key [to where the jewels were stored] was under his father's pillow, and Dama did not disturb him.

The next year, the Holy One of Blessing gave Dama his reward, for a red heifer [an exceedingly rare female cow needed for purification rituals in the ancient Temple] was born in his flock.

The Sages of Israel came to Dama ben Netina. He said to them, "I know that I could ask you for all the money in the world, and you would give it to me. But I only ask of you the amount that I lost for the sake of my father's honor."

1. What differences do you find between the way Rabbi Tarfon honored his mother and the way Dama ben Netina honored his father?
2. Why did the other scholars in the *beit midrash* tell R. Tarfon he had not showed his mother even half the honor he owed her?
3. Why does the Talmud mention that Dama ben Netina was not a Jew?
4. Can we draw any meaningful lessons for our case studies from these stories?

COMMENTS

In these two stories, the Talmud explores the question of whether we have to set our own interests and preferences aside in favor of the mitzvah of honoring our parents.

The tale of Dama ben Netina implicitly asks if we must honor our parents even if doing so costs us money.

Rabbi Tarfon subjects himself to physical discomfort—turning his body into a stepstool—to keep his mother comfortable. Clearly, R. Tarfon thinks well of himself for his behavior. In the *beit midrash*, he brags to the other scholars about how thoroughly he performs the commandment of *kibbud em*, honoring one's mother.

Tarfon's colleagues appear to react mainly to his self-satisfaction in singing his own praises. Could they seriously mean that a son who goes as far as he does fulfills not even half the mitzvah of honor? More likely, they want him not to think so well of himself. Tarfon, like all of us, should remember that we can always try to do more in carrying out the Torah's commands.

At the same time, we can learn something about how to honor parents from Rabbi Tarfon's actions. Even if he does not reach as high a standard as he imagines, he still demonstrates that our parents' needs outweigh our comfort. We need to think about how we might go out of our way to make our parents' lives easier. Susan, the adult daughter in Case Study #2, might consider what she could relinquish to make the end of her father's life more comfortable.

The story of Dama ben Netina offers a different illustration of how far to go to honor one's parents. Dama refuses to disturb his father's sleep, though the refusal costs him a gigantic profit. Interestingly, God rewards him, by giving him an opportunity for the big payday he missed out on. Understanding the value the Rabbis place on a red heifer, Dama ben Netina again demonstrates his high ethical standards by refusing to take advantage of the situation. He knows he can demand any outrageous price for the rare cow, but he makes a point of limiting his earnings to what he lost the year before while he honored his father. The story may suggest that even when we think we lose out by honoring our parents, in the long run we really lose nothing.

It's fascinating—and rare in the Talmud—that the exemplar of the best way to carry out a mitzvah is a gentile. Given the fact that the Talmud often portrays non-Jews as less moral than Jews, we might suspect a kind of invidious comparison at work. The intended meaning could be: If even a non-Jew can go this far for his father's honor, how can a Jew not do at least as much? Possibly the Talmud also hints that honoring parents is a natural law for all human societies. Jews are not the only ones who live by these values expressed in the Torah; all right-thinking people strive to treat their parents with honor. We may not expect the kind of direct and immediate reward Dama receives in the tale; but we can do all in our power to serve our parents' honor.

These stories might suggest that both Daniel in Case Study #1 and Sarah in Case Study #3 must submit to their parents' needs and preferences in ways that make them uncomfortable. Like R. Tarfon and Dama ben Netina, they are to set aside their needs and preferences in order to honor their parents. If the Rabbis' response to Tarfon is not mere exaggeration, we might conclude that almost nothing is too much for parents to demand of their children. Certainly, then, Daniel should give up his college dreams, and Sarah ignore her psychic wounds, in favor of parental honor.

However, these stories are not the last word in Jewish tradition about the extent and limits of the duties children owe their parents. We turn again to Maimonides.

HOW FAR DOES THE mitzvah of honoring one's father and mother extend? Even if they take one's purse of gold coins and throw it into the sea in his presence, one should not embarrass them, shout at them, or show anger at them. Instead, he should accept the Torah's decree and remain silent.

QUESTIONS FOR INQUIRY

1. How does the *Mishneh Torah* describe how far we must go to honor our parents?
2. What would be a modern equivalent of what Maimonides describes?

COMMENTS

In describing the extent of the mitzvah of honor, Rambam here uses an example that appears first in the Talmud (Text 9a, the sages' retort to Rabbi Tarfon). Even if the parent throws away an item of immense value belonging to the child, the child must swallow his or her natural angry reaction. The child must remain silent, accepting the "Torah's decree" that honor for parents goes this far.

As we have seen before, the halakhah establishes standards that can test how far we are willing to go. Few of us would readily accept this kind of treatment, even from a parent, without a word of protest. Let us next examine the *Mishneh Torah*'s summary of the extent of the mitzvah of reverence as we consider whether there is any limit to the treatment a child must accept from a parent.

Text 9c — *Mishneh Torah*, Laws of Rebellion 6:7 (continued)

HOW FAR DOES THE mitzvah of revering them extend? Even if one was wearing fine clothing and sitting at the head of the community, if one's father or mother came, ripped the clothes, struck him on the head, and spit in his face, he should not shame them. Rather, he should remain silent and revere and fear the King of kings who commanded him to act this way. Were a mortal king to decree something which would cause him even more suffering, he would not be able to move even a limb in protest. How much more does this apply when the command comes from the One who spoke and caused the world to come into existence as God desired it.

QUESTIONS FOR INQUIRY

1. Does the commandment of reverence extend as far as the commandment of honor? Does it extend even further? What evidence do you find in Texts 9b and 9c?
2. What comparison does Rambam make to drive home his point about how far we must go to demonstrate reverence for our parents? How is this idea reminiscent of texts mentioned earlier in this chapter?

COMMENTS

As we saw in analyzing Laws of Rebellion 6:7 (Text 9b), the halakhic tradition requires children to carry the mitzvot they owe their parents to an almost unimaginable level. Here in the continuation of the paragraph, the law demands that the child accept public humiliation from a parent in silence. One may be seated in a place of honor as a leader of the community, but if the parent embarrasses him at that moment, he must submit to it as a further decree of the one who commanded him to revere his mother and father — namely God.

By invoking God, the text appears to recall passages from the earlier Rabbinic tradition that compare honor and reverence for parents with honor and reverence for God (see Texts 4a and 4b from *Kiddushin*). Anyone who shows reverence for parents also shows reverence for God. This idea may also recall that God is the "third partner" in creating each person.

Here, Maimonides also shows one of the meanings of the metaphor of God as king. Writing in a time when most societies were ruled by kings, he knew well that a royal decree could not be questioned, let alone disobeyed.

If one would give that kind of obedience to a human king, it follows that one should give the same to the divine ruler of the universe. Therefore, if God commands that a child revere a parent who displays contempt for him in front of others, that child must still obey God's commandment.

The public nature of the parents' actions described here points out an important difference between the commandments of honor and reverence. Most of the challenges of honoring we have seen involve financial loss to the child—a purse thrown into the sea, for example. The texts give no indication that anyone but the parent and the child know what happened (the case of Dama ben Netina is an exception). The challenges of reverence, in contrast, involve things that happen in public. Children must quietly accept being embarrassed even in front of many people who respect them. Thus, reading these sources together, we see that the tradition requires us to do our utmost for our parents, both in private and in public.

The next paragraph of the *Mishneh Torah* shows that the traditional Rabbis were aware of how hard it would be to live up to the standard they recorded in the halakhah.

Text 9d— *Mishneh Torah*, Laws of Rebellion 6:8

EVEN THOUGH THESE COMMANDS have been issued, a person is forbidden to lay a heavy yoke on his children and be particular about their honoring him to the point that he puts an obstacle in front of them. Instead, he should forgo his honor and ignore any slights. For if a father desires to forgo his honor, he may.

A person who strikes a son who has reached the age of majority should be placed under a ban of ostracism, for he is transgressing the mitzvah, "Do not place a stumbling block in front of the blind" [Leviticus 19:14].

QUESTIONS FOR INQUIRY

1. How does this paragraph complete the thoughts about the extent of the commandments regarding parents found in Texts 9b and 9c?

2. If a parent strikes an adult child, what commandment in the Torah does Rambam say the parent has violated? Why is this a violation of that specific commandment?

3. What implications does this law have for our case studies?

COMMENTS

Here the *Mishneh Torah* turns from the children's responsibility to the parents'. Maimonides acknowledges how few people would be able to reach the standard he sets for honoring and revering their parents. Given that, he writes, parents should not put their children in positions that will test their ability to silently absorb poor treatment from them. That is the meaning of the metaphor of the "heavy yoke." Parents should avoid giving a child a burden that is difficult to carry. Indeed, the halakhah goes a step further. Even if the child slips and offends the parent, the parent should let it go; parents should not always insist on their honor.

For children, reading this paragraph may come as a relief. The halakhah recognizes life's realities: few could absorb insult and abuse, even from their parents, without striking back in any way. Thus the halakhah stipulates that parents and children must share responsibility. While the children must, in theory, take whatever their parents dish out, the parents must not make unreasonable demands.

This part of the *Mishneh Torah* offers further insight into Sarah's situation (Case Study #3). For all that the halakhah requires of Sarah, the law also obligates her mother to bear responsibility for her actions. The mother should not expect her daughter to put up with more than might be endured by a normal person. Parents cannot claim the right to subject their children to verbal and physical abuse. As a result, Sarah's duty to honor her mother may have reached its limit.

Discussing situations where parents insist too strongly on their right to receive honor leads Maimonides to broach the question of physically striking an adult child. To understand what he does here, we must recognize that in Rambam's world, parents hitting their minor children was accepted disciplinary practice. We might imagine that this would end when the child reached majority, but in that era children above the age of majority often remained under their parents' authority until they married.

Today as well, college students who are legally adults may live at home, or college graduates may return home to their childhood bedroom for a certain period of time. Thus Rambam included a caution not to strike one's child who has reached the age of majority.

Notice that he does not use the language of "it is forbidden" to strike such a child. Instead, he establishes a rule that expresses disapproval of such behavior by placing the parent "under a ban of ostracism." The Hebrew term used is *niddui*. Invoking *niddui* means that fellow Jews will keep their distance and minimize their contact with the ostracized individual. In the small, closely knit Jewish communities that existed in the Middle Ages, this was a significant punishment.

Again, the *Mishneh Torah* does not claim that the Torah forbids a parent from striking an adult child. If the Torah did so, the offender would receive a direct, court-imposed punishment, not just ostracism. Instead, the *Mishneh Torah* generalizes this offense: "Do not place a stumbling block in front of the blind." The Talmud understands that verse (Lev. 19:14) as a metaphor. One of its meanings is presenting individuals with a situation that tempts them to sin. (Chapter 7 presents more information on this mitzvah.) Here, the parent hitting an adult child might cause the child to strike back. The natural reaction to a blow might well be to strike a blow in return. Since Exodus 21:15 reads, "One who strikes one's father or mother shall be put to death," the parent in this case would potentially subject the child to the death penalty. That is a large stumbling block indeed!

Of course, the death penalties prescribed in the Torah and elaborated in the Talmud are no longer enforced (if they ever were). But the *Mishneh Torah* here teaches a valuable lesson. Parents, no less than children, need to reflect carefully on the effects of their conduct. Inasmuch as parents have the right to hold their children to behavioral standards and to discipline them when they fall short, they also have the responsibility to recognize the limits of their authority.

This idea also offers us the opportunity to reflect on Case Study #1 from the perspective of children's independence. First, when does that independence begin? In our society, has an eighteen-year-old on the verge of high school graduation who could not put himself through university without his parents' support fully reached the "age of majority"? Second, how far should that independence reach? If his parents insist on having their way now, might Daniel's resentment build to the point that he reacts without consideration of the honor and reverence he owes them?

Indeed, in the next set of texts, we see that Rabbinic tradition considers fulfilling the commandments to honor and revere our parents one of the most difficult challenges in Jewish tradition.

Text 10a — Midrash *Tanḥuma Eikev* 3

RABBI SHIMON BAR YOCHAI taught:

The Holy One revealed the reward for two mitzvot. One is the easiest of all the easy ones, and one is the hardest of all the hard ones.

Which ones are they?

The easiest of all easy ones is sending away the mother bird. There it is written, "you will have a long life" [Deut. 22:7].

And the hardest of all the hard ones is honoring father and mother. About that mitzvah it is written, "that you may long endure" [Deut. 5:16].

QUESTIONS FOR INQUIRY

1. What idea that we explored earlier appears in this midrash?
2. How does Rabbi Shimon bar Yochai characterize the commandment to honor parents?

Text 10b — *Kiddushin* 31b

RABBI YOCHANAN SAID:

Happy is the person who never saw his parents.

Rashi comments:

For it is impossible to honor them as much as needed, and the child gets punished on their account.

1. Setting aside Rashi's explanation for now, how do you understand Rabbi Yochanan's claim?
2. How does Rashi explain Rabbi Yochanan's comment?
3. Does Rabbi Yochanan's idea make sense? Is honoring our parents as difficult as that?

COMMENTS

Text 10a, from a midrash on the book of Deuteronomy, notices that only two commandments in the Torah describe the reward for keeping them, and in both cases the reward is the same: long life. The midrashic author also distinguishes sharply between the two mitzvot. One he considers among the easiest commandments to fulfill and the other among the hardest.

"Sending away the mother bird" describes a situation in which a person finds a mother bird in a nest with her eggs or her baby birds. If one wishes to take the eggs or baby birds, one must first send away the mother bird. Commentators disagree, but the reason may be that we must spare the mother the pain of seeing her children taken from her. According to Rabbi Shimon bar Yochai, fulfilling this mitzvah is quite easy. All the individual must do to get the desired eggs or baby birds is to first chase away the mother bird. For this small act, the Torah promises long life.

Far harder to accomplish, as we have seen, is to honor one's parents properly. For this mitzvah, too, the Torah promises us long life. But in light of what we have learned, we must wonder if anyone can earn the reward. Through stories and halakhic discussions (Rabbi Tarfon, Dama ben Netina, and others in Texts 9a–d), the Talmud establishes how very far we must go to show our parents honor. Fulfilling the commandment completely seems hopeless. We can imagine Rabbi Yochanan throwing up his hands. Better never to meet one's own parents than to have to try, and inevitably fail, to honor them!

Perhaps R. Yochanan is using a common Rabbinic technique called *guzma*, meaning "exaggeration." He may not mean us to take his point literally—surely it's better for people to know their parents—but offers it as a means of acknowledging how very difficult it is to do all we can to honor our parents. Even children whose parents have treated them lovingly experience times when doing what their parents ask, or otherwise showing them respect, interferes with something they would rather do. In Case Study #1, for example, bowing to his parents' wishes out of duty does not come easily for Daniel. Parental abuse exacerbates these considerations. Sarah (Case Study #3) would readily agree with R. Yochanan that honoring her mother would be the hardest mitzvah Judaism could possibly impose on her.

One such challenge arises when parents disapprove of their children's choice of life partner. In earlier times, arranged marriage was the norm. Hence, the biblical and Rabbinic literature we studied so far in this chapter assumes that parents will choose their children's spouses or play a substantial role in that choice. In our time, by contrast, Jewish adults choose their own partners (though in some Jewish communities, especially among *haredim*—the traditional communities often referred to as ultra-Orthodox—parents still have considerable influence over their children's marital choices). Even in the thirteenth century, parents and children sometimes came into conflict over such choices. In the following text from his book *Love Your Neighbor as Yourself*, Rabbi Elliot Dorff, a modern Conservative rabbi, cites a halakhic decision by Rabbi Solomon ben Adret (Rashba), an important Sephardic authority of that period.

Text 11a—Dorff, *Love Your Neighbor as Yourself*

RABBI SOLOMON BEN ADRET (Rashba) [Responsa Part 7, #147] used the principle that divine commands supersede parental ones to permit a man to violate his parents' wishes in marrying the woman he loves, even if that means that the son would be precluded from providing the range of services prescribed as part of the honor and respect due to parents. . . . The man has the right to do this, according to Rashba, to fulfill the commandment "Be fruitful and multiply," for which marriage is a legal prerequisite.[2]

1. What two reasons does Rashba use to allow adult children to disobey their parents' wishes in choosing whom to marry?
2. Does Rashba's reasoning help Daniel (Case Study #1) or Sarah (Case Study #3) make their decisions?

COMMENTS

Rashba's ruling relies on the principle articulated in the *Mishneh Torah* (Text 7c) that since both parent and child must obey God's commandments, a child is exempt from honoring the parent when the parent wants the child to violate God's will. Rashba argues that the son (in this case) must fulfill the commandment of having children. Legally, he cannot do so unless he marries. Therefore, Rashba reasons, the son must be free to ignore his father's instruction not to marry a certain woman, so that he (the son) may carry out God's command to "be fruitful and multiply."

The logic of this responsum seems to support a decision to marry a partner of one's choice, regardless of one's parents' preferences. While following it may well lead to conflict between parents and their children, it appeals to our modern sense that adults (at least) ought to be able to make important life choices without interference. We generally believe that romantic love trumps family responsibility. While the younger generation certainly should do all in their power to maintain good relationships with their parents, they need not sacrifice what they see as their chance for love to a strict understanding of the halakhot of honoring parents.

In our time, many Jews face a dilemma the ancient and medieval sources could hardly have anticipated: how to honor the religious practices of non-Jewish parents. Our communities include many more Jews by choice, people raised in another religion who converted to Judaism. They often struggle to honor the traditions of their families of origin without betraying their chosen loyalty to the Jewish people and its traditions. To take a common example: Can you join your non-Jewish family for Christmas celebrations at their homes after you adopt Judaism? What about after you have your own children, whom you wish to raise as Jews?

Anita Diamant is a novelist who also wrote several books about contemporary Jewish life and practice. In *Choosing a Jewish Life: A Handbook for People Converting to Judaism* (2007), excerpted in the next section, she offers advice that may help us think through these challenges.

Text 11b — Diamant, *Choosing a Jewish Life*

EVEN IF THEY HAVE no theological objections to your choice, family members — especially parents — may perceive your decision to convert as a rejection of them and everything they believe in. Although all parents have to let go of their children and accept their independence, religious conversion is an unexpected form of separation. . . . Your family may worry what your becoming Jewish will do to your relationship with them, and wonder what it means for you to become one of "them" rather than one of "us."

You can help reassure your parents by stressing the ties that will always bind you together. . . . The bottom line is that while you may be choosing a different religion, you are not converting out of your family.[3]

QUESTIONS FOR INQUIRY

1. What aspect of the problem of honoring parents does this source address?
2. How does the author suggest that adult children can honor parents while making their own choices?

COMMENTS

The last sentence of this text may be the most important. Converting to Judaism represents a religious choice. It means giving up any prior beliefs and joining a new people. But it does not ask the convert to give up one's family of origin. Most rabbis supervising conversion students advise them to show their parents the same honor and reverence that born Jews are commanded to demonstrate to theirs. Jews by choice can negotiate ways to honor their parents' traditions without compromising their new identity. Even if the occasion is a Christian holiday, there should be no objection to joining together to renew family ties and enjoy a festive meal.

Now that we have explored the nature and extent of what children must do for their parents, we move on to a series of texts that consider what Jewish tradition requires parents to do for their children.

Text Study #3: Parents' Responsibilities to Children

Text 12a — *Kiddushin* 29a

OUR RABBIS TAUGHT:

The father is obligated to his son

to circumcise him;

to redeem him [if he is firstborn of his mother];

and to teach him Torah;

and to marry him off;

and to teach him a trade.

And some say: Also to teach him to swim.

Rabbi Yehudah says: Anyone who does not teach his son a trade teaches him thievery.

—Do you really mean thievery?!

Rather: It's as if he teaches him thievery.

QUESTIONS FOR INQUIRY

1. What does each of these parental obligations contribute to the child's growth toward adulthood?
2. Does learning to swim fit into this list or not?
3. If you rewrote the list for modern times, what would you add to it? What would you remove from it?
4. How do you understand Rabbi Yehudah's idea and the Talmud's objection to it?

COMMENTS

We might sum up the Talmud's understanding of a parent's primary duty to a child as giving the child the ability to live a full Jewish life. The birth of a son specifically brings with it the obligation to fulfill certain mitzvot. The father (typically; the Talmud does not mention the mother) must enter the boy into the covenant of circumcision. "Redeem him" refers to an obligation the Torah imposes on Israelite parents who are not descendants of *Kohanim* (priestly families) or Levites (members of the Levi tribe). Originally, the Torah intended every firstborn son to serve in the priesthood. After the sin of the Golden Calf, when only the tribe of Levi remained loyal to God, God rewarded the Levites with the exclusive privilege of carrying out the sacrificial rites of worship. Male children born to other tribes had to "buy out" their obligation to serve God: their fathers would exchange five silver coins with a *Kohen* to redeem them. As the children grew up, their fathers had to teach them Torah or see that they learned Torah.

The responsibility to arrange a marriage reflects the centrality of family in Jewish life. The son must ultimately continue the cycle by marrying and having children of his own. Even teaching him a trade can fall into this category, since that will enable the son to eventually support a family of his own.

Today, daughters are usually given these responsibilities as well. In liberal Jewish communities, most families hold ceremonies, at home or in the synagogue, to welcome baby girls into the Covenant of Abraham and Sarah. Growing up, girls study Torah in the same way and to the same extent as boys. Almost all parents today want their daughters to have a trade or profession, as much as they want that for their sons. Given these facts, we can readily add the word "daughter" to the text in our minds as we read it.

What about the additional thought, "Some say: Also to teach him to swim"? That might not seem to fit in with the rest of the parental responsibilities listed here. Rashi postulates that this is a matter of preserving the son's life. At some point he might need to travel by boat, and if the boat went down, his life would be endangered if he could not swim. Rashi's plausible understanding is that the Talmud asks the parent to make sure children can take care of themselves in a variety of situations, including dangerous situations in the water.

Rabbi Yehudah's comment on the responsibility to teach one's son a trade comes as a surprise. Every reader probably begins with the question the Talmud itself asks: Do you really mean that a father who does not make sure his son learns a trade teaches him to steal? After all, as Rashi puts it, the father did not take any positive action; he did not give the child lessons in thievery. He simply refrained from teaching his son a productive way of earning a living.

The Talmud responds to the objection by adding the phrase, "as if." R. Yehudah does not literally accuse the father of teaching his son thievery. However, by not giving his child a means to support himself, he puts the son in a position where he may believe he needs to steal in order to survive.

Most of the examples in the *baraita* still make sense in modern life. Jewish parents can accept the responsibilities of circumcising their newborn sons (though not all Jews in twenty-first-century America are comfortable doing so). Many will perform the ritual of *pidyon ha-ben*, redemption of the firstborn, ritually buying out their baby's obligation to serve as a priest from a *Kohen*. We can restate "teach him Torah" as "provide him and her with a Jewish education." We might reinterpret "teach him a trade" as providing the child with the kind of general education that leads to the ability to earn a living.

Here we might think further about Case Study #1. Daniel's parents could say that they willingly perform all of these mitzvot. They just have a different idea than their son about where he should pursue his college education, which they will finance. This forces us to answer the question: How much control over decisions relating to that responsibility should the parents have? Does it matter that Daniel is closer to being an adult than he was when he started school?

Few today would argue that parents should not make sure that their children can swim. Some of my students extend the idea of swimming to other forms of physical activity as well. Modern parents, they say, should teach their children to live actively, and in that way contribute to their lifelong health. Others interpret the sentence more broadly, saying that parents must make sure children know how to take care of themselves in a variety of situations.

One modern consideration is the absence from this *baraita* — and, notably, from the Torah in general — of the commandment to love. The Torah does not command children to love their parents, or for parents to love their children. The Torah's omission of a commandment to love one's parents or children may come as a surprise when we consider the kinds of love the Torah *does* command. We are instructed to love God (Deut. 6:5), to love our neighbor (Lev. 19:18), and to love the stranger (Deut. 10:19 and elsewhere). Why, then, would the Torah refrain from mentioning love in the primary human relationship?

Perhaps the answer lies in understanding the verb "to love," the Hebrew root a-h-v, as used in the TANAKH. In his explanation of Deuteronomy 6:5, "You shall love YHVH your God with all your heart and with all your soul and with all your might," the Bible scholar Jeffrey Tigay observes that "in ancient Near Eastern political terminology, 'love' refers to the loyalty of subjects, vassals, and allies." As a king's subjects must demonstrate their loyalty through specific actions, so too "Israel's duty to love God is inseparable from action and is regularly connected with the observance of [God's] commandments."[4]

If we say that parents should love their children, we face the same question presented by the verses "Honor your father and mother" and "Each of you shall revere his mother and his father." How, specifically, must parents show love? In a sense, to answer that question we would need to create new versions of the Talmud sections we have been studying. While it's hard to argue against asking parents to love their children, it's also daunting to imagine delineating that request in terms of specific obligations. How many statements of affection, how many kisses and hugs and presents would suffice? The questions multiply, and good answers are few.

Some might argue that parents demonstrate love through the actions we have been discussing in this section. Helping children learn and find their way into adult lives of productive activity and loving partnerships—these acts express love. Perhaps parents best show their love when they teach their children values and prepare them to live on their own and make their own choices.

That idea has extensive implications especially in the case of Sarah, whose mother appears not to love her child, or at a minimum does not allow her daughter to feel loved. Given that the halakhah does not require parental love—at least not in its contemporary sense—Sarah may not be able to use her mother's apparent lack of love for her as a halakhic justification to remove her mother from her life.

The subsequent passage, drawn from a book by the Conservative rabbi Daniel Nevins describing how the Conservative movement in America encourages living life according to halakhah, tries to explain the absence from these texts of a discussion of love. The author quotes Rabbi J. B. Soloveitchik (1903–93), a leading scholar of Orthodoxy in the twentieth century.

Text 12b — Nevins, "Between Parents and Children"

RABBI JOSEPH B. SOLOVEITCHIK . . . distinguishes between the external norms and the internal experience of filial piety. The halakhah, he observes, does not attempt to regulate the emotional side of the parent-child relationship. It rather establishes norms of conduct to ensure that parents attend to the needs of their children, and that children reciprocate when they reach the proper age. Ideally there will be confluence between external devotion and internal love, but the halakhah is realistic in its requirement that children demonstrate reverence and honor for their parents through their behavior, not that they love them. Love can and does flower, however, within the supportive environment of honor and reverence.[5]

QUESTIONS FOR INQUIRY

1. What is the difference between the external norms and the internal experience of children honoring their parents?
2. What does halakhah regulate and not regulate in the parent-child relationship?
3. Why does Rabbi Joseph B. Soloveitchik argue that this aspect of the halakhah is realistic?

COMMENTS

When our society thinks about the parent-child relationship, the first consideration is usually the love parents feel for their children, and the second the love children, in turn, develop for their parents. But the Jewish legal tradition focuses its attention elsewhere. Whether describing what parents owe children or what children owe parents, it lists specific actions and behavioral norms. It never tells us what either parent or child should feel.

Here, Rabbi Soloveitchik distinguishes between the external and the internal. The halakhah prescribes what we must *do*, our visible behaviors toward our parents or children. Halakhah does not prescribe what we must *feel* about what we do, or the people we do it for. Those feelings represent the internal. Only the individual knows how he or she feels. We can do the right thing, while hiding negative feelings we harbor toward the beneficiary of our actions. The halakhah cares only that we do what we should.

Rabbi Nevins teaches that while ideally both parents and children will feel good about fulfilling their obligations to each other, and will do so out of love, the halakhah establishes a framework to ensure that each side has its needs met regardless. We hope that both parents and children will feel truly devoted to each other out of love; but as Jews, we do not wait for the positive feelings before doing the right thing. More optimistically, Nevins suggests that the experience of devotion created by following the rules of halakhah creates an environment conducive to love. In other words, by providing for each other's needs, parents and children may develop feelings of love for each other.

The Torah's definition of love (provided in the comments to Text 12a) supports Soloveitchik's suggestion. What matters to the Torah is not the kind of emotional attachment that we associate with love. The Torah cares about what Jews *do*. When the Torah commands love for God, or one's neighbor, or the stranger, it expects us to act in specific ways: studying God's Torah, treating our neighbor fairly, showing kindness to the person who is not part of our community. Similarly, the Torah wants children and parents to take specific actions for each other. The doing may lead to the feeling, or it may not. In this understanding, the doing *is* the loving.

Thus these texts also recognize that the relationship between parents and children is not always lovingly ideal. We now turn specifically to texts that address parent-child relationships that do not work as intended.

"THE FATHER IS OBLIGATED to his son to circumcise him"—and where his father did not circumcise him, the court is obligated to circumcise him, as it is written [Gen. 17:10], "every male among you shall be circumcised." And where the court did not circumcise him, he is obligated to have himself circumcised, as it is written [Gen. 17:14], "And if any male who is uncircumcised fails to circumcise the flesh of his foreskin, that person shall be cut off." ...

"To redeem him"—and where his father did not redeem him, he is obligated to redeem himself, as it is written [Num. 18:15], "you must be sure to redeem." ...

"And to teach him Torah." And where his father did not teach him, he is obligated to learn on his own, as it is written [Deut. 11:19], "You will learn."

QUESTIONS FOR INQUIRY

1. What problem unites the three examples the Talmud discusses here?
2. What solution does the Talmud propose in each case? What do the solutions have in common?
3. What lessons can we draw from this text about what happens when parents fail to carry out their responsibilities to their children?

COMMENTS

In considering the *baraita* that enumerates what parents owe their children, the Rabbis of the Talmud naturally wonder what happens if parents fail to meet their responsibility. They therefore take up three of the obligations mentioned in the *baraita*: circumcision, redemption of the firstborn, and teaching the child Torah.

Each of these cases lends itself to a simple solution. The child can simply fulfill the obligation later in life. In the case of circumcision, the local court has the first duty to step in if the father (or parents) do not act. But if the son reaches adulthood, he must arrange for his own circumcision. Similarly, an adult son can redeem himself from a *Kohen*, and he can arrange to study Torah.

The obvious conclusion, then, is that if parents neglect their duties to their children, responsibility falls either to the community's representatives, or to the children themselves. That idea works well enough for many situations. If (to take another example mentioned in the *baraita*) my parents do not arrange my marriage, I can find a partner myself.

Yet adult children cannot fix other forms of parental neglect so easily. If (in our terms) the parents fail to arrange an adequate education, the children may not easily find the means to pay for it, which might leave them without a way to earn their living. Even worse, some parents inflict emotional or physical abuse on their children. The next, and last, set of texts in this chapter directly considers the cruel or abusive parent.

Text Study #4: Problems in the Parent-Child Relationship

Text 14 — Shulḥan Arukh, *Yoreh De'ah* 240:18

EVEN IF ONE'S FATHER was wicked and sinful, the son honors him and shows him reverence.

Note: But there are those who say one is not obligated to honor a wicked father, unless he has repented.

QUESTIONS FOR INQUIRY

1. What limit to the commandments to honor and revere parents does the Shulḥan Arukh suggest?
2. How does Rabbi Moshe Isserles, who added Ashkenazic practice to the halakhah in the Shulḥan Arukh, disagree with Rabbi Yosef Karo, the author of the Shulḥan Arukh?
3. What implications does this halakhah have for Sarah, the daughter of an abusive mother in Case Study #3?

Interestingly, when considering what halakhah requires of a child whose parent is unworthy, the two authorities whose work appears in the Shulḥan Arukh disagree. Karo baldly states that the child owes even a wicked and sinful father both honor and reverence. Isserles notes that at least some authorities do not require honoring and revering a wicked parent. If the parent has repented, then the child's obligation resumes. But just as we saw that the child need not follow a parent's command to violate the Torah, the child need not honor and revere a parent who consistently flouts the Torah.

One way to analyze Sarah's situation would be to look at whether or not her mother repented for the ways she wronged her daughter. While Karo would expect Sarah to show her honor regardless, Isserles would put the onus on the mother. In this view, she deserves honor and reverence only if she repents her sins. That would require at a minimum asking Sarah's forgiveness and resolving never to repeat those actions.

In the next selection, the contemporary scholar Mark Dratch, an Orthodox rabbi who has drawn the Jewish community's attention to issues of domestic violence, argues that this opinion releasing the child from the commandments toward a wicked parent helps us decide the child's responsibilities if the parent abuses the child.

Text 15 — Dratch, "Honoring Abusive Parents"

WHILE MANY ACTS OF honor make demands on a child's time, emotions, and energies, the emotional and psychological burdens imposed on an abused child in order to honor an abusive parent far surpass any appropriate . . . filial responsibility. In addition, children are not obligated to honor parents when the expressions of that honor support sinful acts.

Those who violate any Torah prohibition that qualifies them for [punishment by] lashes are in the category of *rasha* ["wicked person"], and thus a parent who abuses a child is considered a *rasha*. . . . The sexual violation of one's children is a severe violation of biblical and rabbinic law. . . . The physical abuse of children is prohibited. . . . Emotional abuse . . . is prohibited by the verse, "You shall not wrong one another; but you shall fear your God; for I am the Lord your God" (Lev. 25:17). . . . Child neglect, another form of abuse by which parents ignore the basic needs of food, clothing, shelter, and protection of their children, is also prohibited. Parents have an obligation to support their children.[6]

QUESTIONS FOR INQUIRY

1. Which authority in the Shulḥan Arukh does Rabbi Dratch follow?
2. What logic does Rabbi Dratch use to support his argument that children need not honor a parent who abuses them or neglects them?
3. Does this argument lead to a convincing resolution of Sarah's dilemma?

COMMENTS

In this article, Rabbi Dratch upholds the approach of R. Moshe Isserles: the child need not honor or revere a parent who so terribly violates the Torah's norms and values. He argues that any child abuse—physical, sexual, or emotional—places the abuser in the halakhic category of *rasha*, the wicked person who is not owed any honor or reverence. Referring to the Talmud's enumeration of parental responsibilities to children (Text 12a), he reminds us that "parents have an obligation to support their children." Those who neglect that duty forfeit the right to their children's honor and reverence.

Rabbi Dratch shows special sensitivity to the emotional impact the halakhah may have on the child, and helps us to see that the halakhic tradition has enough flexibility to deal with significant challenges to its ideals. Declaring that "the emotional and psychological burdens imposed on an abused child in order to honor an abusive parent far surpass any appropriate . . . filial responsibility," he then shows that halakhic terms can be defined in ways that release an abused child from the mitzvot of honor and reverence for the abusive parent. In short, asking a child to honor such a parent is asking too much. Therefore, parents who abuse their children lose the privilege of receiving their children's honor and reverence.

If Rabbi Dratch is correct, Sarah has a strong argument that her mother forfeited her right to her daughter's honor and reverence. Sarah may properly end contact with her mother.

Our next text addresses a contemporary need. We have seen the Rabbinic and medieval sources focus on questions about when a child must support a parent—usually when the parent has become impoverished in old age (see Text 8a); in our times, the converse issue may arise about parents' financial support of their adult children. Economic forces require many adult children to accept continuing financial help from their parents well past the stage of life when they are expected to become independent. Tensions can arise when parents feel that the financial support they continue to willingly provide allows them to continue to dictate their children's behavior. Grown children naturally chafe against what they experience as parental interference in their lives. They feel caught between their need for help and the desire for their parents to finally treat them as adults.

This issue surfaced when a couple approached the Reform movement's Responsa Committee asking for an outline of their responsibilities to their parents after they married. Following a review of some of the sources we have studied and the early modern responsa literature, Rabbi Walter Jacob, for many years chair of the Responsa Committee, reaches the conclusion excerpted here.

Text 16a—Jacob, "Responsibility of Children to Their Parents"

EVERYTHING WAS DONE [IN halakhah] to balance the interest of the older and younger generations. Normative Judaism encouraged freedom for the younger generation. The children remained responsible for the maintenance of their parents and were to look after their physical and psychological needs, but the children were not to be subjected to every whim and desire of the older generation. Through this, the full personal development of the younger generation was constantly encouraged.[7]

1. What questions does Rabbi Jacob respond to?
2. What does his answer tell us about adult children's responsibilities to their parents?
3. How realistic do you find his response?

COMMENTS

Rabbi Jacob argues that while the younger generation retains responsibility for the parents' physical welfare, they need not accede to every demand their elders make. Showing parents honor and reverence does not mean relinquishing one's right to make decisions as an adult.

While this responsum reaches a conclusion that respects the needs of the older and younger generations alike, it provides only a general guideline. When conflicts arise, Rabbi Jacob leaves it to readers to determine how best to balance parents' needs for a say in their children's lives and children's needs for "full personal development."

In the next excerpt, taken from *The Observant Life* (2012), a volume of essays describing the Conservative movement's ideals for living a Jewish life, Rabbi Daniel Nevins addresses the difficulties parents encounter in balancing respect for their children's independence with the desire to express their point of view about how the child lives.

Text 16b—Nevins, "Between Parents and Children"

JEWISH LAW DOES NOT obligate parents to provide ongoing material support for the education, housing, food, or entertainment of healthy adult children. One important lesson that a parent must teach his or her children is independence. . . .

Parents may be uncomfortable with lifestyle decisions made by their children. Parents may not be satisfied with a child's profession, marriage plans, parenting techniques, religious practices, healthcare decisions, or sexual proclivities. Significantly harder to delineate, however, is the precise boundary between loving concern and counterproductive nagging, between constructive criticism and devastating censure.

Parents must therefore exercise diplomacy when criticizing adult children. To ignore vulgar behavior or tragically misguided decisions is not allowed—we must seek to strengthen and improve the lives of our loved ones. . . . Yet there is a point of diminishing returns at which a parent's criticism may not benefit the child, but will rather deepen the estrangement between the generations. . . . The Torah's path of criticizing lovingly and effectively is perhaps the trickiest challenge of parenting adult children.[8]

QUESTIONS FOR INQUIRY

1. How is the Conservative approach described here similar to that of the Reform responsum we studied in Text 16a?
2. How realistic do you find the standards proposed here?

COMMENTS

Rabbi Nevins wisely suggests that parents seek a middle way between interfering in their adult children's lives and keeping silent. He points out that any criticism must be expressed in a way that makes it clear it is said out of love. Often parents are unlikely to find a way to express their disapproval without harming their relationship with the child. In these cases, they should refrain from expressing their thoughts.

On the other hand, parents need not abandon their role of guiding their children—even when the children are themselves mature adults. As with any other person we care about, parents have a duty to speak up when they see their children going seriously astray. Then they must call on all the tact and diplomacy they can muster in speaking to their children. Such conversations are never easy. If parents practiced the art of caring criticism as their children grew up, it may be possible for them to strike the right balance. If so, adult children will be able to hear and consider their parents' point of view, whether they agree with it or not.

Conclusion

The material in this chapter shows that Judaism expresses an idealistic view of the parent-child relationship. While parents must provide for their children in certain ways, children bear greater responsibility. Carrying out the twin commandments of honor and reverence for parents imposes both emotional and financial burdens: children must display reverence for parents regardless of their own feelings at any given moment, and they must pay to support their parents if the need arises. While the hope is that love will motivate both parents and children to carry out their duties toward each other, the halakhah focuses on deeds, not feelings. Generally, we must do what is expected of us regardless of our desires.

From one point of view, that might be all we need to know to resolve the case study about Daniel's dispute with his parents over his college decision. Nothing indicates that Daniel's parents have done anything to put them in the legal category of *rasha*, of Jews too evil to deserve their children's honor. Perhaps his duty of reverence, combined with the fact that he remains in the stage of life where his parents support him financially, obligates Daniel to do what they want. He may respectfully explain his preference. He might try the *Mishneh Torah*'s approach for correcting a parent's error by asking them questions about what they value when they think about his going to college. In the end, though, this analysis suggests that if his parents insist, Daniel must concede.

Some might consider Daniel's parents' actions an excessive display of parental authority. We saw in the *Mishneh Torah* (Text 9d) that a parent may not attempt to control an adult child in the same manner as a younger child. Those who believe Daniel has the right to make such an important decision about his future for himself will consider his parents' response overbearing. If Rabbi Jacob (Text 16a) is correct, Daniel's "full personal development" plausibly requires him to attend the best possible college, despite his parents' opposition. Daniel might also argue, based on *Kiddushin* (Text 12a), that allowing him to pursue the education he desires is part of his parents' responsibility to "teach him a trade"—to prepare him to support himself in adulthood. As a counterargument, Daniel's parents might invoke *Kiddushin* (Text 6) and the Shulḥan Arukh (Text 7a) to support the idea that he may not contradict their opinion.

In the situation Susan and Bill face, this chapter's text study demonstrates that while children of declining elderly parents need not bankrupt themselves, they must fulfill the commandment of reverence by providing or arranging for their parents' necessary care. Different voices in the tradition advocate for different choices. The Shulḥan Arukh (Text 8a) codifies children's responsibility to care for an elderly parent at the child's expense if the parent has no funds. It adds that such financial support need not come at the expense of the children's ability to earn a living. The *Mishneh Torah* (Text 8b) rules that if caring for ill or demented parents becomes too burdensome, children may entrust their care to others. Rabbi Golinkin (Text 8c) recommends that even those who hire others to care for their parents arrange for the parents to live in the children's home. Since Susan's father already lives in Susan and Bill's home, they could readily adopt Golinkin's suggestion to hire trained caregivers for her father.

As for Sarah, we saw that some parts of the tradition assume that children owe all parents honor and reverence, regardless of circumstances, whereas others suggest that a parent who habitually violates Jewish ethical standards loses the right to those marks of respect. Here, children's choices concerning how to treat their parents depend on their understanding of what makes someone a *rasha*, a wicked person who loses customary status. The Shulḥan Arukh (Text 14) illustrates a difference of opinion among medieval thinkers. R. Karo, the Sephardic authority, insists that parents never lose their right to the honor the Torah commands. That implies that Sarah must reestablish contact with her mother and do for her what tradition requires. For R. Isserles, the Ashkenazic authority, children do not owe these duties to parents who consistently violate the Torah. Rabbi Dratch, the contemporary writer in Text 15, states definitively that a parent like Sarah's mother falls into this latter halakhic category of someone who is not owed honor or reverence. Sarah would ideally consider each of these points of view in making her decision.

Admittedly, having the halakhic tradition speak to modern parent-child relations can be challenging because of the enormous differences in social attitudes between our time and those that formed the tradition. Most contemporary Jews no longer live based on the assumption that Jewish tradition imposes duties on them regardless of their personal feelings. Without that willingness to carry out our duty, we find ourselves more likely to question what we owe our parents, or whether as parents we really must do everything the halakhah prescribes for our children.

Still, the traditional rules express fundamental values that can guide us through the ordinary challenges of family life. In moments of conflict, we can reflect on how best to live based on these ideals. Parents want to teach their children values, while giving them room to grow independently. Children want to show their parents respect, while leading the lives they choose. With mutual goodwill, Jewish ethics show us a path toward those goals.

2

Honesty

In this time of high-pressure competition for college admissions, students face the temptation of doing anything it takes to earn the highest possible grades. When workloads overwhelm the time available for studying (and even for sleeping), students avail themselves of various shortcuts. While schools teach the fundamentals of academic integrity and the consequences of violating it, students sometimes excuse these as victimless crimes, arguing that by not learning the material or doing the work, they hurt only themselves. Other students may not like seeing their classmates act dishonestly, but they convince themselves that the issue is between the cheater and the teacher. They do not get involved.

The adult world, too, fails to model honest behavior. Corporate misconduct regularly makes headlines. Political figures lie and engage in corruption ranging from favoring donors to accepting bribes. Private individuals are not immune. Many who think of themselves as law-abiding cheat on their taxes in what they consider minor ways. In 2019 federal authorities charged a group of wealthy parents with paying bribes and falsifying applications to gain their children admission to prestigious universities. Numerous public figures have been caught making false claims on their resumes and plagiarizing work to earn advanced degrees — adult versions of cheating in school.

All of these activities call upon us to make core ethical judgments. Indeed, in different forms at various stages of our lives, each of us confronts questions of how honest to be. Does the duty to tell the truth have any limits? Are there situations that justify withholding part of the truth? May we ever push the boundaries of the rules?

This chapter explores traditional and modern texts that confront these dilemmas in academic settings and other areas of life.

Case Study #1: Cheating on an Exam

Sydney chose an ambitious course load for her junior year at a college preparatory high school. At the time it seemed doable: after all, she had worked hard in her sophomore year and earned good grades. How was she to know that her eleventh-grade classes, including several Advanced Placement courses, would demand so much more of her? Now, many days, after classes and athletic practice or a game, she finds herself finishing dinner after 8:00 pm, with hours of homework ahead.

Late one night in December, Sydney drops her head to the desk. She hasn't slept more than four hours any night this week. Even if she can stay awake, how can she complete a lab report and an essay and study for a math test by morning?

At this moment, she decides to try something she's never done before. She records formulas into the programmable calculator permitted during her exam. Sydney knows that if the teacher passes near her desk, she can easily clear the screen or punch keys to hide what she's doing. Just before sleep overwhelms her, she dismisses a guilty feeling with the thought that this is the only way to maintain high grades and get into her first-choice college.

The next day, Sydney uses her calculator to cheat on the math test. Her classmate Eitan, seated to her right, notices and inwardly groans. He knows the school's honor code requires him to report any cheating or dishonesty he witnesses, but he hates the thought of having to "snitch." At the same time, he resents Sydney for taking an unfair advantage. She wasn't up all night studying for this exam, he surmises, whereas he stayed up until 2:00 a.m. to learn the material.

Is Sydney justified in doing what she did? Should Eitan report her?

Case Study #2: Potential Plagiarism

Penn State University asks incoming students to evaluate several scenarios to help them understand the university's academic integrity rules. Here is one scenario:

"Jennifer really enjoys the art history class she is taking this semester. She spends a lot of time on her final project—[she selects] a portfolio of works of art . . . , writes a brief background about the artist, and then describes what she feels about the piece. She is careful to make sure all her information about the artists is correct, and reads several essays on the artists she has chosen. She agrees with most of what the essayists have to say regarding the pieces. She represents some of their thoughts in her project as her own, reasoning that since it is not fact, and instead intangible opinion, and because she agrees with them, then she is not plagiarizing."[1]

Has Jennifer violated the principles of academic integrity?

Case Study #3: Withholding Part of the Truth from a Prospective Employer

Jennifer's professor from Case Study #2 realizes what she has done and reports her to the university's academic integrity board. The board rules that Jennifer did, in fact, plagiarize and suspends her for one semester.

As her suspension begins, Jennifer becomes ill. She recovers in time to return to school the subsequent semester. When she looks for a job after graduation, some employers ask why she took an extra term to graduate. Jennifer explains that illness prevented her from attending college that semester.

Is Jennifer at fault for lying?

These cases raise complex questions about honesty. While we learn in childhood to always tell the truth, in adulthood we come to realize that sometimes the whole truth does more harm than good.

In today's world, the seemingly simple question of who owns intellectual material is complicated. Anyone can find enormous amounts of material on the web with just a few clicks. Whereas a printed book presumably represents the work of the author named on the cover and is clearly protected by copyright, the writing one finds on the internet can appear ownerless. While such work, too, belongs to its author, slogans like "information wants to be free" justify in the minds of many readers using anything they find without payment or attribution.

Interestingly, while the Torah commands us to avoid falsehood, traditional sources confronted many of the same ambiguities we do. As we explore the development of halakhah related to this chapter's case studies, we will see how legal authorities struggled to protect owners of intangible property like words and ideas.

We begin text study with three Torah verses that establish the Jewish value of truthfulness (Texts 1a, 1b, and 1c) and then a commentary by R. Yaakov Tzvi Mecklenburg, a traditionalist German rabbi of the nineteenth century (Text 1d).

Text Study #1: Truth Telling and Its Limits

Text 1a — Exod. 20:13

YOU SHALL NOT BEAR false witness against your neighbor.

Text 1b — Exod. 23:7

KEEP FAR FROM A false charge; do not bring death on those who are innocent and in the right, for I will not acquit the wrongdoer.

Text 1c — Lev. 19:11

YOU SHALL NOT STEAL; you shall not deal deceitfully or falsely with one another.

Text 1d — Mecklenburg, *HaKetav VeHaKabbalah* on Exod. 23:7

"KEEP FAR FROM A false charge [literally, a false matter]"—The Torah phrased this in an unusual manner, not saying "Do not tell a falsehood," because there is no more commonly found sin than lying. . . . Therefore this verse comes to create even greater distance, telling us to keep away from ugliness and anything resembling it.

1. Text 1a: What is the context of the verse? Beyond that context, what does the commandment mean?
2. Text 1b: What is the context of the verse? Beyond that context, what does the commandment mean?
3. What does Text 1c add to our understanding of Exodus 23:7?
4. What problem in Exodus 23:7 does R. Mecklenburg notice in his commentary? How does he solve it?
5. Based on these texts, what can we conclude about the importance of telling the truth in Judaism?

COMMENTS

Truth telling matters enough that it is one of the Ten Commandments all Israel heard (the Torah reports) in the divine voice at Mt. Sinai. The verse's context is the courtroom; it warns against false testimony. However, it supports the larger emphasis Judaism places on truth telling in all situations. "False witness" metaphorically represents any untrue or misleading statement.

Chapter 23 of Exodus also speaks to people involved in a court case. It warns against bringing false charges or making false claims. God will not absolve anyone who wrongs another in this way.

As commonly happens in traditional Torah interpretation, many later readers took the word *davar*—here translated as "charge"—in its more general sense of "matter." They read the verse as warning us to keep our distance from any "false matter." Together with Leviticus 19:11, which tells us not to "deal deceitfully or falsely" with one another, the verse in Exodus teaches a larger lesson. We are to live in such a way that we keep our distance from anything false—not only in bringing cases before a court, but in all our interactions with other people. Truth must form the basis of all our relationships.

A simple understanding of this commandment would instruct us to tell the truth and not to lie. Writing in the nineteenth century, Rabbi Yaakov Tzvi Mecklenburg noted that the Torah does not take the straightforward approach of commanding, "Do not tell a lie." He noticed that the verse instead says, "Keep far from a false matter." Mecklenburg suggests a psychological explanation of this word choice. Nothing is more common, after all, than lying. Everyone lies. The Torah must go one step further than forbidding lying. It stresses the harmfulness of lying by ordering us to keep our distance from anything that even resembles it. (Later in the chapter, we will explore the possibility that this commandment has limits: not every situation demands the whole truth and nothing but the truth.)

These brief texts open a window on what Jewish ethics contributes to our case studies. We can easily define cheating on an exam as a "false matter." In Case Study #1, Sydney allows the teacher to think her test demonstrates her understanding of the material—a misrepresentation of the truth. She deceives the teacher, violating both Torah verses. R. Mecklenburg would agree that she failed to distance herself from unseemly behavior.

Case Studies #2 and #3 require subtler analysis, as neither presents a straightforward lie. In Case Study #2, only if we decide Jennifer's actions amounted to plagiarism has she violated the edicts in these texts by misrepresenting someone else's work as her own. In Case Study #3, Jennifer has told part of the truth to a prospective employer—the part of the truth that presents her in the best possible light. That, after all, is what every job candidate strives to do. Jennifer likely believes that her single violation of the university's academic rules—an arguable violation at that—would not affect her future employer or her ability to do a good job for the company.

Both Sydney and Jennifer propose justifications for their falsehoods. We must consider the possibility that some such arguments are valid, meaning that we may ethically lie under certain circumstances.

To determine whether these scenarios violate R. Mecklenburg's admonition to remove ourselves from anything even resembling falsehood requires us to explore the boundaries of the rules established in Texts 1a–1c. To begin, we study a famous debate in the Talmud about the tension between truth and people's feelings.

Text 2—*Ketubot* 16b–17a

OUR RABBIS TAUGHT: HOW do we dance before a bride?
The school of Shammai say: The bride as she is.
The school of Hillel say: A beautiful and graceful bride.

The school of Shammai said to the school of Hillel: Suppose she was lame or blind, do we say about her, "a beautiful and graceful bride"? But the Torah said, "Keep far from a false matter"!

The school of Hillel said to the school of Shammai: According to your idea, if someone made a bad purchase in the market, should we praise it to him or condemn it? You must say that we praise it to him.

Based on this, the Sages said: A person should always be empathetic with people's feelings.

QUESTIONS FOR INQUIRY

1. Offer a reason to support the school of Shammai's argument.
2. Offer a reason to support the school of Hillel's argument.
3. What general principle does the Talmud derive from the debate between the two schools?
4. What does this debate add to our understanding of truth telling?

COMMENTS

This text records the Talmud's classic debate over the role of the white lie. The schools of Shammai and Hillel, a renowned pair of leaders from the early Tannaitic period, generally take opposite sides on every halakhic question. Here they dispute how to fulfill the commandment to bring joy to a bride and groom at a wedding. When dancing in front of a bride, how should we sing her praises? The school of Shammai proposes literal truth telling: describe the bride exactly as she is. The school of Hillel argues that we are to praise every bride as beautiful and graceful.

What exactly does the school of Shammai have in mind? Is Shammai saying that as wedding guests, we should explicitly tell the bride she is unattractive? Possibly "describe the bride exactly as she is" means that we are to praise her good qualities without mentioning the beauty or grace she lacks. It could also mean that if the bride really has few pleasing qualities, we are to say little in order to keep away from falsehood.

The school of Hillel does not consider the wedding party a time for worrying about the literal truth. As the saying goes, every bride is beautiful.

At the least, she is beautiful to her husband. Therefore, we can justifiably sing about her beauty and gracefulness.

The ensuing dialogue, in which each side critiques the other's approach, adds to our understanding of the lessons about truths and lies. The school of Shammai stresses that we cannot tell categorical falsehoods. A lame bride, in their eyes, cannot be described as graceful. That violates the rule laid down in Exodus 23:7. The school of Hillel responds with a rhetorical question. Consider the common situation in which a friend asks you to admire a new purchase that he's proud of. It's obvious to you that he made a bad bargain, but it's a done deal. What do you do? Surely, the Hillel side argues, you would praise the item and reassure the friend. The empathetic approach is to resort to the small lie.

The final remark ("Based on this, the Sages said: A person should always be empathetic with people's feelings") shows that the Rabbinic tradition prefers the school of Hillel's approach to the situation. We are to prioritize the kindness of sparing people's feelings — on their wedding day, when they are proud of their purchase — over the rigor of sticking to the absolute truth. Maintaining relationships takes priority over the whole truth. The Talmud's conclusion adds nuance to our understanding of the mitzvah to avoid false matters. By way of the school of Hillel, it teaches us to consider the feelings of those affected by what we say.

We need not conclude that the school of Shammai advocates truth at the expense of all relationships. They may propose only that the Rabbis not make a general decree that could mislead people into straying from the Torah's admonition to avoid falsehood. The exception must not become the rule.

The debate about the bride demonstrates that the halakhic tradition recognizes exceptions to the rule that Jews must stick to the truth. The next set of three Talmud excerpts identifies several other exceptions.

Text 3a — *Yevamot* 65b

R. ILAI SAID IN the name of R. Elazar son of R. Shimon: A person is permitted to deviate from the truth in the interest of peace, as it is said [Gen. 50:16–17], "Your father left this instruction: So shall you say to Joseph, 'Forgive, I urge you, the offense and guilt of your brothers'." . . .

They taught in the School of R. Ishmael: Great is peace, for even the Holy One changed the truth for its sake. For at first it is written, [Gen. 18:12], "with my husband so old?" But at the end [Gen. 18: 13], "Then YHVH said to Abraham, 'Why did Sarah laugh, saying, 'Shall I in truth bear a child, old as I am?'"

Text 3b — *Bava Metzia 23b–24a*

FOR RAV YEHUDA SAID that Shmuel said: In these three matters, the Rabbis' practice is to change the truth: in regard to a tractate, a bed, and hospitality.

Text 3c — *Mishnah Nedarim 3:4*

ONE IS PERMITTED TO make a vow to murderers, plunderers, and tax collectors that the produce they wish to seize is *terumah* [permitted only to priests], even though it is not *terumah*; or that the property they wish to seize belongs to the royal house, even though it does not belong to the royal house.

QUESTIONS FOR INQUIRY

1. Read chapters 18 and 50 of Genesis for background on Text 3a. How do the verses show that one may bend the truth? For what reasons?
2. Text 3b names three topics on which a rabbi may say something different than the truth. What are they, and why may the rabbi avoid the truth in each case?
3. Text 3c permits a Jew to take certain false vows. Why does the Mishnah allow these falsehoods?
4. What principles can we derive from these sources about when we may deceive others?

5. In what ways do you find these rules helpful? Might following them cause unintended problems?

The passage from *Yevamot* (Text 3a) uses two stories about familiar biblical characters to derive an important exception to the requirement of truth telling. First, it cites Joseph's brothers' fear: Now that their father Jacob has died, what if Joseph exacts revenge for the way they mistreated him in childhood? The brothers invent a deathbed instruction from Jacob, hoping Joseph will believe their fiction and refrain from harming them; in response Joseph cries and reassures them that he harbors no hidden resentment against them. The Talmud's understanding is that the brothers did right in telling Joseph something that did not happen, because they did it to keep peace within their family.

The teaching from R. Ishmael daringly claims that even God lies to make peace. Here the context is Sarah's reaction to the announcement that in her tenth decade, she will give birth to a long-awaited son with Abraham. She laughs, wondering how she can conceive so late in life, and notes that her husband, too, is old to father a child. Speaking to Abraham about Sarah's skepticism, God changes the phrase "with my husband so old." Imagine the conversation between husband and wife if Abraham heard about that! To spare Abraham's feelings, and to promote marital harmony, God reports instead that Sarah said, "old as *I* am."

These examples from the Torah's narrative establish that one may change the truth to preserve peace. In this they add something important to the exception we saw in Text 2. *Ketubot* 16b–17a showed that we may resort to white lies to maintain smooth relations when we interact directly with someone. From the stories of Joseph and his brothers as well as of Sarah, God, and Abraham, we learn that we may also prevaricate to keep the peace for others, such as siblings and marital partners. Preserving these important relationships sometimes matters more than the truth.

Text 3b refers specifically to rabbis, but its ideas have wider application. First, one may lie about a "tractate." When rabbis are asked whether they know a certain volume of the Talmud well, they may say no even if they have studied it. Such a lie can be viewed as a matter of modesty:

one should not brag about one's accomplishments. Better to pretend to less knowledge than one has. The second permissible lie is about a bed. Several commentaries take this to mean that one should lie for the sake of modesty. If asked whether one has "used the bed," a rabbinic euphemism for sexual intercourse, one should lie and say no even if one did. The third permitted lie concerns responding to a query regarding the generosity of hosts who have welcomed you as an overnight guest in their home. The commentaries advise downplaying the hosts' generosity, explaining that the lie is for the good of the host. If you say that they welcomed you and fed you generously, other guests might overwhelm their ability to extend hospitality.

Each of the three examples in Text 3c describes an interaction with an immoral person: someone who kills, someone who plunders, and a tax collector. Most commentaries agree that in this scenario the tax collector is someone who pays the government a fee for the right to collect taxes and then imposes unreasonable taxes on the public. (The Roman authorities regularly auctioned off the right to collect taxes to ease the difficulty of collections in their far-flung provinces, including Judea.) Thus in situations where the individual faces a significant financial loss and a lie is likely to protect one's resources, the Mishnah determines that the lie is morally acceptable.

To summarize, Rabbinic law provides several exceptions to the rule of keeping away from falsehood. These include: (1) to spare someone's feelings, (2) to preserve peace, especially within the family, (3) for the sake of modesty about one's accomplishments, (4) for personal privacy, (5) to spare someone who has shown kindness in hospitality from being unduly burdened by it, and (6) to save one's property from immoral people.

These exceptions complicate our moral analysis of our case studies as well as our own everyday choices. Lying for purposes of modesty (or, more specifically, of avoiding the appearance of arrogance), exception 3 above, seems inappropriate in other contexts, such as a job interview. Modestly pretending to less accomplishment than we have—"I don't know that tractate"—rarely leads to a job offer.

While Jennifer in Case Study #3 cannot use this idea to validate the partial truth she told the interviewer (it did not concern her qualifications for the job), we might wonder if she can justify her actions based on *Mishnah Nedarim* (Text 3c). Perhaps Jennifer protects her financial interests through the small lie she tells. If withholding the fact of her suspension from college helps her get a job, might that be a legitimate way to ensure she has an income?

Despite the partial analogy, the careful reader will notice that the Mishnah does not create a general rule that we may always lie to improve our finances. It speaks only of protecting our resources from those who would commandeer them. An employer who chooses to hire someone else does not meet this description.

We now turn our attention to a set of texts that inform an ethical analysis of how to respond when we see wrongdoing. The first source, the Tosefta, defines a category of deceit that halakhah warns us to avoid via the example of Absalom, the eldest son of King David. Absalom's attempts to usurp the throne in David's lifetime set off a civil war that had lasting consequences for the king and his family. (See 2 Sam. 12–19 for details.)

Text Study #2: Whistleblowing and Rebuke

Text 4 — *Tosefta Bava Kama* 7:3

THERE ARE SEVEN CATEGORIES of thieves. First among them is one who steals other people's minds. . . . For anyone who steals other people's minds is called a thief, as it is written [2 Samuel 15:6], "Thus Absalom won away [literally, stole] the hearts of the men of Israel."

QUESTIONS FOR INQUIRY
1. In what sense is deceit a form of "theft"?
2. What might this law tell us about cheating on schoolwork?

COMMENTS
This Tosefta excerpt defines the sin known in Rabbinic law as *geneivat da'at*, "stealing someone's mind." In this form of deceit, people use

information they have to take advantage of those they know are less informed. The theft involves depriving those who are ill informed of the option of acting with complete information. As when stock traders use inside information for financial gain, *geneivat da'at* involves taking unfair advantage of other people.

By cheating on her math test, Sydney in Case Study #1 commits *geneivat da'at*. She "steals" her teacher's mind in the sense that she allows her teacher to think that her score represents her understanding of the material; instead, of course, it represents her abilities to record the necessary formulas and hide the fact that she referred to them during the test. Cheating on the test also blatantly violates the verse, "Keep far from a false matter" (Exod. 23:7). While we may sympathize with the pressures that led to Sydney's decision, the Jewish ethical tradition does not defend cheating.

What, then, are the responsibilities of other students who know about the deception? As in our first case study, school honor codes often require students to report violations, but many students hesitate to report on their peers. We turn next to halakhic sources that shed light on the issue of reporting wrongdoing to authorities.

Before we begin, know that, generally speaking, talking about what other people do violates the broad category of halakhah called *lashon ha-ra*, "evil speech." (We will study these laws in more detail in chapter 3.) In general, Jews are not supposed to tell a third person what a friend or classmate did. Thus, thinking about Eitan's responsibilities in Case Study #1 requires looking at some exceptions to that rule. We begin with a *teshuvah* written for the Committee on Jewish Law and Standards of the Conservative Movement. The author, Rabbi Barry Leff, refers to rules established in a famous compilation of the halakhah of speech from the early twentieth century called *Chofetz Chaim*.

Text 5a—Leff, "Whistleblowing"

CHOFETZ CHAIM . . . [STATES] THAT if someone sees someone doing something wicked to another . . . it is permissible to tell people to help those who have been transgressed against. He goes on to list . . . conditions that should be met. . . .

1. It should be something he saw himself, not based on hearsay;
2. He should reflect carefully that he is certain the behavior he saw met the requirements of being considered theft or damage;
3. He should first gently rebuke the wrongdoer;
4. Don't exaggerate;
5. He should be clear about his motives— . . . to benefit the one who was sinned against, and that the one who is reporting the matter is not going to benefit . . . , or that he is doing it because he hates the transgressor.[2]

QUESTIONS FOR INQUIRY

1. How do you understand each of the rules for reporting wrongdoing?
2. Which of them would you keep on the list? Which would you remove? What rules that do not appear would you add?
3. What do these *halakhot* tell us about Eitan's obligations in the case study?

COMMENTS

While his *teshuvah* concerns whistleblowing, reporting wrongdoing by an employer, Rabbi Leff provides a helpful summary of the halakhah governing informing someone about harm a third party did to them. A student reporting an honor code violation fits into this category. Academic dishonesty harms the teacher, as we have seen, and also harms other members of the school community, including other students taking the same assessment. Considering this list of requirements helps us think about Eitan's choices.

Halakhah does not accept hearsay evidence, a witness reporting what someone else said. One may only testify about what one personally saw or heard. The rule protects the accused from false testimony by people who might wish them harm. As such, in our situation, Eitan may tell the teacher what he saw Sydney do, but if Eitan told another friend about it, that third party would have no right to share the information with the teacher.

The second rule, along with the fifth, asks that people who want to disclose someone else's misbehavior begin with a careful examination of their own motives. Students should share the information only out of a desire to uphold the honor code and maintain a community based on fairness and honesty. Any improper motive, such as personal hostility, should give one pause.

The fourth rule on the list limits embellishments to the story. In reporting on a third party, one must recount only what happened.

If all of those conditions are met, we still confront the third requirement on the list. The *Chofetz Chaim* suggests that the witness may not report wrongdoing to the person harmed or to the authorities before "gently rebuking" the wrongdoer.

He has in mind a commandment in Leviticus known as *tochecha*, rebuke. Let us now study that Torah verse that commands rebuke (Text 5b), as well as the Rambam's halakhic expansion of this law (Text 5c).

Text 5b — Lev. 19:17

YOU SHALL NOT HATE your kinsfolk in your heart. Reprove your kin but incur no guilt on their account.

Text 5c — *Mishneh Torah*, Laws of Personal Qualities 6:7

IT IS A MITZVAH when one sees his fellow sinning or following a bad path to return him to what is right and let him know that he harms himself with his evil deeds, as it is said, "Reprove your kin" [Lev. 19:17]. One who rebukes his fellow . . . must rebuke him privately and speak to him kindly and gently.

---

1. How many mitzvot does Leviticus 19:17 contain?
2. Who must we rebuke? Why?
3. According to Text 5c, what purpose does the commandment of rebuke serve?
4. How should we act when giving rebuke?
5. Why does the *Mishneh Torah* emphasize these aspects of giving rebuke?
6. What do these sources add to thinking about Case Study #1?

COMMENTS

The verse from Leviticus presents the commandment to rebuke others, meaning to let them know when they do wrong. Commentators differ over the purpose of the introductory phrase that exhorts us not to hate others in our heart. Some consider it a commandment in its own right. Others think it provides the rationale for the mitzvah to rebuke: tell the other person what offense they committed so that you will not end up hating them for an offense they are not aware of. Interpretations of "kin" and "kinsfolk" (in Hebrew two different words, *ahikha* "your brother" and *amitekha* "your fellow") also vary. Some argue we must rebuke only those who are close to us. Others, including the author of the *Mishneh Torah*, extend the obligation to rebuke to everyone with whom we interact, especially our fellow Jews.

The ambiguity of the last clause in Leviticus 19:17, "but incur no guilt on their account," gives rise to an important rule the *Mishneh Torah* establishes here and that Text 5a repeats in a different context. These laws understand the caution not to incur guilt as meaning that the person fulfilling the command to rebuke can violate other values by not delivering the rebuke correctly. Rebuke must be given in private to avoid embarrassing the guilty party in front of other people. It must also be expressed as gently as possible. Giving in to one's anger might also lead to embarrassment. It almost guarantees the failure of the rebuke, since the recipient will more than likely respond defensively to the anger instead of to the content of the reproof.

These texts provide the background to the *Chofetz Chaim*'s ruling that a person who wishes to report another's misdeed to the person harmed must first rebuke the wrongdoer directly. We can readily grasp the motivation for this halakhah. A kind reproof might lead the person to confess and try to make amends. That would effectively restore the damaged relationship.

In Case Study #1, Eitan's responsibility under the school honor code complicates the analysis. Honor codes typically require reporting violations to an appropriate authority. Speaking directly to Sydney may protect Eitan's personal relationship with her and assuage his guilt over reporting a fellow student to school authorities, but it does not fulfill his obligations under the school's code and will not set matters right with their teacher and the school administration. Only if Eitan's gentle rebuke motivates Sydney to confess to the math teacher might he fulfill his responsibility in this way.

We have no reason to think Eitan would report Sydney out of any improper dislike for her. He would not benefit directly from getting her in trouble. Possibly his grade will improve if the teacher constructed a curve including Sydney's inflated result, but that is not clear, and everyone else in the class will receive the same benefit. Since there is no question that the behavior Eitan saw violated the honor code, he can legitimately report what Sydney did. Doing so fulfills both his obligations under school rules and his ethical obligations.

The main impediment to Eitan's acting as these sources suggest he should is his general reluctance to be a student who reports another to the teacher. Children in our society absorb that social norm from an early age. For better or worse, this attitude persists into adulthood; adults, too, resist causing trouble for those around them even when they have the opportunity to correct wrongs. Few willingly run the risks involved in blowing the whistle on wrongdoing in the workplace.

Jewish tradition pushes back against the common tendency to avoid reporting wrongdoing. The commandment to give reproof exhorts every individual to take responsibility for righting the wrongs of every other person. Halakhah provides exceptions to its strict regulation of speech so that Jews can point out and hopefully correct wrongdoing. These traditions suggest that in an ideal society, each of us considers the welfare of everyone around us for the good of the group as a whole. That imposes an obligation on Eitan to speak up.

Halakhic tradition proposes another ethical value that provides an additional reason for Eitan to overcome his reluctance to report Sydney's wrongdoing. Our next text study (5d), from the Holiness Code of Leviticus, introduces the notion of a "stumbling block before the blind." Immediately following (5e) is a *midrash halakhah*, a rabbinic interpretation that develops the meanings of the verse in practice.

Text 5d—Lev. 19:14

YOU SHALL NOT INSULT the deaf, or place a stumbling block before the blind. You shall fear your God: I am YHVH.

Text 5e—*Sifra Kedoshim* 2:14

"OR PLACE A STUMBLING block before the blind"—[meaning], before someone blind about a matter. . . . If someone asks advice, do not give unsuitable advice. Don't tell him, "Leave early" so that bandits will attack him, or "leave at midday" so that he will get heatstroke.

Don't tell someone, "Sell your field and buy a donkey" because you're plotting to take that field away from him.

QUESTIONS FOR INQUIRY

1. What is the *pshat* (contextual) meaning of Leviticus 19:14?
2. How does the midrash in the *Sifra* extend the meaning of the word "blind"? What moral rule does it read into the verse?
3. What light does this rule shed on the decision Eitan must make in Case Study #1?

In this verse from the Holiness Code of Leviticus and its interpretation in halakhic midrash, we encounter the rule that became known as *lifnei iveir*, "before the blind." Taking metaphorically the Torah's command not to put something on the ground to trip up the blind, Rabbinic tradition teaches a broader moral lesson: we must never take advantage of another person's relative "blindness" or lack of awareness of something we know. The examples in the *Sifra* tell us not to take unfair advantage when someone asks for help. The wider understanding of the mitzvah also implies that we are not to allow others to remain morally blind when we could enlighten them. (We will explore this rule in a different context in chapter 7, "Medical Ethics at the End of Life.")

Eitan, then, violates *lifnei iveir* if he fails to report Sydney's cheating. His silence would allow her to think she acted appropriately; silence implies approval. Sydney would learn the wrong lesson, that she can cheat without suffering consequences. As the only person in a position to do something about it, Eitan is responsible for seeing that Sydney does not trip over the temptation to continue her dishonest practices.

In sum, then, it is hard to make a case based in halakhic norms to excuse Eitan from acting in this situation. Because the honor code requires it, because stopping cheating benefits the school, because Sydney deserves *tochecha*, and because of the principle concerning "a stumbling block before the blind," Eitan needs to overcome his natural reluctance and speak up.

One other value from Jewish tradition complicates the picture. A rule dating back to the Talmud forbids reporting a fellow Jew to the authorities, even for wrongdoing. The rule applies specifically to non-Jewish authorities, not to rabbinic enforcers of halakhah. One who reports on fellow Jews is called a *moser*, an informer. We will look at the law as recorded by R. Yosef Karo in the sixteenth century in the Shulḥan Arukh.

Text 6 — Shulḥan Arukh, *Hoshen Mishpat* 388:9

IT IS FORBIDDEN TO hand a Jew over to gentiles, whether the Jew's person or property. This applies even if the Jew was wicked and sinful, and even if he causes [the other Jew] continual problems.

QUESTIONS FOR INQUIRY

1. What might motivate a Jew to want to turn a fellow Jew over to the authorities?
2. Why does the halakhah forbid handing a Jew to gentile authorities?
3. What does this halakhah add to our thinking about Eitan's choices in Case Study #1?
4. What dangers could this halakhah have in modern times?

COMMENTS

According to the halakhah presented in this passage, disputes that arise between Jews must be kept within the Jewish community. No matter what a fellow Jew does, another Jew may not involve non-Jewish authorities. While the Rabbis might have enacted this ruling in part to preserve their own authority, the law clearly reflects the Jews' historical distrust of gentile governments. Our ancestors had little experience of fair treatment at the hands of non-Jewish authorities. In this light, we can readily understand their reluctance to subject fellow Jews to possible mistreatment by outside forces. Indeed, many modern halakhists declare that the law of *moser* does not apply to a just government. If that modern argument is correct, then reporting a Jew for misconduct to non-Jewish authorities would not violate the halakhah in North America today.

Perhaps this concept from Jewish tradition excuses Eitan from reporting Sydney's cheating. If the two do not attend a Jewish school, then Eitan's disclosure to the school administration—theoretically a non-Jewish authority—might violate the halakhah by making him a *moser*. Of course, that argument presumes that we consider the administration equivalent to an unjust government.

Even if we find the comparison between a school's leadership and a government convincing, other aspects of the law of *moser* may give rise to discomfort. Some tradition-minded, isolationist groups within the

Jewish community use this idea to hide serious crimes committed by their members. They may refuse to call the authorities even to protect children from molestation. We must apply the halakhah of *moser*, if at all, with great caution.

Fortunately, the halakhah recognizes an important exception to this law. Rambam summarizes it in his code, the *Mishneh Torah*.

Text 7 — *Mishneh Torah*, Laws of Robbery and Lost Objects 11:3

A JEW IS PERMITTED to keep an object lost by a gentile that he finds, as the Torah says [Deut. 22:3], "anything that your fellow Israelite loses." . . .

If one returned it to sanctify God's name, so that people will praise the Jews and understand that Jews are trustworthy, that person deserves praise.

In a situation where keeping it would lead to a desecration of God's name, keeping the gentile's object is forbidden and one is obligated to return it.

QUESTIONS FOR INQUIRY

1. Why would the halakhah make an exception so that we do not have to return lost items to gentiles? (For background on the mitzvah of returning lost articles to their owners, read Exod. 23:4 and Deut. 22:1–3.)
2. What do "sanctifying God's name" and "desecrating God's name" mean in this context?
3. How could we apply this exception to the decision Eitan faces?
4. Does the analogy to Eitan's situation work well? What weaknesses does it have?

COMMENTS

An exaggeratedly literal reading of Deuteronomy 22:3 leads Rabbinic tradition to the idea that the mitzvah of returning lost objects does not apply to gentile owners. The verse exhorts Jews to return any lost articles we find. It specifies "anything that your *fellow Israelite* loses." Because the verse says "your fellow Israelite" (in Hebrew, *ahikha*, literally, "your brother"), the Rabbis exclude anything lost by someone who is not a fellow Jew.

However, the halakhah recognizes that adherence to this rule might have a social cost. Non-Jews who notice that the same Jews who expend great effort to return lost objects to their Jewish owners also keep the lost property of gentiles for themselves might understandably feel angry. They might consider Jews greedy. That would harm the reputation of the Jewish people.

To prevent such an outcome, the halakhah uses a concept called *kiddush ha-shem* and its inverse, *hillul ha-shem*. *Kiddush ha-shem*, sanctification of God's name, refers to acts that make others think well of the God of Israel and God's followers. *Hillul ha-shem* desecrates God's reputation by making Jews, and by implication their God, look bad. Therefore, Maimonides writes, if one chooses to return a lost item to a gentile so that everyone who sees the act will think well of Jews and trust them, that person deserves praise. He goes a step further and rules that if keeping the article will directly result in a desecration of God's name—a blow to the Jews' reputation—the law changes and one is obliged to return the item to its non-Jewish owner.

This exception to the halakhah provides another way for us to think about whether Eitan's reporting on Sydney's cheating would violate the law of *moser*. Cheating in any area of life damages the cheaters' standing. Others who learn about their wrongdoing may rightly conclude that these cheaters are not as moral as they pretend. Sydney may thus be guilty of at least a potential desecration of the divine name. It would not do for people to think that Jewish students allow themselves to cheat whenever they see an advantage. If so, Eitan would have a responsibility to reduce the damage by reporting what she did and obliging Sydney to face the appropriate consequences for her act.

Let's pause for now and return to our other two case studies. First, let's explore *halakhot* concerning ownership of intellectual property and plagiarism. Like secular law, halakhah requires that individuals receive credit for their original work and ideas. The earliest statement of this moral rule appears in a midrash on the Torah from the eighth or ninth century.

Text Study #3: Crediting Others for Use of Their Intellectual Property

Text 8 — *Tanḥuma Bemidbar 22*

R. HIZKIYAH SAID THAT R. Yirmiya bar Abba said in the name of R. Yochanan:

Anyone who repeats a teaching without giving the name of the one who [first] said it — about him Scripture says, "Do not rob the wretched because he is wretched" [Prov. 22:22]. . . .

But anyone who repeats a teaching in the name of the one who [first] said it deserves to have the People Israel redeemed on his account. From whom can you learn this? From Esther, who heard the matter from Mordecai, and as a result Israel was redeemed by her actions.

QUESTIONS FOR INQUIRY

1. In what sense is failure to give credit a kind of robbery?
2. How does Esther become a model of giving proper credit?
3. Should the value of giving credit rank as highly today as it does for Rabbinic tradition?

COMMENTS

Rabbinic tradition recognizes how tempting it can be to share an interesting idea without acknowledging that someone else said it first. Allowing our audience to think the idea is ours makes us look clever. All of us (or at least the vast majority of us) sometimes succumb to the desire to take more credit than we deserve.

This tendency explains why the sources warn in such strong terms against taking unearned credit. Hiding the identity of the owner of the idea amounts to theft. It denies the owner the acknowledgments deserved. It deprives the individual of multiple intangible benefits.

To encourage giving proper credit, the tradition exaggerates the advantages of doing so. A number of other texts parallel the midrash from *Tanḥuma* in claiming that crediting the person who first said something brings redemption to the world. The model is Queen Esther. She heard of Haman's plans from Mordecai, and the Megillah records that she told the king "in Mordecai's name." The Jews of Persia were saved because Esther reported what she knew in the name of the person who told her. The moral is that we should do the same.

Students and scholars well know similar rules from outside Jewish tradition. Anyone who does research is taught how to properly cite the sources referenced in their work: enclose the words someone else wrote in quotation marks and provide the reference. In many cases authors need to pay for permission to use parts of earlier published works in their books.

These procedures form the basis for the prohibition of plagiarism. Like the classical Rabbis, academics today believe that individuals must receive credit for their ideas. Claiming others' work amounts to stealing their property—American law uses the term "intellectual property" to distinguish it from tangible property like a house or car. Plagiarism also represents a lie on the part of the person who commits it: unattributed use implies an assertion that "this is my work," when in fact someone else did it.

Jennifer, the undergraduate in Case Study #2, argues that her actions do not amount to plagiarism. She believes that mere opinion does not deserve the same protection, or exclusive credit to the author, as new facts or findings. She points out that she did not borrow wording without giving credit. Her situation will require analysis beyond the general moral rule that requires us to name those from whom we learn.

We begin by studying halakhic texts that delve further into the nuances of giving credit when using others' work. The Talmud (Texts 9a and 9b) and the Tosefta (Text 9c) consider nuances that complicate situations where people want to use work belonging to others.

Text 9a — *Gittin* 10b

SHMUEL SAID, THE LAW of the land is the law.

Text 9b — *Berakhot* 5b

FOUR HUNDRED BARRELS OF wine belonging to Rav Huna spoiled. . . . The Rabbis came to him and said, "Let the master think over his actions."

He said to them, "Do you suspect me of wrongdoing?"

They said to him, "Do you suspect the Holy One of acting unjustly?"

He said, "If anyone knows anything against me, let him say it."

They said to him, "What we heard is that you did not give your tenant farmer a share of the cut grapevines."

He said to them, "Does he [the tenant] leave me anything? He steals it all!"

They said to him, "That's the meaning of the folk saying, 'One who steals from a thief gets a taste for thieving.'"

Text 9c — *Tosefta Bava Kama* 7:3

ONE WHO SNEAKS BEHIND a Torah scholar and repeats his teaching, even though he is called a thief, still earns himself merit, as it is said [Prov. 6:30], "A thief is not held in contempt / For stealing to appease his hunger."

QUESTIONS FOR INQUIRY

1. What idea from Text 9a might inform a Jewish view about plagiarism?

2. In Text 9b, what does Rav Huna do wrong? What message do the Rabbis impart by quoting the folk saying about "one who steals from a thief"?
3. What does the Tosefta teach about repeating someone else's ideas?
4. Which of these texts contributes to deciding if Jennifer committed plagiarism? In what way(s)?

COMMENTS

The excerpt from *Gittin* 10b (Text 9a) presents a general principle that has broad application. Few Jews, if any, ever lived entirely under Rabbinic law. Shmuel, one of the first generation of Amoraim in Babylonia, articulates the rule that Jews must follow the law of the land in which they live. Outside matters of ritual, Jews who follow halakhah must also obey local civil laws.

In our context, "the law of the land is the law" implies that as Jews, we must obey the copyright laws of the nations where we live. No one can claim an exemption on the grounds that our religious tradition handles such matters differently. That law may well include the rules of academic honesty promulgated in school. If so, the only remaining question is whether Jennifer's actions did in fact break those rules.

The story about Rav Huna (Text 9b) helps us analyze Jennifer's claim that she did not actually misappropriate anyone's original work. Rav Huna hired a tenant farmer. Usually, such a tenant undertakes to cultivate a piece of land for its owner in exchange for a portion of its crops. Apparently, this tenant did not hand over Rav Huna's share of the grapes he grew in the rabbi's vineyard. Rav Huna paid himself back, as it were, by not providing the tenant farmer his due share of the cut vines to plant next season.

Rav Huna's actions come to light when he suffers the significant financial loss of four hundred spoiled barrels of wine. His colleagues suggest he examine his conscience. Perhaps God found a reason to punish him. Rav Huna claims innocence. When the Rabbis persist, he acknowledges what he did to "reimburse" himself for his tenant's misconduct. But, Rav Huna insists, he only took back what was owed him. The others remind him of a trenchant folk saying implying that anyone who imitates a thief ends up a thief too. Rav Huna may believe he only paid himself back; indeed, in principle he may not have done anything wrong. But, the Rabbis are saying, Rav Huna went about seeking reimbursement in an unethical manner. Being the victim of theft does not entitle anyone to steal.

We must bear in mind that Rav Huna did not actually steal, if stealing means taking an object in someone's possession. Until his wine spoiled, he had no sense he did anything wrong. That feeling of unwarranted righteousness highlights the comparison to students who make use of other people's work without authorization. Tradition teaches that we must avoid not just the sin, but anything close to it. Thus even if Rav Huna did not steal from the tenant, his actions were a breach of contract. By analogy, even if Jennifer did not copy someone else's words, her use of others' opinions in her writing without acknowledgement was a form of plagiarism.

The Tosefta (Text 9c) provides another applicable analogy to Jennifer's conduct. The student in this source peeks at a scholar's work without his knowledge and then repeats the teaching. While the student receives credit for learning and teaching Torah, he nevertheless is considered a thief. He took the ideas without making their originator aware, and repeated them without giving proper credit. While for her part Jennifer read the online sources only to help her articulate her own feelings, she ended up repeating what she read without extending credit. She had better options. Jennifer could have quoted and cited the writers she found online, and explained why she agreed with them. If the Tosefta is right, while Jennifer may have completed her assignment, she nevertheless behaved inappropriately. In many academic settings, she would face the consequences of plagiarism.

Another halakhic category teaches more about improper use of others' property. A commandment in the Torah forbids interfering with others' property. Rabbinic tradition expands the law to include interfering with someone's ability to earn a living.

YOU SHALL NOT MOVE your neighbor's landmarks, set up by previous generations, in the property that will be allotted to you in the land that your God YHVH is giving you to possess.

Text 10b — *Bava Batra* 21b

RAV HUNA SAID: IF one resident of an alley set up a mill, but then a second resident came along and set up another next to him, the law is that the first can stop the second. He can say to him, "You are cutting off my livelihood."

Let us say that a *baraita* supports him: Fish traps must be distanced from [someone else's] fish traps the distance that a fish will travel.

QUESTIONS FOR INQUIRY

1. What does Deuteronomy 19:14 literally forbid?
2. What rule do the two situations in *Bava Batra* 21b establish? How is this rule an extension of the law in Deuteronomy 19:14?
3. What does this idea add to our analysis of plagiarism?
4. Do you find the comparison convincing? Explain why or why not.

COMMENTS

Deuteronomy presents itself as speeches Moses delivers to the Israelites shortly before his death. Verses like the one before us teach the people how they are to live in the Promised Land. After conquest, Israel will divide the territory among the tribes and the tribes among their various families. The mitzvah in 19:14 seeks to ensure that every family will maintain possession of their allotted share of land. No one may stealthily move a landmark to enlarge one's own property at the expense of a neighbor.

The laws first established in the Talmud in Text 10b extend this rule into the area of business competition. In many circumstances, the Rabbis forbid opening a new business competing directly with an established one. Thus if someone opens a small mill to earn money grinding flour for his neighbors in the alley, another resident of the same alley may not deprive him of his living by opening a competing mill. The *baraita* establishes a similar rule for those who spread nets to trap fish. If one person sets up traps in a given spot, no one else may intrude there.

These *halakhot* became known by the phrase in Deuteronomy 19:14, *hasagat gevul*, literally, "moving a landmark." Metaphorically, the landmark represents something of value whose ownership is already established. Just as one may not move the boundary of a neighbor's property, one may not encroach on the area in which the other person does business.

For our context, the question arises: If someone makes a living from intangibles, does this rule apply? We understand how a retail business like milling grain or catching fish can lose out to unfair competition. If, however, the income derives not from exchanging goods for money, but from the production of something immaterial like words or images, we might wonder what "landmark" has been erected that others may not disturb. To put the question another way: Does using others' words or ideas without permission violate the principle of *hasagat gevul*?

This problem arose in its modern form with the invention of printing in the fifteenth century. An author might hire a printer to produce and sell his book, and share in the profits, but unscrupulous competitors would set the same text in type and sell it without the author's permission, keeping all earnings for themselves. Out of this problem grew the laws of copyright in Europe and North America. Such laws protect creators' rights to their original works, including all forms of what we now call intellectual property. Depending on the given circumstance, the words, images, or ideas in the form imagined by their creator is the "landmark" that no one else may move.

Even though the halakhic tradition grew for centuries by disseminating ideas old and new in manuscripts and in printed books, authors' rights to intellectual property within Jewish law took some time to develop. The next set of texts demonstrates how changing conditions provoked a change in established halakhah. The sixteenth-century Shulḥan Arukh reproduces a law from the Talmud. In the nineteenth century, Rabbi Yechiel

Michel Epstein wrote an updated code, following the Shulḥan Arukh's structure, cleverly titled the Arukh HaShulḥan, that tackles intangible property. The third in this set of texts, an unsigned responsum of the Reform movement's Responsa Committee, addresses copyright questions raised by the internet.

Text 11a — Shulḥan Arukh, *Hoshen Mishpat* 203:1

ANYTHING THAT DOES NOT have a physical existence cannot be legally acquired.

QUESTIONS FOR INQUIRY

1. Give examples of "things not having a physical existence."
2. What does it mean to "legally acquire" something? What difference does it make if something cannot be legally acquired?
3. What implications does this law have for Case Study #2?

Text 11b — Arukh HaShulḥan, *Hoshen Mishpat* 212:3

IN COUNTRIES WHERE IT is the law or the established custom, things that do not have a physical existence can be legally acquired [even under halakhah].

QUESTIONS FOR INQUIRY

1. How does the nineteenth-century code (Text 11b) modify the law from the Shulḥan Arukh (Text 11a)?
2. On what basis does the author make this modification?
3. What implications does this law have for Case Study #2?

Text 11c — CCAR Responsum, "Copyright and the Internet"

IT SEEMS TO US, however, that while information technology has become more sophisticated, the ethical issues that led to the creation of copyright laws remain the same. If it is wrong to print a book or copy a painting without obtaining the permission of its creator, it is just as wrong to download literary and artistic creations as files without the consent of those who authored them or who own the rights to them. . . . We continue to shoulder a duty, under Jewish tradition as well as under the law of the state, to honor, protect and safeguard the rights of authors and publishers to the works they create.[3]

QUESTIONS FOR INQUIRY
1. What is the main point of the responsum?
2. What implications does this reasoning have for Case Study #2?

COMMENTS

Halakhah struggled to deal with intangible property. The Talmud and the medieval sources that develop its ideas elaborate laws covering real property and movables, a category covering both objects and livestock that can be sold, lent, and otherwise exchanged. As late as the time of the Shulḥan Arukh, however, these *halakhot* excluded intangibles. Text 11a summarizes the rule: if it has no physical existence, a person cannot legally acquire it. Ownership cannot be firmly established. While commentaries illustrate the rule with examples like the scent of flowers or a promise to keep someone company, this law also excludes abstractions like words and ideas.

Later halakhists recognized the importance of protecting what we now call intellectual property, those creations of the mind that can refer both to inventions and to artistic works. By providing authors, for example, with the exclusive right to produce and reprint their words and ideas, copyright laws encouraged the publication of new ideas. In theory, authors would share their insights with the reading public, secure in the knowledge that no one else could claim credit for the ideas. Many rabbis deciding cases in this area were themselves published authors. They understood at first hand the importance of protecting their published ideas. They also saw that the theft even of intangibles caused concrete financial damage.

Rabbi Yechiel M. Epstein, the author of the nineteenth-century code Arukh HaShulḥan, acknowledges the need for a form of copyright protection. Relying in part on the principle of *dina de-malkhuta*, that Jews follow the law of the land (see Text 9a), he writes that if local law protects intangible property, the halakhah follows suit. In so doing, he overturns the Talmudic ruling excluding intangibles from protection. Going forward, halakhah would now protect intangible property in any country where local law protects it.

The Reform responsum (Text 11c) points out that while technology has changed, the reality of authors' need to protect their work has not. Just as halakhah protects printed material, it protects ideas transmitted through newer means such as the Internet. The ease of downloading and copying does not excuse us from the obligation to respect property rights, including creators' rights to intellectual property in all its forms.

The expansion of halakhah beyond its talmudic origins bears on our analysis of Case Study #2. While Jennifer maintains that her actions did not amount to unauthorized taking of intellectual property, because opinions are not the same as academic creation, later Jewish tradition calls for protecting intangibles, and the Talmud stresses the need to give credit for an idea to the person who originates it. As we saw, one midrash (Text 8) hints that withholding credit is akin to robbery; a similar comparison appears in *Tosefta Bava Kama* 7:3 (Text 9c). Thus intangible opinions, too, deserve protection as intellectual property.

Conclusion

Jewish tradition prefers truth to lies, honesty to deceit. Despite the nuances in the case studies, not much room remains for compromise on these principles. As much as possible, without causing unnecessary harm or interpersonal tension, Jews are to speak truthfully.

Sydney (Case Study #1) does not uphold the Torah's requirement to keep far away from falsehood. Her false representation of her knowledge of the exam material and ensuing deception of her teacher violate the Torah's commandment in Leviticus (Text 1c); some would also suggest that she committed *geneivat da'at*, taking advantage of her teacher's ignorance of her true actions (Text 4). While halakhah recognizes situations when we may lie or tell partial truths, Sydney cannot draw upon any of the tradition's sanctioned rationales for misleading others: acting out of empathy for someone's feelings, as the school of Hillel recommends (Text 2); trying to keep peace in a family (Text 3a); displaying modesty either about her achievements or her private life, or protecting a hospitable host from being taken advantage of (Text 3b); or behaving to avoid threats of violence or a predatory tax collector (Text 3c). As much sympathy as we may feel for overburdened students like Sydney, the only ethical advice we can offer her is not to cheat. Having cheated, she will have to accept the consequences of her lapse.

Sydney's classmate Eitan, too, is challenged by her cheating. As we've seen, Leviticus (Text 5b; the detailed rules are in the *Mishneh Torah*, Text 5c) commands him to rebuke her for her wrongdoing. The school's honor code requires him to report her. The halakhah of *moser* does not offer Eitan a way out, given the justice of the school's policy, assuming that administrators enforce it fairly (Texts 6 and 7). Rabbi Barry Leff (Text 5a) adds that halakhah requires Eitan to be certain he harbors no animus toward Sydney before reporting her to the authorities. While Eitan resents Sydney for cheating when he worked hard to earn his grade, he does not "hate her in his heart," as Leviticus warns us to avoid. It follows that Eitan must carry out his responsibilities under the school's honor code and report Sydney.

While the halakhah on this point is not perfectly clear, likely Eitan should perform *tochecha* first—that is, approach Sydney privately and speak gently to her about her offense. In addition to fulfilling an important mitzvah, rebuking first offers Eitan the advantage that Sydney might then take responsibility for her choice and confess to the teacher herself.

As an undergraduate, Jennifer (Case Study #2) believed that personal judgments like responses to works of art could not be considered intellectual property in the same sense as original ideas. Yet Jewish tradition stresses the need to credit an idea to the person who originates it. Midrash *Tanḥuma* (Text 8) hints that withholding credit is akin to robbery. A similar comparison appears in *Tosefta Bava Kama* (Text 9c). In language signifying the importance tradition ascribes to proper behavior in this area, midrash *Tanḥuma* adds that giving the proper credit brings redemption to the world.

The ready availability of online material creates challenges for many of us, young and old alike. A principal conclusion from the texts in this chapter is that Jewish ethics do not condone unauthorized taking of other people's work, regardless of its form of publication.

In Case Study #3, Jennifer cannot claim support from most of the sources that permit dissembling. In withholding her suspension from college from a potential employer, she too does not seek to save anyone's feelings or to maintain peace between family members. She might attempt an argument based on *Mishnah Nedarim* (Text 3c), but the Mishnah does not articulate a general rule allowing misleading speech in any situation involving finances; moreover, an employer who might hire another applicant does not compare to the unscrupulous tax collector in the Mishnah. As challenging as it is within the high-stakes atmosphere of a job interview, Jewish ethics would have Jennifer tell her prospective employer the whole truth.

Jennifer might find a way to turn adhering to the norm of truthfulness to her advantage in her job search. She could explain the circumstances of her suspension from college and use them to illustrate her ability to learn and grow from experience. Depending on the employer, her candor would not necessarily ruin her chances of getting the job; in fact, some employers might find her forthrightness and ownership of her wrongdoing refreshingly honest and impressive. In a way, such a course would exemplify the Jewish value of *teshuvah*, repentance and turning to the right way of living (see chapter 3).

As these cases show, the ideal of honesty is difficult to practice. Although competing values like the need to strengthen interpersonal relations and save lives and property may sometimes call for digressions from truth, these exceptions do not provide broad grounds for ignoring the Torah's basic rule, "Keep far from falsehood." They offer narrow conditions for compromise. In principle, we are enjoined to stick to the truth.

The Psalmist expresses the ideal (Ps. 15:1–2): "LORD, who may sojourn in Your tent, who may dwell on Your holy mountain? / One who lives without blame, who does what is right, and in his heart acknowledges the truth." Honest people share the truth with others and tell the truth even to themselves.

3

Social Media

Contemporary social media use presents a fascinating challenge to the study of Jewish ethics. In traditional sources one will not find direct reference to phenomena such as "liking" on Facebook or sharing photos on Instagram. Yet Judaism claims to speak to its adherents in all times and situations. If it does, then values and ideas within the tradition ought to be able to help us make our way through the new technological landscape.

Rabbi Jonathan Sacks, the late chief rabbi of Great Britain, captured the primary ethical challenge of social media when he wrote, "Technology gives us power, but it does not and cannot tell us how to use that power. Thanks to technology, we can instantly communicate across the world, but it still doesn't help us know what to say."[1] In other words, new technologies may give us new powers that we — individually and collectively — may not know how to use well. Social media can easily distract us from asking "what is worth saying?" as well as "what is worth knowing?"

This chapter explores several ethical concepts developed by the talmudic Rabbis for guidance on ethical dilemmas relating to sharing messages and pictures, looking at other people's activities and information, bullying, maintaining privacy, and engaging in social deceptions.

Case Study #1: Social Media Insults

A Jewish school was in the midst of a heated student government election when the principal spotted an email in her inbox with the subject heading "Please read — Snapchat problem." The text of the email from Jonathan, the current student body president, read:

> Max sent me a Snapchat last night that I think is really inappropriate. In case you don't know, Snapchat is an app where you can send someone a picture with your phone, but the picture deletes itself

after 10 seconds. My friends use it to send funny pictures that they don't want anyone to keep. You know that Max is running against Elizabeth for class president. Last night, Max sent a Snapchat of a campaign sign with a picture of Elizabeth and a really offensive slogan: Elizabitch.

I took a screenshot of it because I thought someone should know about this. As the current class president, I take these elections seriously and I think it's really inappropriate for someone to use campaigning to bully or defame someone.

Because of the way Snapchat works, Max got a notification that I took a screenshot. He texted me right after to find out why I did that. I told him it was a really bad idea to Snapchat a picture like that. He said it was just a joke, and that he only sent it to me and three other people in our class. I'm not sure if I believe Max about the number of people he sent it to, and I'm not sure if he'll stop doing things like this. I think this is really bad for student government elections and our school, and it needs to stop. — Jonathan

The email and screenshot struck the principal as an example of the very behavior the school wanted to prevent—and, in fact, was actively working to prevent. Recently, faculty members had cocreated with the student government a set of *midot* (core values) for the student community. The school had also held assemblies on bullying and had trained several students to help mediate when issues arose.

Considering the situation, the principal realized that Elizabeth was unlikely to be aware of the insulting campaign sign. The incident had taken place outside of school during after-school hours. While the school had established a "zero tolerance" policy toward bullying in school, there was no established policy about cyberbullying or about bullying that occurred outside of school grounds or school hours.

The principal decided to suspend Max for three days to demonstrate that such behavior would not be tolerated. Shocked, Max and his parents protested that they did not believe his actions deserved such a response. While Max understood that the school took the no-bullying policy very seriously, he and his parents did not think that a Snapchat message sent to four friends after school was an act of bullying. Max contended that the picture was a private communication, and that if anyone was to be disciplined, it should be Jonathan, who had no right to share this Snapchat with the school administration.

Max was adamant that he was the one who was wronged. He asked, Isn't Jonathan's email *lashon hara*, an act of speech about other people forbidden by Jewish tradition? In fact, Max argued, the suspension had now made things much worse, and far more public. Whereas originally only Max's four friends had known about the Snapchat, once the other students heard about the suspension, they started talking about it. That's when Elizabeth found out about it as well. Max and his parents demanded that the school erase the suspension from Max's permanent record.

This case asks us to consider who is the wrongdoer and who is the injured party. Did Max engage in bullying—or violate any other Jewish ethical principle—by sharing the doctored photo of Elizabeth? Does Jonathan deserve praise for trying to stop mistreatment of a fellow student, or should he be held responsible for violating Max's privacy in a way that led to Elizabeth's learning about the insult? Did the principal respond appropriately and for the right reasons?

Case Study #2: Online Privacy

A true story: After a Pennsylvania school began monitoring Apple laptops on loan to students by activating their built-in cameras remotely, high schooler R. filed an invasion of privacy lawsuit, alleging that the school district had taken hundreds of secret photos of him over a two-week period. His family had discovered this when a teacher accused R. of dealing drugs based on one of the photos. (He claimed, though, that he was popping Mike and Ike candies, not pills.)

The school denied any active spying, saying that security software activated for laptops suspected of being stolen kicked in automatically and took photos every fifteen minutes. That seemingly reasonable defense was made shaky by the school's possession of more than fifty-six thousand Webcam shots. Ultimately, district officials decided to settle the case. They voted to pay R. $175,000, his lawyer $425,000, and a second student $10,000.[2]

Many school districts struggle with the problem faced in this case study. If the district provides students computers to use in schoolwork, how can it make sure the computers are used only for their intended purposes and avoid losing expensive equipment to theft? How can it balance the need to protect the district's property and its students' privacy? How far should—and does—an individual's right to privacy extend? Some values in halakhah provide guidance.

To help sort out the complexities of these cases, we begin with classical and modern sources that address the Jewish ethics of speech. Our first sources on permitted and forbidden speech come from the Torah and Rashi's comment on the verse.

Text Study #1: Permitted and Forbidden Speech

Text 1a—Lev. 19:16

JPS 1962 TRANSLATION: Do not deal basely with your countrymen. Do not profit by the blood of your fellow; I am the Lord.

JPS 1917 TRANSLATION: Do not go up and down as a talebearer among thy people; neither shalt thou stand idly by the blood of thy neighbor; I am the Lord.

QUESTIONS FOR INQUIRY

1. What differences can you identify between the two translations of the verse? Can you identify the Hebrew phrases that lead to these very different versions?
2. What connections could there be between the two commandments in this verse?
3. Why does the verse add "I am the Lord" at the end?

I SAY WE SHOULD understand this phrase on the basis that all those who sow strife and relate gossip go into the houses of their neighbors to spy out what evil they might see, or what evil they might hear to retell in public. They are called *holkhei rakhil*, which is the same as *holkhei ragil*, meaning "people who go around spying."... Similarly, the *rokhel*, the peddler, is one who goes around and searches for all kinds of merchandise. And also, every seller of perfumes that women wear, because they always go around in the towns, is called *rokhel*, which means the same as *rogel*.... It seems to me that their practice was to eat something in every house where people accepted their gossipy talk, and this served to confirm the truth of the statements he made.

QUESTIONS FOR INQUIRY

1. What two meanings does Rashi give for the Torah's word *rakhil*?
2. Do the two translations in Text 1a conform to either of the understandings Rashi offers?
3. How is a merchant a metaphor for someone who spreads gossip and slander?
4. Does gossip today spread in the same way as Rashi describes?

COMMENTS

This verse from Leviticus forms the basis of the area of halakhah called *lashon ha-ra*. Literally meaning "evil speech," the phrase refers generally to gossip. It generally prohibits talking about third parties — two people discussing an absent third person — even if the story shows the person in a positive light.

The area of *lashon ha-ra* has many subcategories of prohibited speech, along with a number of exceptions when speaking about another person is permitted. The interpretation of this verse hinges on the word *rakhil*. The more recent Jewish Publication Society version of the Torah translates it in line with the context of this chapter in Leviticus, giving the *pshat* meaning: "Do not deal basely with your countrymen," meaning, do not treat them in an immoral fashion. The translation from 1917 follows the rabbinic midrash on the verse cited by Rashi in Text 1b, "Do not go up and down as a talebearer"—that is, do not go from one person to the next telling tales about your "countrymen." The halakhic term for this activity is *rekhilut*.

The word *rakhil* allows for two such dissimilar translations because the midrashim that guided the 1917 JPS Torah translation relate it to a root that means "peddler." Specifically, it refers to a peddler who goes from door to door offering his wares. Rashi explains that the best comparison is to a peddler selling perfumes. As a peddler walks from one house to the next, showing each person his merchandise, people who gossip tell the same story to each person they meet. Additionally, just as the smell of the perfume lingers after the peddler leaves the house, a story once told lingers in the listener's memory. Once spoken, words do not disappear.

Here the Torah sets a very high standard for limiting our conversations. Almost all of us share a fascination with what other people do and say. We often see or hear something and immediately plan how we will share it with others. Yet retelling the story is the very definition of *rekhilut*. Taking this commandment seriously requires us to eliminate this kind of material from our speech. That means not circulating any information that shows another person in a bad light. The halakhah permits sharing good news. We may also praise a third party, as long as it's not the kind of praise that can cause that person trouble—the Ḥafetz Ḥayyim (a collection of laws of speech by the nineteenth- and early twentieth-century Polish scholar Rabbi Yisrael Meir Kagan) gives the example of extolling someone's hospitality to the point where others may overwhelm the host with requests for food and drink (*Ḥafetz Ḥayyim* 9:3). Within these limits, we may speak kindly about others.[3]

One of the complicated issues in our first case study concerns *lashon ha-ra* and *rekhilut*. Max claims that Jonathan committed *lashon ha-ra* by relating the story of what he did to the principal. To decide who, if anyone, did in fact engage in *lashon ha-ra* or *rekhilut* we need to consider the prohibition against telling tales and injuring reputations.

Another midrash adds to our considerations a lesson about the power of speech.

Text 2 — Arakhin 15b

RABBI HAMA SON OF Rabbi Ḥanina said:

What is the meaning of the verse (Prov. 18:21) "Death and life are in the power [literally, 'hand'] of the tongue"? Does the tongue have a hand?

It teaches you:

Just as the hand can kill, so the tongue can kill.

QUESTIONS FOR INQUIRY

1. What surprises Rabbi Hama son of Rabbi Ḥanina about the language in Proverbs?
2. What lesson does Rabbi Hama son of Rabbi Ḥanina find in the verse? Is the lesson meant literally? What is the rabbi trying to say?
3. What does this passage teach the characters in Case Study #1?

COMMENTS

This brief excerpt from the Talmud contains one of the most famous rabbinic comments about *lashon ha-ra*. The lesson relies on a careful reading of the verse that is at once literal and figurative. Proverbs uses the word *yad*, meaning "hand," to describe the tongue's power. Rabbi Hama son of Rabbi Ḥanina therefore concludes that just as the human hand can take life, so, too, can the tongue.

That is the literal part of the *drash*, Rabbi Hama son of Rabbi Ḥanina's reinterpretation of the verse. But the literal-minded reading simultaneously depends on figurative understandings of both the words "hand" and "tongue." The rabbi has in mind not an actual tongue, but the words that the tongue forms — tongue in the sense of "language." He understands "hand" in the verse as a metaphor for "power." From the ensuing meaning of the verse, "Life and death are in the power of speech," he draws the conclusion that the ways we speak about other people are just as much a matter of life and death as what we may do to people physically.

It is hard to imagine a stronger warning to guard our tongues. It may seem that Rabbi Hama exaggerates, and perhaps he intentionally overstates the case to drive his lesson home. And yet rumors can ruin reputations, and young people have taken their own lives in the aftermath of online bullying.

How might we evaluate Max's insult of Elizabeth in Case Study #1 in this light? The Talmud warns Max of the harm his casual use of insulting words may cause Elizabeth. Yet before making a final determination that Max is the person most at fault, let's consider the halakhah governing improper speech as codified in Maimonides' *Mishneh Torah*.

Text 3a—*Mishneh Torah*, Laws of Personal Qualities 7:2

WHO IS A TALEBEARER (*rakhil*)? One who carries things and goes from one to another and says, "This is what x said; such and such I heard about x." Even though it is the truth, he destroys the world.

There is a much greater sin than this—and it is included in this negative commandment—and that is evil speech (*lashon ha-ra*). That is the one who speaks disparagingly about his fellow, even though it is true.

But one who speaks falsely is called "one who gives his fellow a bad reputation" (*motzi shem ra*).

QUESTIONS FOR INQUIRY

1. Identify the three categories of forbidden speech in this passage. What are the key differences among these categories?
2. Why is it forbidden to speak badly of another person, even when one is telling the truth?
3. In what ways might these types of forbidden speech "destroy the world"?

In this section of Maimonides' codification of the halakhah we find the basic definitions of the types of forbidden speech the classical Rabbis created through the processes of *midrash halakhah*. More than one way of speaking about others violates Rabbinic ethics. To analyze the rights and wrongs of Case Study #1, we need to distinguish carefully among the types of *lashon ha-ra* and decide which, if any, have been violated.

Rambam begins with the category familiar to us from Texts 1a and 1b. *Rekhilut* involves going from person to person, telling the same deprecatory story about a third party. Rambam adds an important element to our understanding of this sin when he writes, "Even though it is the truth, he destroys the world." We may not tell disparaging stories about other people, even if the stories are true.

Who in our case study might be guilty of *rekhilut*? Jonathan seems the most likely candidate. Yes, Jonathan told a true story—Max did create the insulting image of Elizabeth—but we already know that truth does not excuse talebearing. Still, certain exemptions govern the law of *rekhilut*, as we will see later in this chapter. Jonathan's worthy motives for sharing the story—his wish to protect Elizabeth, the integrity of the student government election, and the integrity of the school in general—may in fact exempt him from the law of *rekhilut*.

The next paragraph from the *Mishneh Torah* defines two further categories of forbidden speech. *Lashon ha-ra* (which also serves as a general term for all the laws of forbidden speech) means to denigrate another person. Any slur, any description designed to make someone look bad, is encompassed within this understanding of *lashon ha-ra*. Thus Max may have run afoul of the law of *lashon ha-ra*. Jonathan may also have done so, as Max and his parents claim.

The third definition in the passage covers attempts to destroy someone's reputation by inventing a *false* story. (By contrast, disparagement by *lashon ha-ra* can be true.) For this, the Rabbis adapted a phrase from the Torah, *motzi shem ra*, meaning "to spread a bad name." Max's action may not qualify as *motzi shem ra*, since he sent the Snapchat to four friends and not the whole school. Jonathan surely did not violate *motzi shem ra*, as he told the truth.

Our next text study delves into the means by which one can commit *lashon ha-ra*. It is from *Ḥafetz Ḥayyim* (1873), an influential survey of the halakhah of forbidden speech written by the Polish scholar Rabbi Yisrael Meir Kagan. *Ḥafetz Ḥayyim*, meaning "eager for life," comes from Psalm 34:13, which asks, "Who is the man who is eager for life?" The next verse warns such a person, "Guard your tongue from evil," implying that evil speech shortens a person's life. As sometimes happens in traditional Jewish literature, the phrase *Ḥafetz Ḥayyim* came to refer both to the book and to its author. In the comments, we will sometimes refer to R. Kagan as the Ḥafetz Ḥayyim.

Text 3b — *Ḥafetz Ḥayyim* 1:8

THIS PROHIBITION OF *lashon ha-ra* applies whether speaking about someone verbally, or writing about him. [The rule] does not distinguish between telling it explicitly or just hinting at it—in every form, it falls into the category of forbidden speech (*lashon ha-ra*).

QUESTIONS FOR INQUIRY

1. How does this text add to our understanding of what constitutes *lashon ha-ra*?
2. How do these additional details help us analyze the issues in Case Study #1?
3. Would manipulating a person's image (such as someone's photograph) fall into this category of forbidden speech?

COMMENTS

An important idea for our first case study is the Ḥafetz Ḥayyim's ruling that forbidden speech need not be verbal speech. While the author refers to writing, for our times the rule would extend to messages sent via email, text, and other formats. The language of the prohibition—"in every form, it falls into the category of forbidden speech"—implies that the prohibition against *lashon ha-ra* would also apply to images, like the one Max created that insulted Elizabeth.

The Ḥafetz Ḥayyim adds a fascinating detail to the law. Not only may we not directly denigrate another person, but we may not even hint at something negative. We all know how easily we can convey our meaning to another person without speaking words out loud. The "hint" can come from a tone of voice, or a gesture as simple as a raised eyebrow. If the listener gets the point about the third party, the speaker engages in forbidden speech.

Possibly this text convicts Max of violating the law against *lashon ha-ra*. But what of his defense that he was only joking? The Ḥafetz Ḥayyim addresses that question directly.

Text 3c — Ḥafetz Ḥayyim 3:3

THE PROHIBITION OF *lashon ha-ra* is so serious that even if one does not speak it out of hatred, and does not even intend the story to denigrate the other person, but said it only in jest or humorously—even so, since it in fact is negative information, the Torah prohibits it.

QUESTIONS FOR INQUIRY

1. What does this passage add to our understanding of *lashon ha-ra*?
2. What circumstances does this law warn us to avoid?

COMMENTS

The halakhah here tells us that humor does not excuse us from the rules of forbidden speech. Even comments made without animus or hostility constitute *lashon ha-ra*. "I was only joking" is not a justification. In fact, actual feelings often hide behind jokes. The victim may suspect that the other person really meant the comment and used the idea of a joke to escape responsibility for giving offense.

This text casts Max's "joking" behavior in a negative light. While he may have amused some of his friends with the doctored campaign poster and caption, the tradition would hold that he violated *lashon ha-ra*.

Did Jonathan also violate *lashon ha-ra* by bringing Max's Snapchat to the principal's attention? The next few texts will help us think about that problem.

Text 4 — Yoma 4b

HOW DO WE KNOW that when someone tells his friend something, the latter may not repeat it until the person says to him, "Go and say it"?

As it says (Lev. 1:1), "God spoke to Moses from the Tent of Meeting, saying."

Rashi: "The latter may not repeat it" — "Saying" [in Leviticus] is *leimor*, which we can read as *lo emor* — "do not say" these things unless he gives him permission.

QUESTIONS FOR INQUIRY

1. What problem of interpersonal relations does the Talmud address here?
2. According to Rashi's explanation, how does the verse from Leviticus "prove" that one may not repeat what a friend shares without permission?
3. Can we ever repeat negative speech without violating the law of *rekhilut*?

COMMENTS

Clearly, the Talmud here values keeping confidences. If someone tells a friend something, the friend does not automatically have permission to share it with anyone else. The information may only be shared if the friend receives explicit permission to do so.

The Rabbis of the Talmud liked to find a "prooftext," a verse from the Torah that through the tools of midrash demonstrates their teaching.

Here the Talmud references the beginning of the book of Leviticus. As God begins to instruct Moses about the rules the priests will follow in conducting sacrificial worship, God calls to Moses from the Tent of Meeting. The verse ends with a verb that means "saying." At the *pshat* level, the "saying" (in Hebrew, *leimor*) simply introduces God's words that begin in the next verse.

The proof relies on a *drash* understanding. Rashi's commentary on the Talmud suggests that the *drash* depends on reading *leimor* as if it were two words, one *ending* with the *alef* and the other *beginning* with the same letter. That yields the words *lo emor*, meaning "do not say." God's verbal instructions to Moses, "Do not say," models correct behavior for us. Unless our friend tells us otherwise, "do not say": do not repeat anything the friend tells us.

This law implies that Jonathan would need Max's permission to repeat what he said (or, in Max's case, shared via an image). Jonathan did not have that permission. Logically, the use of Snapchat, where images quickly disappear, implies that the sender wants the recipient to see the image and do nothing further with it. While the sender would know that the recipient may take a screenshot, that is not the usual expectation. Max's response to Jonathan attests to his intention that no one else would see his message about Elizabeth. The Talmud in *Yoma* clearly disapproves of Jonathan's decision to share the information.

Yet that conclusion does not end our analysis of Jonathan's role in the situation. As the next texts show, there are exceptions to the prohibition against *lashon ha-ra* which merit consideration.

Text 5 — Ḥafetz Ḥayyim 10:1

IF A MAN SAW someone harming another person . . . or causing him damage, whether the [victim] knew of it or not—or if he shamed him or bothered him, or wronged him with words . . . he can relate it to others in order to help the one who was wronged and to condemn these evil deeds before people.

1. What exceptions to the prohibition against speaking about third parties does the Ḥafetz Ḥayyim identify here?
2. What is the reason for the exceptions to the rule?
3. What light does this halakhah shed on Jonathan's decision?

Here, the Ḥafetz Ḥayyim describes an exception to the prohibition against *lashon ha-ra*. In a situation where one person intends to harm another physically, financially, or emotionally, the person who finds out may warn the intended victim. Because the motive is to save an innocent person from harm, such an act does not violate the prohibition against speaking badly of third parties.

We might wonder if Jonathan's report of Max's Snapchat to the principal fits under this law. Jonathan does not protect the principal from Max; he hopes to save someone else, Elizabeth, from emotional distress. In telling the principal, Jonathan cannot avoid making Max look bad, which usually constitutes *lashon ha-ra*. Reading the Ḥafetz Ḥayyim passage literally might suggest that Jonathan should go directly to Elizabeth, but it is not clear that Jonathan would in fact be saving an innocent person from harm. Without Jonathan's involvement, in fact, Elizabeth might never have been hurt by the Snapchat image.

On the other hand, what if informing the principal was the best method Jonathan had to protect Elizabeth? In Jonathan's mind, the issue is broader than this specific incident. As student body president, Jonathan believes he must protect both the integrity of the election and the values of the school. By holding Max accountable for violating the school's values, he hopes to shield Elizabeth from being subjected to further nastiness. A broad reading of this halakhic passage would allow him to take the step he took in order to prevent Max from doing further harm.

Halakhic tradition prohibits causing others emotional harm. The Rabbis call this prohibition *ona'at devarim*, a phrase literally meaning "oppression using words." *Ona'at devarim* outlaws speech that causes another person emotional distress, whether said directly to the victim or to third parties.

A contemporary Orthodox rabbi, Gil Student, writing in a magazine published by the Orthodox Union, proposes *ona'at devarim* as a category for promoting ethical behavior online. His suggestion, Text 6, allows us to think about another aspect of Case Study #1.

Text 6 — Student, "A Torah Guide for the Digital Age"

THE TORAH FORBIDS CAUSING emotional distress to others (*ona'at devarim*). This effectively prohibits insulting and bullying. Do not let the anonymity of the Internet lull you into more aggressive patterns of speech. Words hurt and often cause real damage beyond the computer screen.[4]

QUESTIONS FOR INQUIRY

1. How does Rabbi Student define *ona'at devarim* so that it includes a prohibition on bullying?
2. What implications does his definition have for our case study?

COMMENTS

Rabbi Student interprets the halakhah of *ona'at devarim* to encompass bullying and insulting another person. If we adopt his definitions — keeping in mind that this article does not carry halakhic authority — it remains true that Max has not bullied Elizabeth, but Max has violated the halakhah of *ona'at devarim* by insulting Elizabeth, even if Elizabeth is unaware of the insult. We have already noted the irony that Jonathan's attempt to uphold the school's values and protect Elizabeth was the only reason Elizabeth found out about the insult. Even if she never knew, in the light of this text study Max's violation stands because of the group of friends who saw what he said about Elizabeth.

Before resolving the matter, let's turn our attention to other areas of Jewish ethics. Some of these will shed further light on our initial case study; others will help with Case Study #2.

Text Study #2: Privacy

Both case studies in this chapter raise issues concerning privacy. What should other people be able to find out about someone else? On the receiving end, do we bear any responsibility to avoid certain material that we have the capacity to see? How might our findings pertain to Case Study #2, in which students accuse a school district of invading their privacy? We begin with a Mishnah and part of the Gemara on it that establish a basic value of personal privacy.

Text 7 — Mishnah Bava Batra 3:7; Bava Batra 60a

Mishnah

ONE MAY NOT OPEN a door into a jointly owned courtyard directly opposite another's door, or a window directly opposite another's window. If the window was small one may not make it larger; if it was a single window one may not make it into two.

Gemara

FROM WHERE IN THE Torah is this rule derived?

Rabbi Yohanan said, As the Torah says [Num. 24:2], "As Balaam looked up and saw Israel encamped tribe by tribe." What did he see? He saw that the doors of their tents did not directly face one another. Balaam said, "These people are deserving of having God's presence resting upon them."

QUESTIONS FOR INQUIRY

1. What ethical idea can we derive from the Mishnah's rules?
2. What ethical idea can we derive from the midrash the Gemara cites?
3. In what ways can others "see" our private business, other than actually looking into our houses?

The housing arrangements the Mishnah describes are different from our own. In the ancient Near East many houses were arranged around courtyards. Individual families owned each house, and all the families shared ownership of and responsibility for the common space of the courtyard. A single entryway led from the courtyard to the public street.

Nonetheless, the text addresses neighborhood difficulties still common in our times. A family wants to remodel their house as they see fit—perhaps open an additional window, enlarge an existing one, or open an entirely new door. The new or larger door or window may allow the residents of one house to see more easily into others. One or more neighbors may object on the grounds that they will lose privacy, and they deserve to be able to maintain privacy in their own home.

The Mishnah's sympathies lie with the second homeowner(s). Favoring privacy rights over property rights, the Mishnah rules that one may not open a new door directly opposite a neighbor's door. Furthermore, one may not open a new window, enlarge an existing window, or split an existing window into two when it directly faces a neighbor's window.

In examining the Mishnah, the Gemara begins with the question of what biblical source supports these legal rules. As it often does, it identifies a verse that leads to this halakhah only after interpretation through midrash. The background comes from Numbers 22–24. Balak, king of Moab, watches the Israelites under Moses' leadership defeat the Amorites in battle. Afraid of meeting the same fate, he hires the prophet Balaam to curse the Israelites, believing this will allow him to defeat Israel. But each time Balaam tries to invoke curses on the Israelites, he winds up blessing them instead. The words of blessing culminate in the famous words, "*Mah tovu*, How fair are your tents, O Jacob, / Your dwellings, O Israel!" (Num. 24:5).

In Numbers 24:2, the Torah reports, "Balaam looked up and saw Israel encamped tribe by tribe." It appears that seeing how Israel encamped inspired his poetic words of blessing. The midrash naturally asks, "What did Balaam see?" What did he notice about the Israelite camp that impressed him so much? The answer: "He saw that the doors of their tents did not directly face one another." In short, the Israelites allowed one another as much personal privacy as possible, even on their long march through the wilderness.

The midrash makes explicit the assumption behind the Mishnah's rulings. We are to respect privacy by allowing others to go about their business without being observed. All of us deserve a degree of protection from being seen when we are unaware, or when we do not wish to be seen.

Placing this much value on privacy carries important implications for behavior on social media. It asks us to pause and consider what we look at online, especially if the individual poster has not specifically invited us to look. Perhaps we should think twice about looking at photos or other materials belonging to friends of friends. Instead we could allow them more privacy.

Text 7 may suggest another analogy to "opening an additional window." The school district in Case Study #2 attached software that used each computer's internal camera to track students' activities. While the district may have the right to confirm that students use its property only for schoolwork, the Mishnah and Gemara here suggest that it does not have the right to "see" what else happens in the student's room. This source would support the students' claims against the school district.

One might ask if being seen really harms a person. A discussion at the beginning of tractate *Bava Batra* in the Talmud sheds some light on this question. The contemporary author Ilana Kurshan wrote a blog while she participated in an international *daf yomi* (page of the day or daily folio) project in which participants studied a folio page of the Babylonian Talmud each day and completed its study in a little over seven years. In Text 8a, an excerpt from her blog, Kurshan summarizes a complicated debate among Amoraim about the consequences of being seen against one's will.

Text 8a — Kurshan, Comments on *Bava Batra* 2a–b

HEZEK RE'IYAH LITERALLY MEANS "damage done by seeing," and refers to the notion that the invasion of privacy caused by looking at someone else's property is tantamount to physical damage. The term comes up in the opening sugya [passage] of [tractate] Bava Batra, in a discussion about two neighbors who disagree about the construction of a fence. One would like to build a fence so that the other cannot look into his yard, but the other neighbor does not want his yard divided. Is the first neighbor legally authorized to force the second to agree to the fence?

Those rabbis who support the notion that *hezek re'iya* constitutes a genuine form of damage believe that a person can legally prevent a neighbor from gazing into his property by forcing his neighbor to assist in the expenses of building a fence. They argue that damage done through sight is indeed understood as real damage.

On the opposite side . . . are those rabbis who argue that the damage of being seen is not real damage, and therefore the neighbor who desires privacy cannot force his neighbor to join in the expenses of building a wall.

Ultimately, the Talmud concludes that yes, there is indeed a notion of *hezek re'iya*—the damage of being seen constitutes a very real form of a damage, and people have the right to protect their own privacy.[5]

QUESTIONS FOR INQUIRY

1. Which side of the debate do you find more convincing? Is being seen a genuine form of damage or not?
2. Why do you think the Talmud concludes that being seen is a real form of damage?
3. What does this debate add to our understanding of the value of personal privacy?

COMMENTS

Tractate *Bava Batra* examines at length how someone who harms another person compensates the injured party. We might readily understand the need for compensatory payments for bodily and property damage, but here the Talmud asks: Does seeing someone when the individual does not wish to be seen constitute damage requiring compensation?

As Kurshan's summary indicates, the question provokes debate in the Talmud. Some Rabbis plausibly argue that we should not categorize *hezek re'iyah* as damage. Controlling what we see is not always possible. It seems unfair to penalize seeing, especially when it is inadvertent. Nonetheless, the Talmud ultimately concludes that *hezek re'iyah* does fit into the category of actual damages requiring restitution. Legally, this means that the person who sees another person inappropriately must pay, just as if that person had damaged the other person's property. It also means that anyone may take steps to prevent other people from seeing them at times and in places where they want to preserve their privacy.

This debate holds interesting implications about online behavior. If being seen in a private space amounts to damage, everyone has the right to prevent others from seeing them without permission. But we must first define "private." In the virtual world, what constitutes a private space?

Every social media platform offers various "privacy settings." Yet it remains hard to prevent postings from being seen. My students point out that allowing a parent to see their Facebook pages (for example) can lead to embarrassment when the parent, by clicking "like," inadvertently makes photos or other materials available to other relatives and family friends.

Information about us online is also nearly impossible to control or wipe clean, sometimes with serious life consequences. Yet another true story: In 2012, a Jewish college freshman, B., was a passenger in his van packed with fraternity house friends on their way to a spring-break rental house when the police pulled the van over (citing a faulty taillight), asked if they could search the vehicle, and the driver said yes. They found six Ecstasy pills in B.'s knapsack, handcuffed him, and placed him under arrest. B. later agreed to enter a multiyear, pretrial diversion program that involved counseling and drug tests, as well as visits every six months to update a judge in the arresting state on his progress. Once B. completed the program, he would wipe his record clean in the eyes of the law. But not in the eyes of anyone who searches for B. online. The mug shot from his arrest is posted on a handful of for-profit websites with names like Mugshots, BustedMugshots and JustMugshots. These companies routinely show up high in Google searches. My own top four search results for B.'s full name were mug shot sites.[6]

Hezek re'iyah, the damage done to us when others see us without permission, helps us think about Case Study #2. If *hezek re'iyah* truly damages the person seen, R. was right to sue the school district for photographing him without his knowledge or permission. The district certainly violated an ethic that prohibits even placing a window where one might chance to see inside someone else's home.

Saying that the school district violated R.'s privacy does not deny its legitimate interest in protecting its property. It does suggest, however, that the district needs to find a different balance between its rights and those of its students. The district needs to work out how to protects its interests without spying on its students.

We can also think about the value of *hezek re'iyah* from the perspective of the individual posting to a social media site. If we do not wish to suffer the damage of being seen, the onus is also on us to take some precautions to control how we might be seen. Often we display ourselves or our activities without stopping to think about who may see us and how. Adopting the Talmud's view that seeing without permission constitutes real damage requires us to reevaluate our social media practices. To not tempt others to view us (or our families) inappropriately involves thinking carefully about what we post and how often.

In his book *Love Your Neighbor and Yourself*, Elliot N. Dorff, a Conservative rabbi and leading contemporary scholar of Jewish ethics, offers a framework for thinking about privacy both from the perspective of the person posting online and of those seeing what is posted.

Text 8b — Dorff, *Love Your Neighbor and Yourself*

THE RIGHT TO PRIVACY is at the core of human dignity. The more our privacy is invaded, the more we lose two central components of our dignity—namely, our individuality and the respect we command from others. When our innermost selves become the subject for the knowledge and criticism of others, the resulting social pressure quickly wears away our individuality. . . . If many of the details of our lives are open to the public, many of us will be afraid to veer from whatever is socially endorsed, lest we be subject to criticism or even attack. That is, we will relinquish our individuality so as to be able to survive within the group.[7]

QUESTIONS FOR INQUIRY

1. In what ways does Rabbi Dorff suggest that privacy is essential to human dignity?
2. Is it true that most of us will not have the courage to maintain our individuality against social pressures to act or think like everyone else?

COMMENTS

Rabbi Dorff identifies privacy as central to the ancient Jewish value of the dignity of each individual. Because the Torah teaches that each human is created in the "image of God" (Gen. 1:27), each person possesses an inherent dignity. We learn to try to do nothing to undermine that dignity.

The same biblical idea implies that each of us is a unique individual deserving of respect. Each of us differs in various ways from everyone around us, and that diversity reflects the infinitude of the Divine. By allowing one another to express their individuality, we honor the different aspects of the Divine reflected in each person. If a sense of always being watched inhibits people from showing who they truly are, then the way we use social media violates our basic humanity.

Rabbi Dorff suggests that when we make too much of our inner selves public, we open ourselves to criticism that creates pressure to conform. His warning reminds us to consider which aspects of our inmost selves to share publicly and which to keep private. He also draws attention to the way those who express unpopular opinions online can find themselves subjected to strong, even threatening responses from those who want to suppress their ideas. We may want to share opinions we feel strongly about regardless of how others may react to them. Dorff urges us to make considered choices about what to share and what to withhold. Knowing what to keep private helps us remain true to our unique selves.

R. in Case Study #2 illustrates the loss of personal dignity we suffer when others observe us without permission. The cameras the school district installed on the computers they issued to their students allowed administrators to invade R.'s privacy. Certainly the schools have a right to make sure students do not misuse district property. R. should recognize the differences between what he might do on his own computer and what is appropriate to do on the school's computer. The fact that our activities may be visible to others is a reality we all must accept and consider when we go online.

Arnold Samlan, an Orthodox rabbi who serves as Chief Jewish Education Officer of the Jewish Federation of Broward (Florida), suggests some worthwhile rules to consider in online spaces.

Text 8c — Samlan, "The Ten Commandments of Social Media"

4. *Construct a Parapet* — Yes, the biblical idea of fencing in a roof so that a guest doesn't accidentally fall off applies in social media. All of us who use social media need to insure that our friends and contacts are safe. Bullies and haters have to be dealt with quickly and decisively. . . .

7. *Engage in Cheshbon Ha-nefesh* — The idea of self-reflection is powerful. Does my current image reflect who I really am and the way I wish others to know me? Do I still have posts from my ancient past that no longer reflect who I am today, and need to be edited? . . .

9. *Tzimtzum* — The Jewish mystical concept of God withdrawing from a space to give room for creations works online. We need to limit our "selfies"; not everyone wants to see our smiling faces every time they come online. On the other hand, there are others online who can use a kind word, a joke, or that latest viral video that's going around.[8]

QUESTIONS FOR INQUIRY

1. What actions does each of Samlan's commandments imply we should take online?

2. What actions does each commandment imply we should avoid online?
3. How do these guidelines help us avoid "damage from being seen" online?
4. What might these guidelines offer to the individuals in this chapter's case studies?

Rabbi Samlan derives his commandments for online behavior from core Jewish teachings. For example, commandment 4, "construct a parapet," draws from Deuteronomy 22:8: "When you build a new house, you shall make a parapet for your roof, so that you do not bring bloodguilt on your house if anyone should fall from it." The homeowner takes responsibility for visitors' safety by building a fence to keep people from falling off the roof. Similarly, we can take steps to keep our friends and online contacts safe from bullying and other harm that may come to them via social media.

Adhering to this commandment leads to an expansive sense of responsibility to protect our contacts on social media. It entails paying attention not only to our own activity but also to the activities of our friends, family, and acquaintances. It may necessitate speaking up when someone acts inappropriately.

This idea offers justification for Jonathan's choice in Case Study #1. Believing that Max endangered both his opponent Elizabeth and the school's value system, he took steps to stop inappropriate behavior.

The idea of *cheshbon hanefesh* in commandment 7 sheds an interesting light on this discussion. It asks us to engage in candid reflection on our own social behavior. Generally, its purpose is to lead to *teshuvah*, which is meant to change our conduct for the better. Here, we are to honestly examine how we present ourselves in social media settings. Asking how closely the online image conforms to the actual person lets us evaluate our self-presentation. If we can be honest with ourselves, we can be more honest with others. This reflection also reminds us of Rabbi Dorff's admonition (Text 8b) not to hide our true selves out of fear of others' responses.

Rabbi Samlan's seventh commandment also encourages us to think about why we want people to see us in a certain way. Some users of image-based sites maintain two accounts. On one they only post images of happiness and fun; the viewer is meant to conclude that everything in the individual's life is wonderful. The other account presents a more varied and nuanced view of the person's real life. What compels us, collectively and personally, to pretend that nothing ever goes wrong? If we can come to realize that perfection is impossible to attain and that in the end we can only be our true selves, we will make better decisions about what we post and when and where we post it.

Rabbi Samlan's ninth suggestion adds the idea that people online do not need to see everything we do all the time. Not only that, they also do not need our reaction to everything they post every time. A little bit of contraction (the meaning of the word *tzimtzum*) leaves room for others to express themselves. At the same time, as Rabbi Samlan mentions, limiting ourselves makes space for us to think about our contacts' needs. Who needs to hear a kind word or receive a funny meme? Asking that question, and acting based on the answer, helps us make more constructive use of social media.

These guidelines may help Jewish social media users find a balance between public and private communication, and between individual and communal needs. While much of Jewish life happens in community, tradition teaches respect for the individuals who make up the whole. Given the realities of public pressure to conform, maintaining a degree of privacy, even in essentially public media, can help us preserve our individuality.

Conclusion

Our exploration of social media illustrates the complexity of using halakhic literature to approach new problems.

One aspect of social media that does fit readily into an existing category is the temptation it presents to speak ill of others. The laws of *lashon ha-ra* and *rekhilut* apply directly to this new context. They caution us to avoid taking advantage of the ubiquity and anonymity of social media by sharing information about others without their permission, regardless of whether the information is true or not.

Max, the creator of the insulting Snapchat image in Case Study #1, likely committed *lashon ha-ra*. Leviticus (Text 1a) forbids negative speech about other people; the *Ḥafetz Ḥayyim* adds that "speech" includes writing and images (Text 3b) and that even jokes violate the prohibition (Text 3c). Max further committed *ona'at devarim* against Elizabeth, according to Rabbi Student's interpretation (Text 6). While he never intended her to know about the insult, she nonetheless suffered emotional harm when the story spread around school.

All in all, it is hard to arrive at a satisfactory conclusion about what Jonathan should have done when he saw Max's Snapchat. The same laws suggest that while Jonathan acted with good intentions, he may not be entirely blameless, since by sharing Max's post with the principal he inadvertently caused the rest of the student body to find out about the insult to Elizabeth. Telling a third person what one person said about another is the very definition of *rekhilut,* the prohibition against telling tales (Text 1b, Text 3a). But complicating this critique of Jonathan's choice is the rule codified in the *Ḥafetz Ḥayyim* (Text 5) that allows sharing stories to protect others from harm, as Jonathan asserts he did. Jonathan might also argue that he followed Rabbi Samlan's fourth commandment (Text 8c) to build a metaphorical fence to protect Elizabeth from harm. He might further point out that Max should have thought about this ethical responsibility before sending his Snapchat.

Yet Jonathan had other options. Jonathan might have had a conversation with Max before taking the issue to the school administration. As we saw — not in this chapter but in chapter 2 — the Torah includes a mitzvah called *tochechah* which requires us to rebuke others when we see them doing wrong. Furthermore, another related value discussed in chapter 2, *lifnei iveir,* concerns our responsibility not to cause other people to "stumble," meaning to lead them to do the wrong thing. As with the question of whether Eitan should report Sydney's cheating in chapter 2, there is the possibility that Jonathan's failure to report Max would leave Max to believe he did nothing wrong. Had Jonathan chosen to gently rebuke Max and explain his concerns, the two boys might have aired out their differences over Max's actions and agreed to protect Elizabeth by keeping the matter between them. That course of action would have achieved Jonathan's goal of upholding the school's values while avoiding the public scandal that resulted when the principal got involved. After such a conversation, Max might have reconsidered his use of Snapchat.

On the other hand, even if he promised Jonathan he would never do something like this again, Max could have simply omitted Jonathan from any similar Snapchat messages in the future. Since none of his other friends reacted badly to his joke about Elizabeth, Max might have continued to misuse social media to harm his classmates. All in all, given the *tochechah* mandate, it seems that Jonathan should have spoken first to Max, and if Max did not acknowledge wrongdoing, then have taken the matter to the principal.

Our text study also suggests that the principal's handling of the incident was not without fault. She did not review the Jewish values emphasized at school that supported her belief that Max deserved punishment and explain them to both Max and his parents. Without the benefit of these considerations, Max, supported by his parents, was left believing he himself had been wronged. Going forward, Max seems unlikely to change his behavior (except for excluding Jonathan from private correspondence).

Furthermore, the principal's choice to suspend Max from school resulted in the unintended but possibly foreseeable outcome of the student body's learning about the insulting name he called Elizabeth. In a sense, the principal's act could be interpreted as telling others what someone did without permission, which the Talmud forbids (Text 4). Her decision inadvertently ended up trespassing on Max's privacy too. Ironically, then, in upholding one Jewish value she violated another (Text 7). She—and we—are left to ponder: what other options did she have to discipline Max? What options grounded in Jewish values would have been less liable to lead to these consequences?

Social media raises important questions about privacy, a core value in Jewish tradition. A midrash (Text 7) imagines the Israelites camping in the wilderness in a way that honored family privacy. From this the Mishnah derives a series of laws that protect people's privacy in their homes (Text

7). According to halakhah, *hezek re'iyah*, being seen against one's will, is tantamount to physical or property damage (Text 8a).

Balancing privacy with security proved ethically challenging as well as costly when a school district monitored R.'s school-owned computer at home. While the district maintained it had a duty to protect its property and students, halakhic sources emphasize each individual's right to privacy (see the Mishnah and Gemara in Text 7). The district's violation of the privacy of R.'s bedroom is certainly a classic instance of *hezek re'iyah* (Text 8a). The question of what schools can appropriately do to safeguard their property without invading students' privacy remains unresolved.

Recent developments suggest that technology is changing Americans' understanding of privacy in ways that differ from halakhic traditions. We do not stop to think about how much personal information anyone who searches our names online can find. We hand over a great deal of personal information without considering who gets it and how they may use it. Data about us represents tremendous potential profit for technology companies. Companies called data brokers aggregate information ranging from social media posts to browsing history, from phone location data to medical records. They profit by selling information to companies that target advertisements to consumers based on their online activity.[9] The ads and discount offers we receive based on our recent activity online hints at just how well technology companies know us and our preferences. Governments also find this data useful. Some use it to identify participants in political rallies.[10] Police have begun using such data in their investigations.[11]

Modern electronic devices all have privacy settings that ostensibly are under the user's control. Yet researchers have found that Google, for example, can track individuals' travels through apps on their phones even after they turn off location history.[12] It seems that simply using a smartphone and participating in social media mean that we no longer have privacy as previously understood. Rabbi Dorff's argument (Text 8b) that surrendering our privacy risks our individuality begins to look out of date. Given how central they are both to work and social life today, most people cannot opt out of using phones and apps. Unless we respond as a society by passing laws limiting the collection of personal data and the ways it gets used and shared, we may no longer have practical options for keeping our personal information private.

Complicating this reality is the fact that each social media site has its own agenda. A well-known adage holds that if you get something for free — most popular social media sites do not charge users — then *you* are the product for sale. Tech companies now use (exponentially improving) artificial intelligence about every one of us, grounded in what we've posted, read, liked, and shared, both to keep us glued to their sites and to give advertisers their most likely customers.[13]

Given the rapid technological changes of our era, the social media landscape may soon look very different from the realities as of this writing. And yet however it metamorphoses in the months and years to come, and however inexactly ancient wisdom may guide real-world situations, we can still call upon core ethical ideals to help us navigate our life choices.

4

Sex and Intimacy

Decisions to engage in or postpone sexual activity require many ethical choices that, by definition, involve other people. When are Jews to give in to their urges, and when are they to resist them? How are we to discuss sexual matters and make consensual decisions with potential partners?

In offering us guidance, Judaism also makes certain assumptions about sexual ethics. As we will see, for the most part Judaism endorses human sexuality as a beautiful part of God's creation. But traditionally, its approval applies only to heterosexual marriage. No apologetics highlighting Judaism's positive attitude toward sex can obscure the fact that it deplores sexual contact between unmarried people. No honest presentation of traditional ideas can conceal their retrograde attitudes toward women's sexuality and toward LGBTQ activity.

A useful modern Jewish sex ethic must account for changes in our understandings of gender and other new social attitudes and scientific findings. It must incorporate a wider array of sexual relationships and identities. This chapter offers a test of the Jewish textual tradition's ability to inform our contemporary ethical decision-making. The case studies allow us to consider a number of possibilities for reinterpreting the tradition's ideas.

Case Study #1: Four Ideas about Jewish Sexual Ethics

Four college friends are chatting in a dorm room when the conversation turns to the kind of sex lives they want to pursue. Since all of them were involved in different Jewish youth groups in their high school years, Tali asks, "Did any of your high school youth advisors discuss this subject?"

Everyone says yes.

Jordan says, "My temple's youth group went on a retreat in ninth grade devoted to sex education and to telling us what Jewish tradition had to say about sex. The leaders, a husband and wife team, both rabbis, said that

Judaism approves of sexual pleasure. We are supposed to make decisions based on respect for ourselves and for the other person, because we are both made in the image of God. That seems like a realistic approach."

Michael says, "My day school's eleventh-grade Jewish studies course included a unit on sexual ethics. I remember reading an article that suggested a sliding scale. While long-term marriage might be at the top of the scale, other relationships could include sex if they conform to other Jewish values, like mutual respect and consent, and if no one takes advantage of anyone else. I like the idea of a Jewish ethics that recognizes something positive in relationships other than marriage, since I imagine it will be a long time before I decide to get married."

Hannah says, "My youth group included a lot of kids whose families belong to Orthodox synagogues. Our leaders told us to act modestly and not display our bodies to the world. Boys and girls at our programs weren't allowed to dance together, let alone touch each other. Leaders stressed waiting for marriage, and they encouraged us to marry young so that we wouldn't face too much temptation to do things we shouldn't. I may not fully live that way now—I have danced at a couple of college parties—but traditional Judaism continues to guide and inspire my choices."

Tali says, "If that's all Judaism has to say about it, I'm not sure why it matters. I want to enjoy myself and give my partners pleasure, too. It's hard for me to see why people shouldn't do anything they like, as long as they don't hurt or exploit anyone else. Any ethical system that doesn't recognize that principle sounds irrelevant. Besides, people like us won't marry very soon—we'll get our college degrees and finish graduate or professional school first. Is Judaism saying we're not supposed to have sex for maybe a decade? Sounds like Jewish tradition has nothing much to teach me about this part of life."

The students in this case study represent four ways of engaging with Jewish sexual ethics. Some temples hold retreats similar to the one Jordan participated in, where adolescents learn that Judaism looks positively on sex and the main moral requirement is interpersonal respect. Michael's class learned an approach from the 1970s that attempts to update traditional ethics to accommodate the views of Jews committed both to Judaism and to contemporary mores. Hannah was taught a traditional view that limits sexual activity to heterosexual marriage and limits temptation by separating unmarried members of the opposite sex. Tali articulates a central question for this chapter: Can Jewish ethics contribute to our decision-making in this sensitive area?

Case Study #2: LGBTQ Orientations

Tali has another friend, David, who identifies as gay. As a teen, David spent time in a more traditional Jewish youth group and never discussed his sexual orientation with his advisers. Knowing that the Torah forbids same-sex male relations, David wonders what Judaism might offer him as he too navigates the college dating scene.

Tali and David's mutual friend Emma is attracted to people of all genders. She wonders what Jewish ethics has to say about bisexuality in college and beyond.

These case studies pose critical questions for modern Jewish ethics. Do traditional Jewish texts, focused on heterosexual marriage as the only setting for sex, have anything to teach a generation that does not accept marriage for all as the ultimate goal? Closely related is the question of whether Judaism can adapt to new scientific findings and social attitudes. While some Jews today remain loyal to the Torah's understandings of gender and LGBTQ identities, they are likely a minority.

This chapter's text study will consider the relevance of traditional norms to those who seek a livable, contemporary Jewish sex ethic. We begin with texts describing biblical and Rabbinic ideas about the nature of human beings and their sex drive. Our first texts are a Torah verse and a comment by the thirteenth-century Spanish scholar Rabbi Moshe ben Naḥman, known as Ramban.

Text Study #1: The Two Inclinations

Text 1a — Gen. 1:31

AND GOD SAW ALL that had been made, and found it very good. And there was evening and there was morning, the sixth day.

NOTHING IN THE HUMAN organs is created flawed or ugly. Everything is created with divine wisdom and is therefore complete, exalted, good, and pleasant.

QUESTIONS FOR INQUIRY

1. What implications does God's finding everything in creation "very good" have for how we are to look at the world?
2. How is Ramban's idea related to this verse?
3. What implications does his approach have for understanding human sexuality?

COMMENTS

The creation story in the first chapter of the Torah establishes a basic outlook of traditional Judaism: the world and everything in it is good. Nothing God made could be fundamentally evil. More than once during the six days of creation, the Creator stops to declare the results "good." In verse 31, at the completion of the world, the phrase becomes "very good."

Based on this chapter, Jewish tradition affirmed the beauty of the world in which we live. Rather than dream of a time when we will no longer face the challenges of living in the real world, we appreciate everything God created for our use. If we find anything lacking in the world, we work to repair it, to restore it to the status of "very good."

The medieval scholar Ramban, writing about sexuality, extends the label of goodness to all parts of the human body. Anything created through "divine wisdom" must by definition be good and complete. Thus every part of the human body, reflecting the Divine image, is "complete, exalted, good, and pleasant." That positive outlook includes the sex organs. Like the rest of our bodies, they are created with divine wisdom. Our bodies in their entirety constitute a wonderful divine gift. The fact that people sometimes do harm using the good things God created does not contradict the basic insight.

Ramban may argue in part against a competing outlook in Jewish tradition that discourages enjoyment of bodily pleasures. Rabbi Eliezer in the Talmud suggests that a man should uncover only enough of his wife's body to make intercourse possible, and to engage in the act "as if a demon forces him to" (*Nedarim* 20b; see also Text 4).

Rabbinic tradition teaches that while sexuality is undoubtedly part of the creation that God sees as "very good," it has its dark side. A classic midrash on the same phrase in Genesis makes the point elegantly. (The midrash is attributed to Rav Naḥman son of Shmuel, an Amora of the third century, not to be confused with the thirteenth-century Spanish author of Text 1b.)

Text 2 — *Genesis Rabbah* 9:7

RAV NAḤMAN THE SON of Shmuel said: "[Found] it very good" — this refers to the good inclination; "And [found] it very good" — this refers to the evil inclination.

But is the evil inclination very good? How so?

Were it not for the evil inclination, a person would not build a house, would not marry, would not have children, and would not engage in business. As Solomon said (Eccles. 4:4): "(All work comes from) man's jealousy for his neighbor."

QUESTIONS FOR INQUIRY

1. In what way does Rav Naḥman son of Shmuel claim that the evil inclination actually leads to good?
2. How do building, marrying and having children, and engaging in business come from our evil inclination rather than our good inclination?
3. Do you believe the sexual urge comes from the dark side of humanity? Do you agree that it nevertheless leads to good results?

Text 2 illustrates a technique the early Rabbis commonly used to derive new meaning from a verse in the Torah. As we have seen elsewhere, they read the Torah assuming that nothing in it is superfluous or merely a matter of style. Each word appears for a reason. The apparently extraneous word here is the conjunction "and." Several times the Torah reports simply, "God found it very good." Why, here, "*and* found it very good"?

According to R. Naḥman son of Shmuel, the word *and* adds a layer of meaning. His lesson, too, appears surprising at first glance. We assume that the good and the evil inclinations (in Hebrew, *yetzer ha-tov* and *yetzer ha-ra*) are to be, respectively, cultivated and shunned, as one drives us to do good, the other, evil. Not so, says Rav Naḥman: the evil inclination, too, leads to good. He identifies three basic areas of human endeavor in which the bad inclination paradoxically leads to good: building a house, marrying and having a family, and engaging in business.

How is each of these activities associated with the evil inclination? Per the Ecclesiastes prooftext, building a house and engaging in business may in fact stem from pride and jealousy: people may want to show how much more wealth they have or how much smarter they are than others. Nonetheless, acting out of selfish motives can yield positive results: a growing and developing society.

The same is true of marriage and childbearing. Sexuality may emanate from the negative quality of lust, the desire simply to use another person for one's own pleasure. Yet when a person sublimates lust into sexual satisfaction with a marital partner, much good follows. The couple creates a new family, and the human race persists for another generation. In the Rabbinic view, family life, too, is necessary for the world to continue developing according to God's plan.

This midrash darkens the rosy picture Ramban paints of the goodness of human sexuality (Text 1b) by acknowledging the dark side of the sex drive. Desire for sex can lead to harm and exploitation—but without it, the human race would die out. Here, too, what comes from our bad inclination winds up serving our best interests. This is a basic idea about human sexuality in Jewish tradition. The sex drive is a powerful, even dangerous force. Left uncontrolled, it can lead to destructive outcomes. Channeled properly in the marital relationship, it instead builds and perpetuates human society.

To understand more about the traditional Jewish approach, we next explore some of its ideas about sexual expression within marriage. We begin with a legal discussion in the Talmud.

Text Study #2: Sex within Marriage

Text 3 — *Mishnah Ketubot 5:6; Ketubot 62b*

Mishnah

A MAN WHO TAKES a vow not to have intercourse with his wife:
The school of Shammai say: [she must wait] two weeks. The school of Hillel say: one week.

Students who leave for the purpose of studying Torah without the consent of their wives [have] thirty days; laborers, one week.

[The law of providing sexual] pleasure [to one's wife] that is stated in the Torah [is as follows]: one at leisure, daily; laborers, twice a week; donkey drivers, once a week; camel drivers, once every thirty days; sailors, every six months — these are the words of Rabbi Eliezer.

Gemara

WHEN IS THE IDEAL time for Torah scholars to fulfill their conjugal obligations? Rav Yehuda said that Shmuel said: The appropriate time for them is from Shabbat eve to Shabbat eve, that is, each Friday night.

QUESTIONS FOR INQUIRY

1. Based on the evidence in this Mishnah, which partner in a marriage is responsible for the other's sexual satisfaction?

2. What rule governs the decisions about how often a man must have sex with his wife?

3. What larger conclusions about sexual ethics could you draw from this Mishnah?

The Mishnah's legislation about the frequency of marital sex follows from the talmudic Rabbis' understanding of Exodus 21:10. The Torah there outlines the responsibilities of a man who frees one of his female slaves in order to marry her. The verse reads, "If he takes another [into the household as his wife], he must not withhold from this [first] one her food, her clothing, or her conjugal rights." The Hebrew word translated as "conjugal rights" is *onah*, a word indicating something that happens at regular intervals. The Rabbis conclude that sexual pleasure is the wife's right, which her husband must provide regularly. The Mishnah before us details how a man carries out his conjugal obligation.

In the first part of the Mishnah, the schools of Shammai and Hillel dispute the case of a man who vows not to have intercourse with his wife. Vows in halakhah must be kept, but must have a limited duration: no one can swear off a given activity permanently. Here the problem arises that if a man vows not to sleep with his wife for too long a time, he would violate the law of *onah*: her conjugal rights. (The commentators on the Mishnah assume that such a vow arises from anger; otherwise, a man would not give up his own sexual enjoyment.) The house of Shammai limits the duration of the vow to two weeks, which may correspond to the time the Torah establishes for the impurity of a woman who gives birth (Lev. 12:5). The house of Hillel rules more strictly: a man may swear off marital intercourse only for a week. The week may correspond to the time Leviticus instructs a husband to keep away from his wife when she menstruates (Lev. 15:19).

The middle of the Mishnah elaborates further on situations where a woman's husband makes himself unavailable to provide her *onah*. If the husband leaves home to study Torah without asking his wife's permission, he may stay away for a month. Husbands who earn their living as laborers may leave their wives, presumably for a job, only for a week.

The rest of the Mishnah details the law of *onah*: what is the minimum necessary to satisfy the wife's conjugal rights? The answer depends on the husband's profession. Those who do not work for a living ("at leisure") have a daily duty. Those whose work takes them to sea for long periods, in contrast, need satisfy their wives only once every six months. The principle asks both husband and wife to consider the other's needs. Since the husband must support his wife financially (also specified in Exod. 21:10), she must allow him to leave home as his work requires. For his part, the husband must pay appropriate attention to his wife, not extending his work absences beyond what the Mishnah considers reasonable.

The Gemara asks about a profession the Mishnah does not discuss: Torah scholarship. A Torah scholar's obligation turns out to be similar to donkey drivers, whose work resembled that of modern teamsters. Delivering a load and returning home might keep them away for a week. Torah scholars receive permission to spend the entire week in their place of study. They must return home to spend Shabbat with their wives, and use that occasion to share sexual pleasure.

Bearing in mind that this entire passage speaks only to married, heterosexual couples, we still may appreciate its recognition that both men and women experience desire and deserve sexual satisfaction. *Ketubot* gives no sense that only men or only women enjoy sex. In contrast to some Western cultures, it centers the discussion of how often sex should happen on women. The wife is the one who has a right to satisfaction of her libido. Halakhah asks the husband to attend to his wife's desire more than to his own.

In this sense, we can understand the halakhah in accordance with modern sensibilities about equality. This passage portrays sexual pleasure as shared between husband and wife. Unusually for early Rabbinic literature, it does not legislate exclusively from the male perspective. While the idea that only men earn a living does not fit our experience, the idea of asking each partner to pay attention to the other's needs does. This piece of the tradition may be useful in constructing a modern sex ethic.

We still require more information about what the halakhic tradition means when it speaks of satisfying a wife's conjugal rights. As we will see, the Talmud does not shy away from discussing what happens in the bedroom in more detail.

Text 4 — *Nedarim* 20a–b

RABBI YOḤANAN BEN DEHAVAI said: The ministering angels told me four matters: For what reason do lame people come into existence? It is because their fathers overturn their tables [*Rashi*: coitus with the woman on top].

For what reason do mute people come into existence? It is because their fathers kiss that place [female genitals].

For what reason do deaf people come into existence? It is because their parents converse while engaging in sexual intercourse.

For what reason do blind people come into existence? It is because their fathers look at that place. . . .

Rabbi Yoḥanan said: That is the statement of Yoḥanan ben Dehavai. However, the Sages said: The halakhah is not in accordance with the opinion of Yoḥanan ben Dehavai. Rather, whatever a man wishes to do with his wife he may do. He may engage in sexual intercourse with her in any manner that he wishes, and need not concern himself with these restrictions.

As an allegory, it is like meat that comes from the butcher. If he wants to eat it salted, he may. If he wants to eat it roasted, he may eat it roasted. If he wants to eat it cooked, he may eat it cooked. If he wants to eat it boiled, he may eat it boiled. And likewise, with regard to fish that come from the fisherman.

QUESTIONS FOR INQUIRY

1. What attitude toward marital sex does each side of the dispute between R. Yoḥanan ben Dehavai and the Rabbis reflect?
2. Does the allegory suggested at the end of the passage add any nuance to our understanding of the Rabbis' attitude?
3. What implications might each view in this text have for forming a modern Jewish sex ethic?

Rabbi Yoḥanan ben Dehavai and the Sages articulate two approaches to marital intimacy that recur throughout the halakhic literature. Yoḥanan ben Dehavai represents a more limited, restrictive, severe view: intercourse may take place only in the missionary position; men may not kiss or even look at female genitals; and marital relations must happen in silence. Some posttalmudic sources, stressing the holiness of the commandment to be fruitful and multiply, will adopt this restrictive view, insisting that marital sex take place in the dark, with minimal conversation, and proceed as quickly as possible to conception.

The Sages—here, notably, representing the majority of talmudic opinion—represent a more liberal view. They assert that the husband may do anything he wishes with his wife. (While this passage does not say so outright, we will see in Texts 5a and 5b that the wife must agree.) The Rabbis rule that a couple may enjoy sexual intercourse in any fashion. They seem to put less stress on the mitzvah of procreation and to acknowledge the simple desire for pleasure.

This attitude toward sexual pleasure recalls the ideas derived from the texts that opened this chapter. If human sexuality is part of God's "very good" creation, and if the sex organs are as wondrous and positive as anything God made, it follows that married couples should use them as they prefer. Sexual intercourse, in all its human variety, within the marital bond becomes another way of appreciating the gifts of God's world.

The allegory proposed to illustrate the Rabbis' position seems innocuous at first reading. Just as people have different tastes in food, it implies, they have different tastes in sexual activity. How one indulges one's sexual preferences within marriage makes no more difference than how one indulges culinary ones.

Rabbi Danya Ruttenberg, an author named by the *Forward* as one of the fifty most influential women rabbis, points out something more. As permissive as this passage appears, "Even here, not everything goes: within certain 'kosher' parameters, one may engage sexually as one pleases, but there are in fact parameters."[1] In other words, the comparison to food implies that just as the system of kashrut governs our eating habits, so must there be laws applying to sex. Just as halakhah limits (for example) what we eat and when we eat it, Jewish law regulates whom we have sex with and when we have it. The Talmud here reminds us that while sex is meant to be enjoyed, like every other human endeavor it must be sanctified within the boundaries established by halakhah.

Further reflection on the nature of the comparison causes discomfort. As Ruttenberg also notes, it is only the woman whom the Talmud compares to meat and fish. She moves from being a partner whose desires her husband must satisfy regularly to an item that he, so to speak, consumes. In modern terms, the allegory treats the wife as a sexual object—someone on whom the husband acts out his desire—rather than a sexual subject, a person with her own likes and dislikes. While we may prefer the opinion of the Sages to that of R. Yoḥanan ben Dehavai, we may remain dissatisfied with the way it seems to diminish women's agency in sexual relationships.

Fortunately, the Rabbinic tradition does not treat women exclusively as sexual objects for men's use. As we have seen, halakhah requires husbands to satisfy their wives' desires. It also forbids them from deciding that the time is right for sex without their wives' agreement. The following two texts develop the halakhic requirement that women, too, consent to sex. The Note in the Shulḥan Arukh represents the Ashkenazic practice recorded by R. Moshe Isserles.

Text 5a — *Eiruvin* 100b

RAMI BAR ḤAMA SAID that Rav Asi said: It is prohibited for a man to force his wife to have sex, as it is written: "And he who hastens with his feet sins" [Prov. 19:2].

Text 5b — Shulḥan Arukh, *Even HaEzer* 25:2

ONE MAY SPEAK DURING intercourse about sexual matters, in order to increase desire. Or if he was angry at her and needs to placate her, he may speak to her to reconcile her and make her want intercourse.

Note: A man can do with his wife whatever he wants. He can have intercourse whenever he likes; kiss any part of her body he likes; and have vaginal or anal intercourse, or stimulate himself with other parts of her body. . . .

He may not have intercourse without her consent.

QUESTIONS FOR INQUIRY

1. What do these texts add to what we learned from Text 4?
2. What do these texts teach about the roles of husband and wife in their sexual relationship?
3. What do these sources contribute to thinking about Case Study #1?

COMMENTS

The Talmud and the medieval halakhah forbid a man to have sex without his wife's consent. Rashi explains that "feet" in the Proverbs verse is a euphemism for sex. Rami bar Ḥama quotes Rav Asi as interpreting the verse that it is a sin to "hasten"—that is, to force—one's wife to have intercourse. This ruling demonstrates that a husband may not treat his wife entirely as an instrument for his own pleasure.

The discussion in the Shulḥan Arukh shows that the tradition adopted the view of the Rabbis cited by Rabbi Yoḥanan in *Nedarim* 20a–b (Text 4). While some halakhic authors quote R. Yoḥanan b. Dehavai, whose view is far more restrictive, Isserles follows the majority opinion, which allows husband and wife to decide what they enjoy. While explaining the law (taking, as is its usual practice, the man's point of view), the Shulḥan Arukh adds the requirement that the wife consent to sex. Including that rule in this context shows that her interests matter, too. Passages like this one make clear that overall, for all its androcentrism, the halakhic tradition understands that women, too, experience desire and have sexual preferences—and, should a woman prefer not to engage in intercourse, the man must respect her preference.

Here we see support in the halakhic sources for Jordan and Michael's perspectives in Case Study #1 that regardless of gender, everyone must agree to engage in any sexual activity. In addition, everyone must recognize their partners' needs as well as their own. That standard would apply to LGBTQ Jews like David and Emma in Case Study #2, as well as to their straight friends. In saying this, of course, we must recognize that we are adapting halakhic rules to a modern Jewish ethic, as the law itself upholds these ideals only in the context of a heterosexual relationship sanctified by marriage.

We've seen that the tradition recognizes the strength of the sexual urge in both men and women. Some of the *halakhot* setting boundaries on sexual expression derive from an awareness that passion is hard to control. Our next text study looks at the power of sexual desire.

Text Study #3: The Power of Sexual Desire

Text 6 — *Kiddushin* 81a

RABBI AKIVA WOULD RIDICULE sinners. One day, the Tempter appeared to him as a woman at the top of a palm tree.

Rabbi Akiva grabbed hold of the palm tree and began climbing.

When he was halfway up the palm tree, the evil inclination left him and said to him:

"Were it not for the fact that they proclaim about you in heaven: 'Be careful with regard to Rabbi Akiva and his Torah,' I would have made your blood like two *ma'a* [an almost worthless amount]."

QUESTIONS FOR INQUIRY

1. Why do you think Rabbi Akiva ridiculed sinners?
2. How did Rabbi Akiva respond to the temptation he faced?
3. What does the evil inclination's comment to the rabbi mean?
4. What lesson or lessons does the story teach?

COMMENTS

In this droll tale, Rabbi Akiva learns the danger of smugness about one's own virtue. He felt so confident of his righteousness that he would make fun of those who sinned. How, he apparently wondered, could they be so weak as to give in to temptation?

That attitude lasted until the day he himself faced a strong temptation.

Note that the Hebrew word from which the English word *Satan* derives has been translated as "the Tempter" to reflect the way that figure appears in the TANAKH and Rabbinic literature. The Tempter sets traps for the righteous, claiming they will not stay on the straight and narrow if tested. Here, the Tempter takes the form of a beguiling woman atop a palm tree. Akiva immediately begins to climb the tree. Clearly, he craves this woman. And yet, should Akiva commit this one sin, it will destroy his reputation. So powerful is the sexual urge, so severe the consequences of giving in to it, that even the renowned Rabbi Akiva would lose the world's esteem if he failed just once.

Fortunately for him, his evil inclination leaves him when he is halfway to his goal. The Tempter lets him know that only Akiva's reputation has saved him from sin. Only because Heaven highly values Akiva's Torah—what he learns and teaches—does the rabbi escape unharmed.

As is often the case with talmudic tales, this story exaggerates to drive its point home. Surely Rabbi Akiva could do *teshuvah* and repent. One mistake does not necessarily undo all his contributions. Apparently, however, we must take sexual sins especially seriously. As we saw, tradition associates the sex drive with the evil side of human nature. We must take special care not to allow the evil to overwhelm the good that can result from sexual urges.

In modern terms, the story has its troubling aspects. Most disturbing is the treatment of the woman. She has no agency. For all that she is not a "real" woman, but the Tempter in disguise, the tale nonetheless reveals underlying Rabbinic attitudes about women. Her only function is to tempt and distract a man. She draws his mind away from Torah, its proper focus, toward his *yetzer ha-ra*, his evil inclination. Merely seeing her makes him react from a primitive part of his brain. While the Tempter scolds Akiva at the tale's end, we cannot help noticing that some of the blame concurrently falls on the woman. Just by being in a place where Akiva can see her, she almost causes his downfall.

Most contemporary Jews would agree that a workable ethic must treat men and women equally as agents in their own sex lives. Women must not bear responsibility for men's self-control. Men must not think of women merely as objects of desire. Each must see the divine image in the other. As in the discussion of marital obligations (Texts 3 and 4), each must take the other's desires into account.

Even so, we might learn two things from this story. One is the need to remain vigilant in dealing with our sexual desires. Indulging them may yield pleasure, companionship, and other goods. It may also yield hurt feelings, regret, and other harms. Context matters. Rabbi Akiva lusted after someone he did not know; he responded only to the woman's appearance. That implies that seeking pleasure solely on the basis of physical attraction may be dangerous. That side of sexuality comes from the *yetzer ha-ra* without the admixture of good.

The story's second lesson is that no one is immune from the kind of sudden lustful urge that leads to trouble. If one of the greatest of the *tannaim* could fall into this trap, any of us may succumb to temptation. Just as Rabbi Akiva should not have ridiculed those who sin, we must not imagine that we would never make the mistakes others make. We must not trust ourselves too much; anyone who thinks they are beyond reproach may be setting themselves up for a fall.

For those who want to rebuild Jewish sexual ethics without subscribing fully to the early Rabbis' ideas, like Jordan, Michael, and Tali in Case Study #1, these two cautions build upon the previous two lessons that people of both sexes deserve equal treatment and choice in sexual situations. A modern Jewish sexual ethics might also take into account the power of the sex drive, recognizing both its potential and its dangers. It might encourage us to recognize our weaknesses as well as our strengths in this context. It might teach each of us to monitor ourselves carefully, so that if we do have sex, we can be certain that we are not merely satisfying physical urges.

In effect, in doing so we may be modernizing the talmudic idea of "not having intercourse licentiously" (see Text 7c). If nonmarital sex is permissible in our system—whether it is or not is our next question—we can be assured that it must not be engaged in lightly.

Is it possible to indulge sexual desire outside of marriage without falling into licentiousness? The halakhic view is more nuanced than we may imagine. We begin our study with talmudic debates and the halakhah recorded in the *Mishneh Torah*.

Text 7a — *Mishnah Kiddushin* 1:1

A WOMAN IS ACQUIRED [for marriage] in three ways: . . . through money, through a document, or through sexual intercourse.

Text 7b — *Yevamot* 61b

RABBI ELAZAR SAYS: AN unmarried man who has intercourse with an unmarried woman without intending marriage makes her ineligible to marry into the priesthood [*zonah*, literally: unchaste, licentious].

Rav Amram said: The law does not follow Rabbi Elazar's opinion.

Text 7c — *Gittin* 81b

THE SCHOOL OF SHAMMAI hold: An [unmarried] man will have intercourse licentiously; but the school of Hillel hold: An [unmarried] man will not have intercourse licentiously.

Text 7d — *Mishneh Torah*, Laws of Marriage 1:4

BEFORE THE GIVING OF the Torah, if a man encountered a woman in public and they both agreed, he would pay her and have intercourse with her . . . and this is what [the Torah] calls a prostitute [*kedeshah*].

Since the Torah was given, the prostitute is forbidden, as it is said (Deut. 23:18), "No Israelite woman shall be a prostitute." Therefore, any man who has intercourse with a woman licentiously, without betrothal, is punished.

1. What is the point of the disagreements between Rabbi Elazar and the school of Shammai, on one side, and Rav Amram and the school of Hillel, on the other?
2. What does the debate tell us about the Rabbis' attitude toward sex between unmarried adults?
3. Could a modern Jewish sex ethic interpret any of these texts to allow some unmarried adults to have sex?
4. Which view or views expressed in Case Study #1 do the texts support? Consider these four texts along with Texts 1a through 5a.

COMMENTS

Text 7a provides background for understanding the two texts that follow. In Rabbinic law, a man "acquires" a woman when she agrees to marry him. To accomplish the betrothal, either he gives her something of value — money or a legal document — or they have intercourse for the purpose of marriage. While the *amoraim* prohibited betrothal through intercourse, the original law stated in the Mishnah technically remained in force.

The fact that intercourse creates a marriage led directly to the question of two unmarried adults who have sex without intending to marry. Is such a sex act permitted because it could establish a marriage, or is it forbidden as unchastity? Rabbi Elazar and the school of Shammai believe that all intercourse outside the context of marriage is by definition licentious behavior. Rav Amram reports that the law does not agree with R. Elazar's view. At a minimum, that means that a single woman who has intercourse with a single man would not be disqualified from later marrying into a priestly family.

The school of Hillel take the opposing view. By stating that "An [unmarried] man will not have intercourse licentiously," they teach that intercourse between two single adults always reveals the intention to marry. If so, the man must give the woman a divorce document (in Hebrew, a *get*) before she may marry anyone else.

Some modern readers suggest that we extend the school of Hillel's view beyond the immediate legal context, meaning that not every sex act outside of marriage is mere immorality. That opens the possibility that

Jewish ethics might, under some circumstances, approve nonmarital sex. Rabbi Danya Ruttenberg writes that tradition "acknowledges the reality of sex outside of marriage, regarding it with some ambivalence," noting that Rav Amram states (in Text 7b) that the law does not follow Rabbi Elazar. That implies that some sex outside of marriage might be permissible.[2]

However plausible we moderns may find Ruttenberg's interpretation, the halakhic tradition did not adopt it. Maimonides summarizes the law in its stringency in his *Mishneh Torah*, Laws of Marriage (Text 7d): any intercourse outside of marriage, or not intended to establish a new marriage, amounts to prostitution. On his reading, we cannot justify any sex outside of marriage.

All of our texts so far offer insights into Case Study #1. Much of the material confirms what Hannah recalled from her youth group: Jewish tradition approves of sex in the context of heterosexual marriage. Meanwhile, the halakhic tradition also offers some support to the ideas the youth group leaders taught Jordan and Michael. Rabbi Ruttenberg's expansive reframing of select sources is one means of rethinking Jewish sexual ethics from within the texts to allow sex in certain situations outside of the ideal context of marriage. Ruttenberg proposes that even the Talmud does not write off every woman who engages in intercourse outside of marriage. This understanding might be coupled with Judaism's approval of sex as a "very good" part of God's creation, and with the halakhic recognition that both men and women have the right to fulfill their desires.

Careful students of this chapter will have noticed that with the exception of Texts 1b and 2, the halakhic sources explain sexual ethics in terms of behavior: what a person may or may not do. Rabbi David Teutsch, a leader of the Reconstructionist movement, points out that this is an area where contemporary Jews differ from those who came before us. "It is important to remember that contemporary thinking about sexual ethics does not begin with norms—what one must or must not do. It . . . begins with values and ideals."[3] Teutsch's formulation suggests that constructing a modern Jewish sex ethic may involve making ethical decisions differently than our ancestors did. Focusing exclusively on the norms detailed in halakhah would lead many liberal Jews to Tali's conclusion: Jewish tradition has nothing further to teach. A values approach is more consistent with our way of thinking, and we would do better to consult the values embedded in Jewish tradition to guide our behavior.

First, let's take note of values about sexuality explicitly mentioned in Rabbinic traditions. We begin with excerpts from the wedding ceremony.

Text Study #4: Sexual Values

Text 8a — *Birkat Eirusin*, Betrothal Blessing
from the Wedding Ceremony

BLESSED ARE YOU, YHVH our God, Who rules the universe, Who sanctifies us with Your commandments and commanded us about forbidden relations, prohibited the betrothed to us, and permitted those who are married to us by means of the wedding canopy and the betrothal ceremony [*kiddushin*].

Blessed are You YHVH, Who sanctifies the people Israel by means of the wedding canopy and the betrothal ceremony.

Text 8b — Blessing Six of the Wedding Ceremony

GRANT PERFECT JOY TO these loving companions, as You gave joy to Your creation in the Garden of Eden. Blessed are You YHVH, Who creates the joy of groom and bride.

QUESTIONS FOR INQUIRY
1. What key words or phrases do these blessings use repeatedly?
2. What do those words or phrases imply about sex and marriage?
3. Do these ideas have value for contemporary sexual decision-making?

COMMENTS
The betrothal blessing, recited early in the wedding ceremony, names values that tradition associates with marriage. It calls marriage *kiddushin*,

derived from the Hebrew root *k-d-sh*, meaning "holy." This demonstrates two things about the Rabbis' ideas about marriage. First, marrying is a holy act. It is one of the commandments that adds holiness to our lives. Marriage, sanctified by the rituals performed under the *ḥuppah* or wedding canopy, brings holiness to the new husband and wife.

The second idea emerges when we consider the meaning of *holy*. At its base, the word means something set apart, dedicated, or consecrated. By engaging in *kiddushin*, a husband and wife set each other apart from all others. Each dedicates him or herself to the other.

After the betrothal (*eirusin*) comes the second part of the wedding ceremony: *nisuin*, or marriage. It includes a series of seven blessings. The sixth blessing asks God to grant the newlywed couple the gift of joy resembling that of the first humans living together in the Garden of Eden.

Especially notable for the purpose of constructing a modern Jewish sex ethic is the phrase used to describe the nuptial couple: "loving companions." As previously discussed, modern Jewish sexual ethics might best be built on the ideal values rather than the specific practices prescribed by tradition. Here we may deduce that holiness is not the only value tradition finds in marriage. Partners also share love and offer each other companionship.

Thinking about partnerships other than marriage in terms of companionship leads to the recognition that sex may be more justifiable in some relationships than others. This line of thought would appear to rule out sex without any trace of companionship. Anonymous sex, one-night stands, and other encounters between partners who know and care little about each other would be unacceptable. On the other hand, having sex as part of a relationship of two people who offer each other companionship short of marriage might be an ethically acceptable choice.

Many moderns include love on the list of values they consider relevant to sexual decisions. If sex is understood as an expression of love, a Jewish sex ethic might impel us to ask if we love someone before having sex with that person. The values of companionship and love might also apply as much to same-sex couples as to those of the opposite sex.

A related question is whether the sex under consideration would build love between the partners or only satisfy physical desires. Rabbinic tradition always opposed sexual activity merely to satisfy desire. The Talmud (*Sanhedrin* 75a) tells a story about a man who became ill out of lust for a particular woman. Doctors said that the only way to save his life was for the woman to have intercourse with him; the Rabbis ruled it was better for him to die. They said the same to proposals that he see her naked and even that she just speak with him from behind a fence. The severity of their response demonstrates the tradition's opposition to sex for physical gratification alone. It approves only of sex that promotes other important values, such as family life and procreation. In modern times, we might expand this idea to include a broader array of values. The next three texts in our text study suggest ways to accomplish that expansion on the ideals of Rabbinic traditions.

Returning to the wedding ceremony, the third value—holiness—presents greater challenges in practical application than the first two values from the nuptial blessings. "What makes interpersonal relationships holy?" and "What can partners do to foster holiness?" are important questions open to interpretation. Beyond this, it is not easy to decide what relationships other than marriages are, or potentially can become, holy. The traditional Jewish ideal of marriage as a holy relationship raises the question of whether relationships created by those not yet ready to marry deserve the same label.

Nevertheless, some contemporary thinkers propose holiness as a foundation for rethinking Jewish sexual ethics for modern times. They suggest various ways of finding or creating holiness in sexual liaisons outside of marriage. One such effort in the Reform movement came in response to Rabbi Eric Yoffie's Presidential Address at the 2005 Union for Reform Judaism Biennial. "Our kids want to know how sex relates to love and a caring relationship; how to deal with fears and temptations; what is permissible and what is not," he proclaimed to Reform spiritual and lay leaders. "Our kids are frustrated by the combined failure of their parents and their synagogues to offer them practical help here . . . since we have told them again and again that Judaism is an all-embracing way of life."[4] The "Sacred Choices" curriculum for teaching Jewish values about sexuality to teenagers followed in 2007. Its author, educator Rabbi Laura Novak Winer, identified five levels of sexual relationships, each one reaching a higher level of holiness than the previous one.

Text 9a — Novak Winer, *Sacred Choices*

THE FIVE LEVELS OF Sexual Relationships [(1) Conquest without Consent; (2) Healthy Orgasm; (3) Mutual Consent without Exclusivity; (4) Love with Exclusivity; (5) Marriage with Public Commitment] represent a continuum of holiness, the lowest level being the least holy [actually a desecration of the sacred] and the highest level being the most holy.[5]

QUESTIONS FOR INQUIRY

1. What kind of relationship does each of the five levels describe?
2. What aspects of traditional sexual ethics does this text retain, and where does it depart from them?

COMMENTS

Much of this excerpt represents a substantial liberalization of Jewish sexual ethics compared to the classical texts we've studied. It teaches teenagers that Judaism can accept sex in relationships other than marriage.

The first level, Conquest without Consent, cannot be considered ethical; presumably, it refers to one person coercing another to have sex. As we saw in the Shulḥan Arukh (Text 5b), the halakhah requires that both parties agree to sexual relations.

After that, however, *Sacred Choices* finds increasing degrees of holiness in sexual situations that Jewish tradition did not approve. The second level, Healthy Orgasm, apparently means the consensual enjoyment of mutual satisfaction. In the third step, Mutual Consent without Exclusivity, two people capable of consenting agree to have sex, either once or over a period of time, without promising each other fidelity. Interestingly, the Reform curriculum teaches that such relationships partake of a degree of holiness. Better, however, is the fourth level: a loving relationship where partners commit to exclusivity.

The fifth and highest level teaches that marriage remains the best context for fulfilling the goal of finding holiness in sexuality. Partners who marry not only offer each other love and fidelity; they publicly declare their intentions in the wedding ceremony.

In 2001, four years earlier, the Central Conference of American Rabbis' Ad Hoc Committee on Human Sexuality (which had originally formed in 1993 to address issues surrounding homosexuality and then professed broader aims: "It is our belief that Reform Judaism can speak meaningfully to all aspects of our lives, including intimate human relationships"[6]) published in the CCAR *Journal* a list and explanation of sexual values for the Reform movement. This article, written by the committee's leader, Rabbi Selig Salkowitz, goes further than any we have studied so far in approving nonmarital sexual relationships.

Text 9b — Salkowitz, "Reform Jewish Sexual Values"

EACH JEW SHOULD SEEK to conduct his/her sexual life in a manner that elicits the intrinsic holiness within the person and in every relationship. Thus can *sh'leimut* [wholeness] be realized. The specific values that follow are contemporary interpretations of human *sh'leimut*:

1. *B'tzelem Elohim* ("in the image of God")....
2. *Emet* ("truth")....
3. *B'riut* ("health")....
4. *Mishpat* ("justice")....
5. *Mishpachah* ("family")....
6. *Tz'niut* ("modesty")....
7. *B'rit* ("covenantal relationship")....
8. *Simchah* ("joy")....
9. *Ahavah* ("love")....
10. *K'dushah* ("holiness")....[7]

1. How does *sh'leimut* or wholeness unify all ten principles in this document?
2. What does each of the ten principles mean in the context of sexual ethics?
3. Which of these do you find helpful in thinking about sexual decisions?

COMMENTS

The Reform rabbis ground Jewish sexual values on ten traditional ideals, each of which they reinterpret in modern terms.

Since the ten values culminate in *k'dushah,* the document suggests that Jews can realize holiness within the context of sexual expression. The text's charge — "Each Jew should seek to conduct his/her sexual life in a manner that elicits the intrinsic holiness within the person and in every relationship" — derives from the premise that a modern Jewish sex ethic ought to begin with the basic teaching that every person is created in the image of God. In one's sex life as well as in every other area, Jews are to treat one another with all the dignity the divine image deserves. This value implies equality between partners.

The second value, truth, carries other important messages for evaluating the ethics of sexual activity. Partners owe each other honesty, except where complete honesty is liable to lead to hurtful outcomes. (See the discussion of Texts 2 and 3a in chapter 2.) Partners are also to show one another their true and complete selves. Any deceit or manipulation violates this precept. Note that the most common verb for sex in the TANAKH is *y-d-',* which literally means "to know." A modern Jewish sex ethic might require that partners know each other fully, and perhaps learn to know each other better through the exchange of pleasure.

The authors of this statement also use the value of truth to say that "parents should learn how to teach their children both the facts and the physical, emotional, and spiritual consequences of sexual behavior." Sharing truths about sexuality leads to clearer thinking and better outcomes.

The third value reminds us that sexual activity can affect our health profoundly, for good or for ill. It encourages mindfulness of possible dangers.

The authors explain the fourth value, justice, as the need to be sensitive to the use of power and avoid victimization through sexual behavior. Justice precludes "sexual harassment, incest, child molestation and rape." It may also impel us to eradicate discrimination based on gender or sexual orientation.

The fifth value emphasizes the importance Jewish tradition places on family. Sexual expression helps to build families; families build Jewish community and continuity. (Compare the comments on the importance of family in chapter 1, "Parents and Children," and chapter 5, "Medical Ethics at the Beginning of Life.")

A sixth, related value is modesty. One's clothing, speech, and behavior ought to reflect awareness of the tradition's respect for modesty and privacy. Jews are to distinguish between public and private times and activities. Sexual expression belongs to the private realm.

The seventh value of b'rit here means "covenantal relationship." The statement proclaims: "For sexual expression in human relationships to reach the fullness of its potential, it should be grounded in fidelity and the intention of permanence." Note that the term covenantal relationship is broad enough to cover partnerships other than heterosexual marriage.

This statement is the first of the modern attempts at articulating Jewish sexual ethics to include joy and love as central values. In the discussion of joy, the writers note the pleasure people derive from sex. They believe that pleasure can lead to a sanctified kind of joy unique to loving human relationships. We are to conduct our sex lives in consonance with this ideal of love. Partners are to share love with each other, and heighten their existing love through sex. In traditional Jewish language, loving human partners model the love God shows for God's human creations and the people Israel (see Text 8b).

The ultimate purpose of all these values, perhaps, is the tenth one: creating holiness. As the statement points out, k'dushah derives from a Hebrew root meaning "set apart for an elevated purpose." In the traditional context, husband and wife choose each other to be exclusive partners for the shared purpose of building love and a family. A modern Jewish sex ethic derived from this passage would appear to imply exclusivity. Whoever we choose as a sexual partner—spouse or not—deserves our fidelity. Anything less would fall short of holiness.

Feminist ideas have also had significant impact on contemporary Jewish thought. The prominent theologian Judith Plaskow began using the insights of modern feminism to rethink Jewish values in the 1970s. Her influential 1990 volume *Standing Again at Sinai* offers another approach to revitalizing traditional Rabbinic sexual ethics.

Text 10 — Plaskow, *Standing Again at Sinai*

FOR LIBERAL JEWS WHO take their Judaism seriously, there is no area in which modern practice and traditional values are further apart than the area of sexuality. The insistence that legitimate sexual expression be limited to marriage ... and the insistence on boundaries and control as central aspects of an approach to sexuality are thoroughly out of tune with both the modern temper and the lived decisions of most contemporary Jews. Troublesome as inherited sexual values are for Jews of both sexes, however, they are especially troubling for women; for these values are a central pillar upholding Judaism as a patriarchal system, and the stigma and burden of sexuality fall differently on women than on men. ...

To see sexuality as ... part of a continuum with other ways of relating to the world and other people is to insist that the norms of mutuality, respect for difference, and joint empowerment that characterize the larger feminist vision of community apply also—indeed especially—to the area of sexuality.[8]

QUESTIONS FOR INQUIRY

1. What reasons does Plaskow give that Jewish sexual ethics need to change?
2. How does she use feminist thought to recast Jewish sexual values?
3. How might the ideals she proposes work in practice?

Plaskow, writing in 1990, begins with the premise that the sexual life of most Jews today departs farther from traditional values than any other aspect of their lives. Her efforts to reclaim Jewish traditions using the tools of feminism require acknowledging this disparity.

Plaskow objects to specific aspects of Jewish traditional practice that reflect, as she sees it, untenable values. Judaism limits sexual expression to heterosexual marriage. Judaism, in her view, creates artificial boundaries and gives male authorities control over how Jews are to use their bodies. While the same difficulties arise for both men and women, the problems are more acute for women. The Rabbis' patriarchal system defines them as the "other" and seeks to control them. Halakhah treats women's bodies as sources of temptation for men. It also regards their bodies' natural cycles as dangers from which normative society, understood as masculine, must be protected. For example, halakhah requires married women to separate from their husbands during their menstrual periods. Rabbinic law expanded the weeklong separation prescribed in Leviticus to seven "clean" days (with no evidence of bleeding) beyond the end of the period. Only after the woman—not the man—then immerses in a *mikveh*, a ritual bath, can sexual activity resume.

Plaskow proposes a different view of sexuality, grounded in values that feminism proposes for the reconstruction of society generally. First comes "mutuality" or reciprocity: whatever one partner receives, the other does, too; whatever one gives, the other gives in return. Taking mutuality as a basic principle would require abandoning the Rabbinic rule of *onah* discussed in the Talmud (Text 3 above), specifically the implication that one partner (the husband) owes something to the other (the wife), who owes nothing equal in return. For Plaskow, in an ethical sexual relationship each partner gives and takes pleasure in complementary fashion.

Plaskow next invokes "respect for difference." The phrase refers to the feminist call for society to stop considering men the norm and women the exception. Instead, we ought to accept both men's and women's ways as normative for humanity. In heterosexual relationships, this value implies that men and women owe each other understanding of the ways they differ. Neither partner's preferences deserve automatic priority. This reinforces the notion of reciprocal sharing.

Adhering to the value of respecting difference might also help Jewish tradition accommodate those who understand their sexual identities in ways that depart from the standard gender binary. As we will discover below (in my comments on Text 15), the early rabbis understood that not everyone fits into the categories "male" or "female." The feminist call to respect differences may guide us toward a way of incorporating the latest understandings of gender identities into our sexual ethics.

Finally, Plaskow proposes "joint empowerment" as a value to inform sexual decision-making. Neither partner ought to hold exclusive power in the relationship. They should share it equally.

Thinking back to Case Study #1, some of our college students may find Plaskow's suggestions useful for contemplating the choices they face. Some may find it helpful to frame the values Plaskow suggests as questions. Does my partner, or potential partner, want to build a relationship based on mutuality? Do we respect our differences? Does the relationship empower both of us together?

This idea of thinking based on values and ideals rather than norms may also help in considering our chapter's second case study. All the North American denominations of Judaism struggled with how to accommodate emerging new understandings of LGBTQ people. Except for the Orthodox, all eventually found ways to reinterpret traditional prohibitions against homosexual behavior and eventually to ordain gays and lesbians for religious leadership. These changes, as we shall see, often ensued through consideration of underlying values in Jewish tradition that mattered more to liberal Jews than the halakhah prohibiting homosexuality. Our study of this material begins with the normative halakhah.

Text Study #5: LGBTQ Sexuality

Text 11a — Lev. 18:22

DO NOT LIE WITH a male as one lies with a woman; it is an abhorrence.

IF A MAN LIES with a male as one lies with a woman, the two of them have done an abhorrent thing; they shall be put to death — and they retain the bloodguilt.

QUESTIONS FOR INQUIRY

1. Examine the language of the verses closely (in Hebrew, if possible). What act or acts does the Torah prohibit here? Whom do the verses address?
2. What appears to be the reason for this prohibition?

COMMENTS

These verses in Leviticus lay the foundation for the traditional Jewish approach to sex between men, and therefore for all sex other than heterosexual. While much is unclear, the Torah certainly forbids one or more sex acts and characterizes such acts as "an abhorrence." Generations of readers understood these verses to outlaw relations between men. Leviticus 20:13 prescribes the death penalty for both offenders.

Close examination of Leviticus 18:22, especially in the Hebrew, complicates this straightforward understanding. The translation above smooths out some of the difficulties in the language. Read literally, the verse looks like this: "And with a male do not lie the lyings of a woman; it is an abhorrence."

Speaking to a male audience, the verse forbids "lying," a term for sexual relations, with a male. The plural in the third phrase, "the lyings of a woman," makes the meaning harder to grasp. How many "lyings of a woman" are there? The classic understanding holds that the verse forbids a man to have sex involving penetration with another man, as he might with a woman. Therefore, tradition read the verse to forbid anal sex between men.

Let us examine the Rabbinic interpretations of these puzzling phrases in the Torah.

"AS ONE LIES WITH a woman" [literally, "the lyings of a woman"] — the verse teaches you that there are two ways of lying with a woman [meaning, a man who has intercourse with a woman forbidden to him can become guilty for two kinds of intercourse, vaginal and anal]. . . .

We have learned [that this sin carries] capital punishment. Where in the Torah do we find the warning [that must precede capital punishment]?

That is why the Torah says (Lev. 18:22), "Do not lie with a male as one lies with a woman [literally, "the lyings of a woman"], it is an abhorrence."

In that case, we find a warning to the active partner in homosexual intercourse; where do we find a warning to the passive partner [making him, too, liable to execution]?

That is why the Torah says (Deut. 23:18), "No Israelite man shall be a prostitute." . . . This is the opinion of Rabbi Ishmael.

Rabbi Akiva says, It is not necessary to derive the idea from the Deuteronomy verse. The verse in Leviticus says, "Do not lie [*tishkav*] with a male as one lies with a woman." Read it as, "Do not 'be lain with' [*tishakhev*] by a male."

QUESTIONS FOR INQUIRY

1. How does the Talmud explain the fact that Leviticus 18:22 refers to "lyings" of a woman in the plural?
2. What other problem in the Torah's verses about homosexuality does the Talmud raise?
3. What solutions do R. Ishmael and R. Akiva propose? How does each Rabbi support his idea using the language of Leviticus?
4. Does the discussion in this passage offer a way to permit men to share sexual contact of any kind?

COMMENTS

This Talmud passage illustrates how closely the early Rabbis read and analyzed the Torah text. It follows a discussion about various sins for which the Sanhedrin could impose the death penalty. If people are to suffer execution, we must know exactly what crimes permit the court to put them to death.

The first section in this passage establishes what sex acts are blameworthy. That question arises not only for same-sex relations, but for every kind of sex the Torah forbids—incest, adultery, and so on. From the confusing plural "lyings" in Leviticus 18:22, the Talmud concludes that a man can "lie with" a woman in two ways. Commentators agree that this refers to vaginal and anal intercourse.

From there, the Talmud turns to the Torah's stricture against men having sex with each other. The legal problem is that capital punishment may not be imposed unless the wrongdoer was warned that what he plans to do will subject him to execution. Therefore, the Talmud seeks a verse mentioning a warning about the death penalty prescribed in Leviticus 20:13. It finds the warning in Leviticus 18:22, which tells a man not to lie with another man "the lyings of a woman." This passage forbids the sex act without mentioning the death penalty; 20:13 specifies the punishment.

The rest of this excerpt from *Sanhedrin* 54b establishes another aspect of the prohibition against men having sex together. Since Leviticus 18:22 addresses a man, telling him not to engage in the "lyings of a woman" with another man, it seems to speak only to the "active" partner—that is, the one who penetrates his partner. Is the receptive partner equally culpable? Rabbi Ishmael and Rabbi Akiva agree that he is, and find different midrashic ways of proving the point. R. Ishmael derives it from a verse that forbids an Israelite man to be a prostitute. Presumably, like a female prostitute, such a man would allow other men to penetrate him. R. Akiva claims that this prohibition, too, derives from the first verse in Leviticus about homosexuality. Because it uses the plural "lyings," and because Hebrew consonants can be vocalized to yield multiple meanings, Rabbi Akiva understands it to forbid both penetrating and being penetrated by another man.

From these discussions, we can understand why halakhic tradition focused mainly on the prohibition of anal sex between men. On the basis of Leviticus 18:22 and *Sanhedrin* 54b, gay sex came to be called *mishkav zakhur*, "lying with a male." All halakhic authorities prior to recent decades agreed that the Torah forbids it.

However, anal intercourse is only one way that gay men may engage in sex. Beginning in the late twentieth century, some raised the question of whether those who believe themselves gay by nature could be sexually active without violating the Torah if they avoided *mishkav zakhur*, the one sex act specifically outlawed. Our study of contemporary materials (see Texts 17 and 18) will explore possible answers to this question.

As they often do in halakhic contexts, the Rabbis established a number of rules to protect Jews from crossing the line into behavior the Torah forbids. A typical rule seeking to prevent situations that might lead men to experiment with same-sex relations appears in the Shulḥan Arukh. In sixteenth-century Poland Rabbi Yoel Sirkes, whose teacher had studied under R. Moshe Isserles, wrote a commentary on the Shulḥan Arukh called *Bayyit Ḥadash*. Sirkes offers a different view based on the social realities of Ashkenazic Jewry two generations after Joseph Karo's time.

Text 13a — Shulḥan Arukh, *Even HaEzer* 24:1

JEWS ARE NOT SUSPECTED of *mishkav zakhur* [same-sex anal intercourse]. . . . Therefore, there is no prohibition on one man being alone with another. . . . But in these generations, when many are debauched, one ought to avoid being alone with another man.

Text 13b — *Bayyit Ḥadash* on *Even HaEzer* 24:1

IN OUR COUNTRY, ONE does not need to keep that distance from another man as a matter of law; it is only a matter of piety. . . . But two single men may not lie together and we should stop those who do so.

1. Why does the author of the Shulḥan Arukh deem it necessary for men to avoid being alone together?
2. In what way does the author of *Bayyit Ḥadash* rule differently than the Shulḥan Arukh?
3. What attitudes toward homosexuality do these texts reveal?

COMMENTS

The Shulḥan Arukh's discussion here begins with the premise that Jewish men are not "suspected" of engaging in same-sex intercourse. While halakhah requires careful separation of single men and single women lest they yield to sexual temptation, it does not consider men alone with each other an equivalent source of temptation. In principle, men may be alone with each other in ways that men and women may not. However, Rabbi Karo, writing in sixteenth-century Safed, goes on to add that in the corrupt times in which he lives, Jewish men should live more strictly than the law requires. They should avoid being alone with one other man.

The Ashkenazic author of *Bayyit Ḥadash* thinks differently of his fellow Jews in Poland. Where we live, writes R. Sirkes, distancing oneself from other men is not a matter of law. Those who do so act out of a pious desire to be careful. The implication is that men in his time and place do not succumb to the allure of homosexual intercourse. He adds, however, that single men may not share a bed (at an inn, for example). Apparently, that presents too much temptation for any Jew.

We may note an apparent contradiction between the Shulḥan Arukh's statement that Jewish men are not suspected of engaging in same-sex relations and the rules designed to prevent them from succumbing to precisely that temptation. If Jewish men don't do such things, why worry about preventing it? It appears that the idea of gayness as *to'evah*, an abhorrence, made such a strong emotional impact that halakhists took extra precautions to guard against it.

The implied societal differences between Sephardic and Ashkenazic Jewish communities reflected in these sources has implications for our case study. Many of us live in societies that do not consider same-sex intimacy problematic. If so, we can agree with Sirkes that we need not take any measures to discourage it.

Jewish understandings of these issues have changed markedly in modern times. Few if any Jews today believe that merely being alone together leads to sexual experimentation (though certain Orthodox communities still uphold rules forbidding unrelated men and women to be alone together). As we will discuss below, many Jews today also recognize that same-sex attraction is as natural for some people as heterosexuality is for others. In addition, Jews also accept a variety of family structures, including households with children headed by two adults of the same sex.

It is worth noting that the Torah never mentions sexual activity between two women. As we will see in Text 15, the classical Rabbis forbid lesbian relations, too. However, because of the absence of an explicit prohibition in the Torah itself, they put lesbianism in a different category than male homosexuality.

Before turning to this subject, we need to explore another ambiguity in Leviticus 18:22: *to'evah*, the Hebrew word translated as "abhorrence." The Torah prohibits many activities without labeling them *abhorrent*, a word that conveys disgust and rejects a given action in the strongest possible terms. Only a few other commandments in the Torah receive the same label. Why such forceful disapprobation for this sin? A number of answers to this question have been suggested. We begin with a discussion in the Talmud and an explanation of it by the nineteenth-century Lithuanian scholar Barukh HaLevi Epstein, often called by the name of his most famous book, the *Torah Temimah*. In the *Torah Temimah*, Epstein tries to show the ways the Written Torah and the Oral Torah are interrelated.

Text 14a—*Nedarim* 51a with Rashi's commentary

THE TORAH SAYS: "Abhorrence *to'evah*," meaning, you err in this [*to'eh atah bah*].

    Rashi: You err [*to'eh*] in this—a man leaves his permitted wife and instead grasps this degeneracy.

THE MEANING SEEMS TO be that he strays from the ways of the
foundations of creation.

QUESTIONS FOR INQUIRY

1. How does wordplay operate in the Talmud's explanation of
   the Torah's use of *to'evah*, an abhorrence, in the context of
   homosexual relations? (This question requires looking at the
   Hebrew.)
2. What does Rashi identify as the danger inherent in homosexual
   behavior?
3. Does the Torah Temimah's comment explain what Rashi means,
   or extend his idea further? What notions about men, women, and
   society does he express?

COMMENTS

The Talmud here performs a kind of wordplay common in Rabbinic
literature to explicate the rare term *to'evah*. It reads the word as a contraction of the phrase *to'eh atah ba*, "you err in this." That implies that
the problem with the "abhorrent" action is that it leads to error. Sexual
activity between men constitutes some sort of error.

Rashi identifies a specific "error." He explains that homosexual acts
cause a man to abandon the sexual partner the Torah allows him, his wife,
for one that the Torah forbids. The destruction of the marital and family
relationship is what makes this sin particularly "abhorrent" to the Torah.

The Torah Temimah, seeking to explain Rashi's intent, identifies the
problem as "straying from the ways of the foundations of creation." Epstein
has in mind an idea still heard today, that gay sex violates the natural order.
This theory assumes that God created the world for men and women to
desire each other and to come together to propagate the species. Men
who have intercourse with each other abandon this foundational reality
of the world. Gay sex, the argument goes, is unnatural. It tempts men
(especially, but also women) to abandon their proper roles.

Traditional Jewish thinkers apparently feared that homosexuality would undermine the basic family structure on which much of Jewish tradition is built (on this point, see the introduction to chapter 1). Those who have sex with the same gender cannot procreate. Ancient and medieval social structures required women to seek protection and economic support in marriage. If fewer husbands became available, more women would go begging, and the familiar foundations of society would collapse. Tradition found such behaviors abhorrent.

In *The Torah: A Women's Commentary* (2008), a series of commentaries on the Pentateuch written by female rabbis and scholars, the Bible scholar Rachel Havrelock suggests a reading that shows the notion of *to'evah* in a different light.

Text 14c — Havrelock, "Acharei Mot: Boundaries of Rituals: The Sanctuary and the Body"

IT IS AN ABHORRENCE. That is, homosexual sex transgresses the boundary between male and female by penetrating the male body as one does the female body. The priestly writers speak of it as an act of mixture that confused categories in the same way that combining certain foods, seeds, or fabrics confuse categories.[9]

QUESTIONS FOR INQUIRY

1. According to Havrelock, what does the Torah mean when it labels homosexual sex and other transgressions "abhorrent"?
2. What other commandments in Leviticus support her understanding?
3. What implications does this interpretation have for a modern Jewish understanding of LGBTQ people?

COMMENTS

Rachel Havrelock's explanation depends on a basic idea in contemporary scholarship about the Torah. Scholars agree that the Torah is a composite of several ancient documents, one of which is designated the Priestly document (P for short) because it includes many passages describing the rituals conducted by the ancient priesthood. P also displays a concern with classification, dividing people, foods, seeds, fabrics, and more into separate categories and prohibiting the mixture of elements from different categories. For example, seeds of different species may not be sown together, and linen and wool may not be worn together.

Havrelock thereby contends that Leviticus understands anal sex between men as a forbidden mixing of categories. Such an understanding helps explain why the verse says not to lie with a man "the lyings of a woman." The penis may not penetrate a male the way it penetrates a female. Doing so earns the label *to'evah* because it confuses categories.

This commentary helps us understand the verse in Leviticus in its context. Ancient Israelites considered male and female separate, inviolable categories. Men who had sex with each other sinned in much the same way as others who disrupted divinely ordained groupings.

Understanding this background to the Torah's prohibition of same-sex relations allows modern Jews to reconsider the value of these categories in our time. Those who maintain the divisions prescribed in Leviticus—including forbidding the wearing of linen and wool together—will continue to forbid LGBTQ sex. Those who believe in reexamining the categories created by ancient Israelite religion will look for different ways of thinking about sexuality. Behavioral norms may change on the grounds that values and ideals have changed. Since modern Jews no longer draw the sharp lines of separation we find in the priestly sources of the Torah, we need not prohibit same-sex acts in the same way.

Because no verse speaks of women having intercourse as directly as this one speaks about men, traditional halakhah treats lesbianism differently from male homosexuality. Let us examine how Maimonides' *Mishneh Torah*, adapting earlier talmudic sources, summarizes the law.

Text 15 — *Mishneh Torah*, Laws of Intercourse 21:8

WOMEN WHO RUB AGAINST each other: this is forbidden. It falls in the category of "the practices of Egypt" that we were warned against, as it says [Lev. 18:3], "You shall not copy the practices of the land of Egypt." The Sages asked, "What would the Egyptians do? A man married a man, or a woman a woman; or one woman married two men."

Even though this activity is forbidden, the court cannot administer lashes for it, since there is no specific prohibition in the Torah, and there is no actual intercourse involved.

QUESTIONS FOR INQUIRY

1. On what grounds does the law forbid sex between women?
2. On the basis of this passage, how did the halakhic tradition understand lesbianism differently from male homosexuality?
3. Does this text align with contemporary views of lesbianism?

COMMENTS

Rabbinic tradition exclusively describes same-sex relations between women as "women who rub against each other." The phrase is somewhat opaque. It may refer to a full-body embrace. Commenting on the Talmud's use of the phrase in *Yevamot* 76a, Rashi explains it as rubbing the genitals against each other. Whatever the specific sex act, Rambam (Maimonides) codifies the halakhah that forbids women to engage in it.

The fact that the Torah never mentions lesbianism explains the effort we see here to find a legal category to justify the prohibition. The *Mishneh Torah* uses the broad category of "the practices of Egypt" that the Torah warns Israelites not to copy. In this context, Rambam cites a midrash that identifies sexual practices the people Israel must avoid. Two of the examples come from the arena of same-sex relations: a man marrying another man or a woman marrying another woman. The third, marriage of one woman to two men, might seem different. Possibly the midrash imagines that sharing a wife could lead to sexual contact between the two husbands, which would make this example, too, illustrative of the problem of same-sex relations.

While it is clear that the halakhah disapproves of women pleasuring each other sexually, it is not at all clear what the tradition has in mind vis-à-vis lesbian sex. Rashi says that the phrase "women rubbing against each other" refers to genital contact, and Maimonides explains that it cannot be punished by the rabbinic court because "there is no actual intercourse involved." The means by which two women pleasure each other, as imagined by the classical Rabbis, does not involve any form of penetration, let alone by a penis.

Today we hold a broader view of what constitutes sex, including many acts that do not involve penile penetration. We now also understand more about bodies that do not fit into a male-female binary. *Intersex* refers to "a group of conditions in which there is a discrepancy between the external genital anatomy and the internal genital organs (the testes and ovaries)."[10] Intersex individuals' genitals may appear similar to those of males, females, or both, or they may be ambiguous. As early as the time of the Mishnah, rabbinic tradition knew of people who did not fit easily into the categories of male or female. The Mishnah introduces the terms *androgynos*, a person with anatomic features of both male and female, and *tumtum*, one whose gender is unknown because a membrane or skin covers the genitals. *Mishnah Bikkurim* 4:1 rules: "The *androgynos* is like men in some ways, like women in some ways, like both men and women in some ways, and in some ways is unlike either men or women." For our purposes, we need only note that the halakhic tradition always made room for Jews of ambiguous gender identity, the group of conditions we now call intersex.

Aside from these categories, some individuals today understand themselves as both male and female, or as neither male nor female, or as completely outside these categories. People with these identities often describe themselves as *genderqueer*. Many prefer to use the pronoun "they" in place of he or she.[11]

Recent years have brought greater awareness that a person's gender identity may not be the same as the sex assigned to the person by their doctors at birth. A sense that one's actual gender does not match the sex assigned at birth can cause significant distress, a condition now known as *gender dysphoria*. Individuals in this category, whose internal gender identity or whose gender expression (external appearance of gender) differs from societal expectations, usually accept the label *transgender*. Some individuals choose to *transition* to living as the gender they identify with. Transition may happen socially, when individuals adopt a name, clothing, and other markers to align their outward appearance with their internal gender identity. It may also happen through medical and surgical interventions to confirm the individual's gender identity. It is important to note that gender identity is not the same thing as sexual orientation. Intersex and transgender persons may consider themselves straight, gay, lesbian, queer, bisexual, or other categories.[12]

Growing awareness of the variety of gender identities raises questions about how modern Judaism ought to respond. While the *Mishnah Bikkurim* passage cited indicates recognition of people who are neither clearly male nor clearly female, Rabbinic ideas do not match modern definitions of gender identity. In 2006, the well-regarded *haredi* Orthodox rabbi Eliezer Tzvi Waldenberg ruled that "only the actual external organs which are different in the male and the female . . . are determinative in practice."[13] Waldenberg determines gender by the presence or absence of a recognizable penis. That implies that a transgender person who undergoes gender-confirming "bottom" surgery would be recognized as a woman.

In 2017, the Conservative movement's Committee on Jewish Law and Standards approved Rabbi Leonard Sharzer's *teshuvah* that concludes: "A transgender person is to be recognized as their publicly declared gender and to be addressed by their publicly declared name and pronouns. This change takes place when that person has gone through a process of transition, which may or may not include any medical procedures or treatments, and asserts and publicly declares their gender identity."[14] Sharzer's approach, unlike Waldenberg's, does not depend on anatomy but on the individual's "publicly lived gender identity."[15]

Decades earlier, beginning in the early 1990s, the Committee on Jewish Law and Standards (CJLS) had struggled with the Torah's prohibition against sex between men (Text 12), debating, among other issues, how gay and lesbian relationships akin to marriage ought to be acknowledged and whether openly gay and lesbian Jews should be permitted to serve as spiritual and lay leaders in the Conservative movement. In 2006 a majority of CJLS members agreed on an approach based on the halakhic principle of *kvod habriot*, "human dignity," derived largely from an expansive interpretation of the following statement in the Talmud.

GREAT IS HUMAN DIGNITY, for it overrides negative commandments in the Torah.

QUESTIONS FOR INQUIRY

1. What are "positive" and "negative" commandments (mitzvot)?
2. Why would human dignity override a negative commandment
   given in the Torah?

COMMENTS

The Rabbis divide the 613 mitzvot of the Torah into "positive" and "negative" commandments — mitzvot telling the people Israel to do something
specific and those instructing Israel not to act in a certain way. Here the
Talmud teaches that maintaining the dignity of human beings takes
precedence over the negative commandments. We may do something
the Torah forbids when we would otherwise violate someone's personal
dignity. The main idea is that since people carry within them the image
of God, their dignity may at times matter more than other parts of Jewish
tradition.

The concept of *kvod habriot* presents us with a paradox. On the one
hand, Jews must obey the Torah's commandments because we understand
them to be God's will. On the other, *kvod habriot* tells us sometimes to
ignore God's commandments out of consideration for the human beings
who live by the Torah. It seems that God's image within the humans
sometimes overrides God's commandments — especially the negative
commands to avoid certain activities.

The following *teshuvah*, written jointly by three leading CJLS committee members (Rabbis Elliot Dorff, Daniel Nevins, and Avram Reisner)
and approved by the CJLS in 2006, explains the implications of taking a
broad understanding of the rule of *kvod habriot* and applying that understanding to gay and lesbian Jews. Because the Conservative movement
believes that Judaism develops over time through a process of halakhic
interpretation, the Law Committee had to provide a legal justification

before such a significant change could take place. The following *teshuvah*, "Homosexuality, Human Dignity and Halakhah: A Combined Responsum for the Committee on Jewish Law and Standards," thereby frames its conclusions as *piskei din*, legal rulings.

Text 17 — Dorff, Nevins, and Reisner, "Homosexuality, Human Dignity and Halakhah"

OUR UNDERSTANDING [IS] THAT *kvod habriot* [human dignity] describes the dignity of an individual within his or her social context. . . . It is difficult to imagine a group of Jews whose dignity is more undermined than that of homosexuals, who have to date been told to hide and suppress their sexual orientation, and whose desire to establish a long-term relationship with a beloved friend have been lightly dismissed by Jewish and general society. . . .

Piskei Din: Legal Findings: Based upon our study of halakhic precedents regarding both sexual norms and human dignity, we reach the following conclusions:

1. The explicit biblical ban on anal sex between men remains in effect. . . .
2. Heterosexual marriage between two Jews remains the halakhic ideal. For homosexuals who are incapable of maintaining a heterosexual relationship, the rabbinic prohibitions . . . [on] other gay and lesbian intimate acts are superseded based upon the Talmudic principle of *kvod habriot*, our obligation to preserve the human dignity of all people.
3. Gay and lesbian Jews are to be welcomed into our synagogues and other institutions. . . . with no restrictions. Furthermore, gay or lesbian Jews who . . . desire to serve as rabbis, cantors and educators shall be welcomed to apply to our professional schools and associations. . . .
4. We consider stable, committed Jewish relationships to be as necessary and beneficial for homosexuals . . . as they are for heterosexuals.[16]

1. How do the authors apply the principle of *kvod habriot* to gay and lesbian Jews?
2. In what ways do the authors offer gay and lesbian Jews full equality with other Jews? In what ways do they limit it?
3. Do you imagine gay and lesbian Jews committed to Conservative Judaism would find these legal rulings satisfactory? Why or why not?

COMMENTS

The authors of this *teshuvah* provide evidence showing that "human dignity" in halakhah refers to individuals within their social context. While each person deserves *kavod* simply for being created in the image of God, their dignity does not exist in isolation; the people around them uphold (or affront) that dignity.

It is noteworthy and to a degree ironic that this piece presents itself as a *teshuvah*, a response to a halakhic question based on legal sources. For all the halakhic argumentation it presents, the piece nevertheless reaches its conclusion largely on the basis of what David Teutsch terms "ideals and values" as opposed to "legal norms" (see discussion of Texts 7a–d). While conducting a lengthy discussion in halakhic language, the authors base their conclusion primarily on the value of *kvod habriot* and the ideal of a community that offers equal *kavod* to all its members.

The writers suggest that Jewish groups undermine the dignity of gay and lesbian Jews among them in numerous ways, which may involve these individuals hiding their sexuality and not forming the loving partnerships they desire. Their social context denies them the dignity granted to every other member of the group. Because matters of human dignity override even negative commandments of the Torah, the *teshuvah*'s authors believe it is necessary to adjust the halakhah to acknowledge the *kavod* of those who cannot conform to heterosexual norms.

At the same time, the authors do place certain limits on the proposed changes.

Our analysis of Leviticus 18:22 (Texts 11a, 11b, and 12) showed that the verse's prohibition refers to anal sex between men. The *teshuvah* excerpted here demonstrates that this is also the understanding of premodern halakhic literature. It does not overturn this well-established rule. The authors do not consider it a violation of *kvod habriot* to forbid gay Jews to engage in this specific sex act. According to their analysis, since the Torah only outlaws anal sex and places this sexual act alone in the category of *ervah* (the severe prohibitions punishable by death), other sex acts forbidden by later Rabbinic tradition are only safeguards, in order to keep men away from the most severely forbidden act. The authors do not wish to overturn a prohibition established directly by the Torah. Yet because of the stress they place on *kvod habriot*, they overturn other precedents, allowing those who cannot form heterosexual marriages to engage in other forms of sex with committed partners of the same sex.

Strikingly, despite their expressed concern for the dignity of gay and lesbian Jews, the *teshuvah's* authors write that heterosexual marriage remains the halakhic ideal. Their rulings seek only to preserve the dignity of those who cannot enter into such marriages.

Despite the preference given to opposite-sex marriage, the second legal conclusion is quite far-reaching in the context of traditional halakhah. Earlier sources did not allow for any sexual expression between same-sex partners. These Conservative rabbis permit homosexual intimacy (with the exception noted in the first legal ruling). Indeed, their fourth conclusion encourages gays and lesbians to form lifelong partnerships in the same manner as heterosexuals form marriages.

The authors also recognize that their decision welcomes gay and lesbian Jews to full participation in Conservative Jewish life—including as rabbis, cantors, and educators who will help determine the meanings of Torah in the future. By 2006, when the CJLS approved this *teshuvah*, the seminaries of the Conservative movement had struggled for almost two decades over the propriety of ordaining gays and lesbians: In a denomination committed in principle to halakhah, could individuals who violate a commandment recorded in the Torah serve as religious leaders? This *teshuvah* settled the question. Since then, several dozen gays and lesbians have received ordination as rabbis and cantors in the Conservative movement. The same three rabbis who wrote the *teshuvah* have also written rituals for same-sex wedding ceremonies, as have other rabbis within the movement.

Other liberal Jews accepted gay and lesbian Jews more readily and with fewer qualifications than the Conservative *teshuvah*. The Reconstructionist movement, founded by Mordecai Kaplan, led the way. Kaplan argued that when a belief or practice no longer works for modern Jews, we are to "reconstruct" it to allow it to speak to our times. Famously, Kaplan wrote that the past has a "vote"—we should always take it into account—but it does not have a "veto"—it cannot dictate to us against the urgings of our conscience. Halakhah is not binding on Jews today, but when the movement appoints a commission, the guidelines issued "may be understood as responsa, a traditional term for rabbinic application of Jewish teaching to contemporary issues."[17]

The Reconstructionist movement appointed an official "Commission on Homosexuality" in 1993. Years before the Reform and Conservative groups granted Jewish gays and lesbians legitimacy, Reconstructionism affirmed full equality between same-sex and opposite-sex relationships, as seen in the following official statement, which served as its responsum on the subject.

Text 18—Reconstructionist Commission on Homosexuality, "Homosexuality and Judaism"

SEXUAL FULFILLMENT SHOULD BE seen as an obligation for loving partners of any sexual orientation. Jewish tradition speaks of loving partnership as including the divine presence, and affirms sexual intimacy as an integral aspect of fully intimate relationships. We believe that sexual intimacy between loving partners should be viewed as holy. We believe that this holiness is equally available to heterosexuals, gays, and lesbians.[18]

QUESTIONS FOR INQUIRY

1. What claims does the Reconstructionist statement make on behalf of same-sex relationships?
2. Which values from texts studied earlier in this chapter does the statement ascribe to gay and lesbian relationships?

From our study of blessings from the traditional wedding ceremony (Texts 8a and 8b) we saw that Jewish tradition finds holiness in loving partnerships. That holiness extends to the sex life of committed partners. Until very recent times, as noted, Judaism excluded same-sex partnerships from the category of holy relationships.

Strikingly, this official Reconstructionist position goes beyond mere acceptance of same-sex relationships. It insists that same-sex intimacy, too, is holy. Same-sex couples can achieve the same level of intimacy as opposite-sex partners. When they do, they, too, are joined by the divine presence. They, too, bring holiness into the world through their intimate, sexual relationships.

Unlike the Conservative movement's 2006 *teshuvah*, the 1993 Reconstructionist statement sets no limits on gay Jews' sexual choices. Even more, Reconstructionism raises same-sex relationships to an equal level of acceptance as opposite-sex ones, by adopting holiness as its main value for thinking about human sexuality. If homosexual relations carry holiness equal to that of heterosexual relations, then there is no reason to restrict them. On the contrary, denying gay Jews any pleasure would inadmissibly limit holiness and reduce God's presence in the world.

As we saw when we discussed the difference between gender identity and sexuality, thinkers since the 1970s have challenged binary views of gender. Recent ideas extend the challenge to sexual identity, questioning the idea that people are attracted to only one gender. In the following text, published in a Reform movement collection of Jewish perspectives on sexuality in 2014, Reconstructionist rabbi Jane Rachel Litman explores bisexuality within a Jewish framework.

Text 19 — Litman, "'Bisexual' Identity:
A Guide for the Perplexed"

RATHER THAN BLACK AND white, people's sexual identities are a rainbow of colors. In terms of sexual identity, people who do not conform to the hetero/homo categories are often called "bisexual." However, the term "bisexual" is a misnomer, since the defining feature of bisexuality is that bisexual people are *not* binary in their sexual attraction, but rather universal, loving their partners without regard to gender. . . .

It is time for liberal Jews to say that heterosexuality is not morally superior to other sexual identities. What is ethically superior is authenticity. As long as anyone is maintaining a false identity in order to conform to heteronormativity, he or she is doing spiritual damage to herself or himself and others.[19]

QUESTIONS FOR INQUIRY

1. Why does Rabbi Litman argue that the label "bisexual" misrepresents the people it describes?
2. What does she argue should form the basis of Jewish sexual ethics?

COMMENTS

Rabbi Litman's work usefully reminds us that none of the familiar black-and-white categories about human sexuality stand up to scrutiny. Moreover, she contends that every sexuality authentic to a Jewish individual is equally moral. In her view, the central question to ask is "Is this an authentic expression?," and Judaism should correspondingly affirm any sexuality that produces a positive answer.

Conclusion

Our survey of Jewish sexual ethics highlights both the ways the tradition contributes to thinking about contemporary problems and the difficulties of adapting halakhic rules to modern views. We learned that Judaism affirms the beauty of human sexuality (Texts 1a, 1b, 2). It acknowledges the power of sexual desire (Text 6) and that human beings regardless of gender identity want and need sexual intimacy (Texts 3, 4). They derive joy from it (Text 8b). Judaism finds holiness in sexuality (Text 8a).

We also discovered important areas in which most modern Jews' attitudes reject halakhic ethics. Most notably, the traditional approval of sex applies only to heterosexual marriage (marriage, Text 7a; disapproval of same-sex relations, Texts 11, 12, 13, 15). While some contemporary scholars claim to find rationales in Rabbinic law for approving sex in some nonmarital relationships (see Texts 7b and 7c and the suggestion of Rabbi Danya Ruttenberg), a straightforward reading of the tradition allows sex only between married partners of the opposite sex. Yet a majority of Jews today see no problem with nonmarital sexual relations based on mutual consent and reject those traditions as incompatible with modern life.

The chapter's text study showed that one way of reconstructing Jewish sexual ethics for our times is to focus on the tradition's moral values instead of its legal norms. A commission of the Reform rabbinate proposed a list of ten values that build authentically Jewish, ethical sex lives (Text 9b). Feminist values also critique and offer alternatives to received Jewish traditions (Text 10). Substituting values for rules has the virtue of showing a Jewish path toward acceptance of sexual relations outside of marriage and outside of binary, heterosexual norms.

These and the other teachings have implications for our case studies. Jews who agree with Hannah in Case Study #1 will prefer maintaining traditional norms. Jordan, who appreciates having learned about respecting sexual partners as beings made in the divine image, will likely find helpful guidance in the Reform movement materials (Texts 9a and 9b): a scale he can use to evaluate his relationships' potential for holiness and ideals ("Reform Jewish Sexual Values") to strive for until he is ready to marry. Michael, who mentioned one "sliding scale" version of modern sexual ethics, might also derive benefit from the five-step progression toward holiness (Text 9a) and the ten values proposed by the Reform rabbis' committee (Text 9b). These latter values might also show Tali a way that Jewish ideals can in fact contribute helpfully to her thinking.

Attitudes stemming from Leviticus 18:22 (Text 11a) effectively write gay Jews like David and pansexual Jews like Emma in Case Study #2 out of the tradition. Those who wish to find a place for themselves within Jewish tradition may adopt approaches like that of the Conservative rabbinate (Texts 16 and 17) or the Reconstructionist rabbinate's insistence that holiness in sexual relations is available to all Jews, regardless of identity or orientation (Text 18). Emma will likely find some of her concerns addressed by Jane Rachel Litman's argument that seeking partners regardless of their gender identity is an authentic means of self-expression (Text 19); if the divine image Judaism teaches is present in each person, it can find expression in that person's sexuality, too.

These case study characters (except for Hannah) stand in for all who want to redefine Jewish sexual ethics based, as David Teutsch proposes, not on norms, but on values. Our texts presented a number of values useful for such a reimagining. Feminist thought contributes helpfully to this project. Perhaps foremost among its contributions, it teaches that modern Judaism cannot treat women as "other." It must instead evolve a form of ethics that accepts and treats equally all human beings, their bodies included, as created in God's image. Sexual partners who take that ideal as their starting point will, as Judith Plaskow suggests, respect each other's differences, seek mutuality in their sexual activity, and work for mutual empowerment (Text 10).

The Conservative rabbinate found in *kvod habriot*, human dignity, a foundation for reconsidering Jewish tradition's aversion to same-sex relations (Texts 16 and 17). That expansive value, requiring every group in society to respect and preserve the dignity of each individual within it, readily applies to other questions in sexual ethics as well.

A value that arose repeatedly in this chapter is *kedushah*, holiness. We saw in our classical text study that Judaism seeks to infuse sexual activity with holiness. The Rabbis' term for marriage is *kiddushin*, holiness (Texts 7 and 8a). We learned that aspiring toward holiness encourages each individual to commit exclusively to one partner. Additionally, the things we label as holy are those we hold in the highest esteem. If we place holiness at the peak of our sexual values, we strive to remove sex from the base side of human nature (the *yetzer ha-ra*; Texts 1a, 2, and 6). The quest for holiness allows us to bring expression of our sexual desires in line with the higher part of ourselves, the part that reflects God's presence in the world. That explains a famous statement of Rabbi Akiva's about the Song of Songs, a book of the TANAKH composed of erotically charged love poetry: "All of Scripture is Holy, but the Song of Songs is the Holy of Holies" (*Mishnah Yadayim* 3:5). The desire for sexual fulfillment may bring us closer to God than any other human activity.

For a modern Jewish sex ethic to succeed, its adherents must live in a manner consistent with their stated values. The college students in the case studies who choose to uphold a given ethic do not have license to change principles whenever convenient or whenever they realize that the values they profess tell them not to do as they would like. A genuinely Jewish ethic requires that we assure ourselves that the tradition supports our ideals, and that all our choices live up to those ideals.

5

Medical Ethics at the Beginning of Life

Many practices central to Jewish life take place within the family: bringing new children into the covenant (*brit milah / brit banot*), Shabbat rituals around the dining table, the Passover seder, to name just a few. In this chapter, we turn to problems that can arise in forming a family.

Having children is a basic mitzvah, the first commandment God gives human beings in the Torah. But not everyone wants to become a parent, and some who want to have children find that they cannot. Modern medicine provides infertile couples a variety of options unknown to our ancestors for having children. Both men and women can undergo procedures to improve their chances of conceiving. Recent decades have added the possibility of surrogate motherhood: a second woman carries the pregnancy on the infertile couple's behalf, sometimes fertilized with the prospective father's sperm, sometimes using an implanted embryo from the couple's own egg and sperm, and in a few cases with a fetus bearing no genetic relationship to either parent.

Surrogacy and other forms of medically assisted reproduction raise questions unknown at least until the second half of the twentieth century. Exploring these matters will also suggest approaches to such basic questions as: How far should we go in order to carry out a mitzvah? What makes a parent? What creates a family relationship? Does the fact that science enables us to do something mean that we should do it?

Case Study #1: Who Counts as a Parent?

The following story appeared in the *Topeka Capital-Journal* in 2016:

> William Marotta provided sperm to a same-sex couple who posted a Craigslist ad, but he isn't legally the child's father, a Shawnee County [Kansas] District Court Judge ruled. . . .

The Kansas Department for Families and Children has sought since 2012 to have Marotta declared the father so he can be forced to pay child support. Meanwhile, Marotta, through attorney Charles Baylor, has long contended that he never intended to be the child's father. District Court Judge Mary Mattivi declared last week that both women, now separated, are obligated to support the child, not Marotta. . . .

Angela Bauer and Jennifer Schreiner in 2009 posted a $50 ad for a sperm donor to help them conceive a child on Craigslist. Marotta stepped forward and signed a contract waiving his parenting responsibilities. Bauer and Schreiner split up in December 2010, and in October 2012, DFC filed a child support claim against Marotta to care for the girl. . . .

The women decided to inseminate Schreiner at their home, Bauer previously told *The Capital-Journal*, partly because of their previous awkward encounter with the doctor, but primarily because they wanted the act to be more personal.

Last year, genetic testing showed a 99.9 percent probability Marotta is the child's biological father, but in her ruling Mattivi provided ten reasons why he should not be considered the legal father. Among them, she pointed to an ongoing relationship between Bauer and the child, which Bauer wishes to continue. Apart from two meetings over the past five years, Marotta has had no relationship with the child and does not intend to provide emotional or financial support.[1]

At its heart, this case asks what makes someone a parent. If contributing genetic material is enough, William Marotta must be the legal father of the baby conceived with his sperm. But if the acts of raising a child—emotional and financial support—define parenthood, the written agreement Marotta made with Bauer and Schreiner holds up. The two women are the baby's parents.

Case Study #2: Choosing Single Parenthood

A single Jewish woman, Sophia, is approaching forty. Since she's always wanted to have children but never found the right partner, she thinks she should have a baby now before it becomes dangerous or impossible for her to become pregnant. A medically viable option is in vitro fertilization (IVF), a procedure in which doctors collect mature eggs from a woman's ovaries, the ova are fertilized by sperm in a laboratory, and a fertilized ovum is implanted back into the woman's uterus. May Sophia approach a sperm bank to hopefully become pregnant through IVF and raise the child as a single parent?

Further, *must* she? The case presents questions about the extent of the first mitzvah in the Torah: procreation. If a basic purpose of human life is to "be fertile and increase [and] fill the earth" (Gen. 1:28), does that mean that every Jewish woman must avail herself of opportunities to bear children, even without a partner? Finally, Sophia's situation raises questions about parental responsibility in regard to the (presumably anonymous) donor whose sperm she may use to conceive.

Case Study #3: Surrogate Motherhood

In New Jersey in 1985, William Stern entered into a contract with Mary Beth and Richard Whitehead. Stating that his wife, Elizabeth Stern, was infertile, William Stern agreed to pay $10,000 to the Whiteheads in exchange for Mary Beth's bringing to term a baby conceived with Stern's artificially inseminated sperm and turning the child over to the Sterns at its birth.

When the girl was born in March 1986, however, Mrs. Whitehead found herself unwilling to relinquish the infant. William and Elizabeth Stern sued to enforce the contract and to be recognized as the baby's legal parents. This suit became famous as the "Baby M case."

Who should win in court? Who are the baby's rightful parents?

The Baby M case raises painful questions about what makes a parent in a different form than Case Study #1. We can readily appreciate the Sterns's longing to have a child of their own. During the various trials in the case, William Stern testified that as the child of Holocaust survivors, he had no living blood relatives and wanted to pass on his family's genetic heritage. This desire helps explain his choice to seek out a surrogate mother rather than adopt a child. At the same time, it is not hard to understand Mary Beth Whitehead's feelings. Though she originally agreed to relinquish her rights, after carrying the child through pregnancy and seeing her at birth, Mary Beth felt a strong attachment to the newborn. Additionally, as our text study will demonstrate, surrogacy presents legal issues about parental rights and Jewish identity.

Case Study #4: Parenthood through Cloning

Fast forward: we're now in the year 2060. Using IVF, Sophia in Case Study #2 had conceived a daughter, Sonoma, who is now an adult. Like her mother before her, Sonoma finds herself near the end of her childbearing years without the right partner. Not wanting to introduce an unknown donor's genetic material into her family line, Sonoma wishes to clone herself and raise the resulting baby as her daughter. Does Judaism approve her choice?

This fourth case raises provocative hypothetical questions. Other species have been cloned—the first mammal cloned from an adult cell was Dolly the sheep in England in 1996—and though science cannot clone a person yet, the day when it can may not be far off. Before that day comes, it behooves us to think through the ethical conundrums cloning presents. Can Jews fulfill the commandment to procreate by cloning children? What can Jewish tradition contribute to the weighty issues surrounding human cloning?

We begin our survey of classical texts related to medical ethics at the beginning of life by looking at the mitzvah underlying the entire subject: God's command to the first humans to procreate.

Text Study #1: The Mitzvah of Procreation

Text 1—Gen. 1:27–28

AND GOD CREATED HUMANKIND in the divine image, creating it in the image of God; creating them male and female.

God blessed them and God said to them, "Be fertile and increase, fill the earth and master it; and rule the fish of the sea, the birds of the sky, and all the living things that creep on earth."

QUESTIONS FOR INQUIRY

1. Why do you believe "be fertile and increase" is God's first command to humans upon their creation?
2. What relationship do you see between the description of how God created humans in verse 27 and the blessing and commandments God gives them in verse 28?

COMMENTS

These verses narrate the sixth day of the story of the creation of the world. God creates human beings, male and female, as the pinnacle of creation. God blesses them and instructs them to "be fertile and increase"—an update of the familiar translation "be fruitful and multiply."[2] The many descendants of these new beings will rule over the rest of God's creation, as verse 28 specifies.

The immediate instruction to procreate stems in part from the necessity of preserving human life. Like all species, human beings must propagate for their kind to remain on earth. Genesis teaches that the urge to procreate fulfills the divine plan.

The commandment to procreate became an expectation of all Jews. Everyone who could was expected to have children. Community and tradition encouraged Jewish couples to have as many children as possible. Many stories in the Bible and Rabbinic literature portray children as the greatest blessing God can provide. Countless generations of Jews went on to live by what moderns dub family values—raising children to live as Jews, who would in turn grow up to have many Jewish descendants of their own.

As we will see in Text 2, part of the Talmud's discussion of the mitzvah of childbearing, Rabbinic commentators go to great lengths to stress the importance of performing this mitzvah.

Text 2—*Yevamot* 63b

IT WAS TAUGHT IN a *baraita*:
Rabbi Eliezer says, Anyone who does not engage in procreation is like one who sheds blood, as it is said [Gen. 9:6], "Whoever

sheds human blood, / By human [hands] shall that one's blood be shed." And immediately afterwards is written [Gen. 9:7], "Be fertile, then, and increase."

Rabbi Jacob says, It is as if he diminishes the Divine Image, as it is said [Gen. 9:6], "For in the image of God / was humankind made." And immediately afterwards is written [Gen. 9:7], "Be fertile, then, and increase."

Ben Azzai says, It is as if he sheds blood and diminishes the Divine Image, as it is said, "Be fertile, then, and increase."

QUESTIONS FOR INQUIRY

1. What "crimes" do the Rabbis accuse the person who does not procreate of committing?
2. In what sense could failing to have children be compared to shedding human blood?
3. In what sense could failing to have children be compared to diminishing God's image?
4. What is the overall message of the *baraita*?

COMMENTS

The *baraita* exemplifies the Rabbinic attitude toward procreation. It matters so much that the Rabbis compare failing to produce children to serious crimes. Here the three Rabbis seem to try to outdo each other in explicating the grievousness of the fault. Rabbi Eliezer compares it to shedding blood, meaning it is as if one took a human life. Rabbi Jacob ups the ante by comparing the failure to procreate to diminishing the image of God. Not to be outdone, or perhaps simply to combine his colleagues' ideas, Ben Azzai argues that the sin includes both of their suggestions: those who do not have children act as if they commit murder and diminish the Divine.

How is not having children like shedding blood? Rabbi Eliezer does not mean that the person who chooses not to procreate literally commits murder; the phrase "it is as if" (*ke-ilu*) indicates a simile or comparison. Rather, he proposes that passing up the opportunity to create new life has an effect similar to prematurely ending a life. Both acts cut off the potential contributions the individual might make. As the Mishnah suggests elsewhere (*Sanhedrin* 4:5), the murderer ends not only the life of the murdered person, but all the lives that this person might have otherwise conceived. Rabbi Eliezer helps us see that deciding not to have a child deprives humanity not merely of one individual, but of every person who might one day descend from that individual.

Rabbi Jacob takes the discussion in a different direction. He sees harm not only to humanity but to God. The person who refuses to procreate diminishes the Divine. Genesis 1:27, Text 1 above, helps us grasp Rabbi Jacob's idea. God created humans in God's own image. That implies that each person represents a piece of the picture of divinity. Removing any person from the world removes a bit of God's image from the world. Rabbi Jacob extends this thought to include those who are never born. They, too, would bring into the world a bit of God that the world would otherwise never see. The world is diminished by the amount of God's image they represent.

Ben Azzai decides not to choose between the two exaggerated stances of Rabbi Eliezer and Rabbi Jacob; anyone choosing not to have children deserves comparison to both. In the absence of any hypothetical child, the world loses both an entire lineage and an aspect of the divine image.

We need not take this text literally to appreciate the lesson the Rabbis teach. Procreation stands as one of the most important commandments. Jews are to have as many children as possible.

Given this background, we can understand the distress felt by Jews who have had difficulty bearing children: not only the loss of the personal future they dreamed of, but also the inability to contribute their share to the future of the Jewish community. Additionally, through no fault of their own, people around them might view them as terrible sinners. As a result, many Jewish couples want to try any available means to have children of their own.

Before considering assisted reproduction, let's look further at how the halakhic tradition developed and explained the commandment to have children. The first question seems obvious: How many children must a couple have in order to fulfill the mitzvah?

ONE MAY NOT ABSTAIN from procreation unless he [already] has children.

Beit Shammai say: [One must have] two boys, and Beit Hillel say: [One must have] a boy and a girl, as it says, "creating them male and female" (Gen. 1:27). . . .

A man is commanded to procreate but a woman is not. Rabbi Yoḥanan ben Beroka says: About both of them it states, "God blessed them and God said to them . . . be fertile and increase" (Gen. 1:28).

QUESTIONS FOR INQUIRY

1. Why does Beit Shammai define the minimum obligation of procreation as having two sons?
2. Why does Beit Hillel define the minimum obligation of procreation as having a son and a daughter?
3. How do you understand the suggestion that men are obligated to procreate, but not women? Doesn't procreation require both sexes?

COMMENTS

As we have seen in earlier chapters, the halakhic process typically analyzes any commandment in the Torah to spell out the details of how to fulfill it. This Mishnah takes up two basic questions: the minimum number of children needed to satisfy the commandment and who exactly is responsible for procreation.

On the first question, the schools of Hillel and Shammai disagree. In support of having a minimum of both a male and a female child, Beit Hillel offers the Torah verse describing the creation of human beings as "creating them male and female." The followers of Hillel may be saying that just as parents, in a sense, mimic God's ability to create life, parents should copy what God did in the first act of creation: not stopping until they have "created" at least a male child and a female child.

Beit Shammai's alternate standard for procreation, giving birth to two sons, may seem strange at first glance, since reproduction requires both a male and a female. The Talmud's discussion of this Mishnah (*Yevamot* 61b) claims that Beit Shammai bases its theory on the biblical Moses. In 1 Chron. 23:15, we read, "the sons of Moses were Gershom and Eliezer" — implying he had no other children. According to the anonymous theory in the Talmud, Beit Shammai argues that no Jew needs to do more to fulfill the Torah's requirements than Moses himself, the leader who brought the Torah to the Israelites.

Still, Beit Shammai's approach seems sexist to many moderns. Perhaps the school of Shammai valued sons more highly than daughters. Beit Hillel's approach at least hints at valuing members of both sexes equally.

Regarding the second question — does the commandment apply to all Jews, men and women alike? — here again the Mishnah records two contrary opinions. One, presented anonymously, claims the commandment applies only to men. Rabbi Yoḥanan ben Beroka, however, argues that since God's words to the humans (Text 1) are couched in the plural, logically implying that God speaks to men and women alike, both sexes share the obligation to produce offspring.

It is important to recognize that in the Mishnah, anonymous opinions — those not reported in the name of a specific Rabbi or Rabbis — are considered the majority view. The Mishnah does not ascribe them to anyone because the majority of the Tannaim accepted them. As a rule, later Rabbinic tradition considers such majority opinions in the Mishnah to be the law. As such, both of the major medieval codes, the *Mishneh Torah* and the Shulḥan Arukh, rule that the obligation to procreate applies only to men.

Many rabbis rely on this well-established halakhah to respond to situations like Sophia's in Case Study #2. Aside from any other moral qualms they may have about single motherhood, they declare that because women are not commanded to procreate, there is no reason to allow a single woman to become a parent.

However, a subsequent discussion of this Mishnah in *Yevamot* 65b–66a provides conflicting evidence about how we should understand the dispute in the Mishnah. Some Amoraim suggest the possibility that the law follows Rabbi Yoḥanan ben Beroka, meaning that women, too, are subject to this mitzvah. Other participants in the discussion cite Torah verses they claim support the anonymous opinion. The talmudic discussion reaches no conclusion.

This ambiguity in the Talmud's handling of the mishnaic dispute leaves room for us to imagine why the Rabbis restricted the commandment of procreation to men, and what lessons their idea might teach us. Possibly the early Rabbis understood that some women cannot conceive, but did not grasp the possibility of male infertility. In that case, they may not have wanted to subject women to a commandment they might not have been capable of fulfilling.

Many writers on this subject follow a suggestion that originated with Rabbi Meir Simcha Hakohen of Dvinsk (1843–1906, Lithuania and Latvia). In his Torah commentary *Meshekh Ḥokhmah,* Rabbi Meir Simcha wrote that the Torah shows mercy by not obligating people to do things that will necessarily cause them pain. Since childbirth is painful, the Torah does not make it mandatory for every woman. Other modern writers suggest different interpretations. In his work on Jewish medical ethics, Rabbi Elliot Dorff proposes economics as the hidden reason for this law. "Since men were going to be responsible for supporting their children," he writes, "it was against the man's best economic interests to have children, and so it was precisely the men who had to be commanded."[3] Dorff relies on the principle that the halakhah must sometimes force us to do what we would otherwise not choose to do. A man might prefer to limit the number of children he must work to support. That, the argument runs, is precisely why the Torah commands him to be fertile and increase.

What happens, though, if one physically cannot fulfill the mitzvah to procreate? Should a couple feel guilty over their inability to carry out the Torah's commandment? On this point, Dorff notes, it is possible to reassure infertile Jews.

Text 4 — Dorff, *Matters of Life and Death*

IF A COUPLE CANNOT *have children, the commandment to procreate no longer applies,* for one can be commanded to do only what one is capable of. The religious commandment to generate children, which in any case traditionally is incumbent only on the male, ceases to apply to those men who cannot have them, and there is no guilt or shame involved in that. That is just the way God created some of our bodies. . . .

The context, then, for the entire discussion . . . on methods to overcome infertility must be made clear at the outset: it applies only to those couples who *choose* to use them. Jewish law imposes no obligation on infertile couples to employ any of them. . . . Whenever we *can* do something new . . . the moral and legal question of whether we *should* do so then arises, and the new methods of achieving conception come with some clear moral, financial, communal, and personal costs that . . . must be acknowledged and balanced against the great good of having children.[4]

QUESTIONS FOR INQUIRY

1. What are Dorff's main arguments to exempt an infertile couple from the commandment to procreate?
2. What aspects of his argument are strong and convincing? What aspects are not as convincing?

COMMENTS

Sensibly, Torah and tradition command people to do only what they are capable of doing. Logically, then, those physically unable to produce children in the past would be exempt from the commandment, not guilty of violating it. But in our own day, if one cannot procreate through intercourse, and newer means of conception are available, does it now become the individual's responsibility to use those means?

Rabbi Dorff provides a commonsense answer. The Torah does not command anyone to do anything they themselves cannot do. Halakhah includes a category called *ones* that describes a person to whom an unavoidable accident happens, or who does something involuntarily. The principle in the Talmud is *ones raḥamana patreih* — the Torah exempts someone unavoidably prevented (*Bava Kama* 28b and elsewhere). In a sense, an infertile male falls into this category: if he simply cannot carry out the commandment to father children, he is exempt from the rule. Thus Jewish law imposes no obligation on him or his wife to employ any medical means to rectify their situation.

What of those who may prefer not to have children? Before reliable contraception became widely available, few sexually active adults could choose to remain childless, but in recent decades Jews have asked if Jewish tradition approves their preference not to become parents. Not surprisingly, given their commitment to the divine origin of the commandments, Orthodox rabbis have responded unequivocally: every Jew who can must "be fertile and increase." In 1979, the Reform movement's responsa committee, represented by its longtime chair Rabbi Walter Jacob, showed some ambivalence (Text 5a). In contrast, in 2013 Rabbi Michael Panitz, a Conservative rabbi, would come to express sympathy for the point of view of a young woman questioner who could not imagine herself ever bearing or raising a child (Text 5b).

Text 5a—Jacob, "Jewish Marriage without Children"

IF THEY ENTER THE marriage fully aware of the refusal of one or the other to have children—either because of a physical defect or because of an attitude—the marriage can be considered valid.... In light of the Holocaust and the current diminution of the world Jewish population, it is incumbent upon each of us to urge Jewish couples to have two or more children. Although young people may marry reluctantly and late, the marriage at least represents a step in the direction of children. In Jewish law, the marriage is valid, yet given the Reform emphasis on the underlying spirit of the law as a guide to modern practice, marriage without children is very distant from the Jewish ideal of marriage. The letter may permit it, but we must encourage every couple to have at least two children.[5]

Text 5b — Panitz, "Must a Jew Have Children? A Conservative Answer"

NONETHELESS, RABBINIC TRADITION CONSTRUED these words to the first humans as a mandate—humans not only can procreate, but they ought to, under the correct conditions.

That last restriction, "under the correct conditions," may serve as a consolation for the questioner, and also as a spur to further reflection. She might want to explore the psychological roots of her lack of comfort with children—but regardless, if, upon mature consideration, she is convinced that she would not function well as a biological parent, then she may legitimately conclude that this is one commandment that she will not fulfill in its literal sense. . . .

Without in any sense promoting flippancy towards the non-fulfillment of one or another of the commandments, it is nonetheless appropriate to remind ourselves that, in the Rabbinic view expressed at the end of the Mishnaic tractate "*Makkot*," God gave us many commandments to provide many opportunities for the refinement of our character. Instead of seeing "100% as the minimum passing grade" and being disabled by scrupulousness over the non-fulfillment of every last one of them, we ought to fulfill all the mitzvot that we can, and to seek to perform those deeds with both joy and reverence.[6]

QUESTIONS FOR INQUIRY

1. On what grounds does Rabbi Jacob declare a childless marriage halakhically valid?
2. What is his attitude toward the couple's choice not to have children?
3. How does Rabbi Panitz find justification in Jewish tradition for a woman's choice to remain childless?
4. What is his attitude toward the couple's choice not to have children?

Rabbi Jacob, writing for the Reform rabbinate, takes a hard line on the question of remaining childless by choice. He acknowledges that no halakhah forbids a couple from marrying on the grounds that they do not want children. That said, he invokes the idea of the law's "underlying spirit," a set of abstract values that its rulings express. In this case the underlying ideal seems to be the need to preserve the Jewish people's future, especially given the losses the Holocaust inflicted on the world's Jewish population. Therefore, even though rabbis may officiate at weddings of couples who announce they will never have children, the rabbi must try to convince the couple to have children after all. (Rabbi Jacob's ruling that they should have "at least two" children follows the law based on *Mishnah Yevamot*, Text 3 above.)

The more recent responsum by Michael Panitz, a Conservative rabbi, takes a different view. As we have seen in this chapter's classical texts, Rabbinic tradition understood God's words to the first humans, "Be fertile and increase," not only as a blessing, but also as a commandment. However, Panitz describes it as a mandate only under the correct conditions. While presumably he has in mind that Jews should procreate only in adulthood and only with their duly married partners, he expands the idea of "correct conditions" to include psychological willingness to parent. The questioner's statement that she cannot "wrap her head" around children at all demonstrates that she lacks the emotional capacity for parenthood.

Panitz suggests that not every Jew can fulfill every commandment to the same extent. He references a Mishnah from tractate *Makkot* to argue that God asks each of us to do the mitzvot we can do to the best of our ability. If we devote ourselves to those commandments we fulfill and use them as a source of continuous self-improvement, we need not feel badly about the mitzvot we cannot carry out. His argument is similar to Rabbi Dorff's concerning infertile individuals (Text 4): the Torah commands us to do as much as we can. It cannot ask more of us than that.

Still, some infertile people suffer significant emotional pain. Many of them look to modern medicine to fulfill their dreams of having children and contributing to the propagation of the Jewish people. Meanwhile, these new means of conception present new ethical dilemmas in and of themselves. We turn now to exploring the ethics of various means of assisted reproduction.

Before we begin, it is important to note a halakhic problem that may arise in regard to one such procedure—AIH, or artificial insemination by husband (distinguished from AID, artificial insemination by donor)—because of the need to procure the husband's sperm. Generally, halakhah forbids a man to emit semen other than during marital intercourse. Any other emission falls into the prohibited category of *hashḥatat zera le-vatalah*, wasteful destruction of seed. Since Jewish tradition forbade this activity based on the story of Onan in Genesis 38, some rabbis raise concerns about the need for a husband to masturbate to provide semen for use in AIH and IVF (in vitro fertilization). Those who allow the procedure reason that since the purpose is the same as in marital intercourse—to inseminate the wife with her husband's sperm—such masturbation would not constitute an act of "destruction" of the seed and therefore, the husband may masturbate to produce the semen necessary for the procedure.

Notably, a few sources in the classical tradition do speak about insemination other than through marital intercourse. Most halakhic analysis of the issue begins with the following passage in the Talmud.

Text Study #2: Assisted Reproductive Technologies

Text 6—*Ḥagigah* 14b–15a

THEY ASKED BEN ZOMA: A virgin who became pregnant—may she marry a High Priest [who may marry only a virgin]? Do we consider the opinion of Shmuel, who said, "I can have intercourse several times without causing bleeding [from breaking the hymen]"; or perhaps what Shmuel describes is uncommon?

[Ben Zoma] told them: What Shmuel describes is uncommon. We are concerned that she may have become pregnant in a bath.

---

1. What are the two ways the Talmud here suggests a virgin may become pregnant?
2. What analogies can we find in this text to methods of assisted reproduction?
3. What does the text contribute to considering the ethics of assisted reproduction?

COMMENTS

To understand this rather strange discussion on its own terms, let's first review the special rules the Torah applies to the High Priest, the leader among the priestly caste. Leviticus 21:10–13 specifies: "The priest who is exalted above his fellows, on whose head the anointing oil has been poured and who has been ordained to wear the vestments . . . may marry only a woman who is a virgin." That rule is the background to the question posed to Ben Zoma. Supposing a woman became pregnant without physically losing her virginity—that is, without an act of intercourse that breaks her hymen—would she be eligible to marry the High Priest? Is such a woman legally a virgin? Or if semen entered her body and led to pregnancy, is she by definition no longer a virgin?

The anonymous questioners in the Talmud propose two ways of looking at the issue. They introduce a statement by the Amora Shmuel, who claimed he could have intercourse with a woman several times without causing the bleeding that would mark the end of her status as a virgin. If we took that statement seriously, it would follow that the pregnant woman who says she is still a virgin is indeed a virgin, making her eligible to marry a High Priest. On the other hand, if we treat Shmuel as an exceptional case, his experience would not teach us anything about other people's situations. In that case, the pregnant woman would not retain her virgin status and could not marry a High Priest.

Ben Zoma responds that the situation of Shmuel is indeed uncommon. He offers a different explanation for a pregnancy without coitus. We suspect that the woman became pregnant from sperm that a man ejaculated in a public bath before she got into the water. Technically, then, her virginity remains in place.

What Ben Zoma describes is implausible. Sperm are unlikely to survive long in bathwater, let alone manage the trip from the water up a woman's vagina to reach a mature egg in her fallopian tube. Why, then, do modern rabbis discuss this text when they ponder the ethics of assisted reproduction?

This passage provides a way for rabbis both ancient and modern to consider pregnancies that result from insemination by means other than sexual intercourse. Setting aside the weirdness of the details, we recognize an ancient discussion of noncoital insemination. Notably, none of the Rabbis in the Talmud express any concern about the legitimacy of a child born in this manner. As we will see, some modern rabbis found in that fact a reason to permit Jewish couples to make use of artificial insemination.

At the same time, insemination in a public bath differs significantly from the modern, medicalized forms of artificial insemination (AI), which we understand as the direct insertion of semen into a woman's cervix, fallopian tubes, or uterus by means other than sexual intercourse. Since this method enables sperm to take a relatively short trip to fertilize an available ovum, it helps in certain situations: where a man does not produce enough sperm, or his sperm are not strong enough to "swim" through the cervix and into the fallopian tubes on their own.

Also, by contrast to modern AI, the Talmud's "pregnant virgin" likely had no intention of bearing a child. Modern women do have such intentions: they typically pursue artificial insemination only when their attempts to conceive fail or when they have no partner with whom to create a child. Some modern analysts have found grounds in this difference to object to artificial insemination. Further texts from the halakhic tradition will show other reasons why not all writers in recent decades have approved of using artificial insemination and other noncoital means of conception.

Most halakhic ethicists who have examined the issues find it easiest to approve of artificial insemination using the husband's sperm (AIH). AIH spares us two questions that may arise if a married woman is inseminated with another man's sperm. First, there is no doubt that her husband is also the child's legal father (whereas in AID, the sperm donor may have a claim to paternity). Second, AIH does not raise the problem of adultery, since there is no use of semen from anyone but the husband. One traditional text often cited to support this last point comes from a commentary on Maimonides' code of halakhah by Rabbi Judah ben Samuel Rosanes (1657–1727), rabbi of Constantinople. Here in *Mishneh LaMelekh*, a work whose title became an alternative way of referring to the author, Rosanes references the passage in *Ḥagigah* (Text 6) concerning the woman who conceived in bathwater.

Text 7 — Mishneh LaMelekh on *Mishneh*
Torah, Laws of Matrimony 15:4

ABOUT A WOMAN WHO conceived in a bath: Is the child legally the child [of the woman's husband] in every respect?

There is no doubt that the woman is not forbidden to her husband [as an adulteress], because there is no prohibited intercourse. . . .

It is demonstrable that the child is legally the father's in every respect, since we take care that he not marry his half-sister on his father's side.

QUESTIONS FOR INQUIRY

1. What legal problem does the *Mishneh LaMelekh* raise?
2. How does the *Mishneh LaMelekh* demonstrate that the woman in this situation did not commit adultery?
3. What additional halakhic concern does he raise?
4. What implications does the text have for the use of AIH and AID?

COMMENTS

Rosanes — Mishneh LaMelekh — directly addresses the question of whether a wife's conception in a public bath constitutes adultery if the sperm is not the husband's. While it might be argued that introducing sperm into the reproductive tract of a married woman by anyone other than her husband amounts to the same thing as having intercourse with her, the *Mishneh LaMelekh* rejects this suggestion. In the absence of an act of intercourse, she is not "forbidden to her husband," as a woman who committed adultery would be.

The *Mishneh LaMelekh* goes further. Rosanes argues that the child will legally be the child of the woman's husband, even though another man most likely "donated" the sperm from which the infant was conceived. He mentions only a concern that the child not grow up to unwittingly marry a half sister. That is, the child may not marry a daughter of his legal father's by a different mother. The same rule would apply to a child born through marital intercourse, reinforcing the ruling that this child belongs fully to the husband of his mother.

As we saw earlier, this idea of unexpected conception via sperm in a bath was the means premodern thinkers found to consider noncoital insemination. Our sources show that insemination without intercourse is not in and of itself a halakhic problem. Neither the mother nor the child suffers any legal consequences. The woman's husband receives full legal status as the child's father. Given this, the tradition seems not to have any difficulty with the idea of artificially inseminating a woman with her husband's sperm if she cannot conceive through intercourse. Still, that permission does not automatically extend to AID.

From the *Mishneh LaMelekh* passage, we might conclude that halakhah allows AID. After all, the author rejects any idea that the mother sinned, and awards paternity to her husband, regardless of the source of the sperm. Nevertheless, we must take into account the aforementioned differences between noncoital insemination and modern medical procedures. When a couple today opts for AID, the woman's ovum is intentionally fertilized with sperm from another man. That is a different choice than unknowingly entering a bath that contains viable sperm. If the donor is anonymous, as is often the case when women make use of sperm banks, we return to the problem of incest the *Mishneh LaMelekh* raises. When children with an unknown biological father grow up, they will not be able to know if people they meet are half siblings.

Rabbi Eliezer Tzvi Waldenberg, a twentieth-century Israeli haredi who became an expert in the halakhah of medical issues, is one among several modern authorities who have objected to the introduction of sperm into a wife's body unless it is her husband's. Waldenberg wrote numerous volumes of responsa titled *Tzitz Eliezer*, "Eliezer's Frontlet," playing on a phrase in the Torah about the ceremonial garb worn by Eliezer the High Priest. As background to Waldenberg's ruling against AID (Text 8b), we look first at a verse from the Torah as interpreted by the thirteenth-century Spanish commentator Rabbi Moshe ben Naḥman, called by the acronym Ramban.

Text 8a—Ramban on Lev. 18:20

DO NOT HAVE CARNAL relations with your neighbor's wife and defile yourself with her.
Commentary:
The verse literally says "for seed," which appears redundant. Possibly it says "for seed" to stress the reason for the prohibition, because it will not be known to whom the seed belongs. Many abhorrent and evil things will result for both of them.

Text 8b—Waldenberg, *Responsa Tzitz Eliezer*

A CHILD BORN TO a married woman from another man's sperm: logic indicates that the child is at least of doubtful status [and may be illegitimate because of possible adultery].

The very act of artificially introducing semen into a woman's body, even an unmarried woman, is greatly abhorrent and involves serious prohibitions . . . among them, that the child may marry his half-sister on his father's side.[7]

QUESTIONS FOR INQUIRY

1. What anomaly in the phrasing does Ramban notice in the verse? How does he make sense of it?
2. How does Rabbi Eliezer Tzvi Waldenberg use the idea from Ramban to conclude that artificial insemination amounts to adultery?

3. What other concern does *Tzitz Eliezer* have about artificial insemination?

4. In what ways does the comparison between artificial insemination and adultery make sense? In what ways are the two not comparable?

COMMENTS

Understanding Ramban's commentary requires looking closely at the Hebrew of the verse. Translated literally, it says, "Do not have carnal relations with your neighbor's wife for seed" (in Hebrew, *le-zara*). *Seed* in such contexts in the Torah means sperm. Since the command makes sense even without the phrase "for seed," Ramban suggests that the Torah must have a lesson in mind aside from prohibiting adultery. To him, the verse hints at the underlying reason the Torah forbids adultery: no one will know the identity of the resulting child's father. Thus the child could grow up and unwittingly marry a half sibling.

Extending the concern Ramban identifies, Waldenberg holds that even in a medical context, even in the interest of fulfilling the mitzvah to procreate, insemination outside of marital intercourse violates Judaism's moral code. The resulting child is, at the very least, suspected of being the product of adultery—a serious legal debility, which among other things forbids the child to marry a Jew.

This responsum leads us to think about a concern couples considering AI may have. It's true that the resulting baby will come from the "seed" of someone other than the prospective father. In modern terms, the baby will be genetically related to the mother, but not to the legal father. Both partners need to decide they can accept that reality before they undertake AI.

Understanding the concerns that Waldenberg points to, however, does not preclude noticing an additional way in which modern AI in a medical context differs from a discussion in the older sources. Whereas the comment from Ramban that Waldenberg relies on refers to adultery, a married woman wishing to conceive from donor sperm does so with her partner's full awareness and agreement. That fact, in addition to the absence of sexual contact, precludes many of us from interpreting what happens as adultery.

Rabbi Waldenberg's conclusions reflect one side of a debate among Orthodox ethicists about artificial insemination. In Text 9, the Orthodox rabbi and law professor Michael Broyde summarizes several other positions taken by Orthodox experts.

Text 9 — Broyde, "The Establishment of Paternity
in Jewish and American Law"

RABBI [MOSHE] FEINSTEIN [WRITES] that artificial insemination is permitted and that the paternity of the child is established by the genetic relationship between the child and the father. Thus, he who donates the sperm is the father. Furthermore, Rabbi Feinstein is of the opinion that the act of artificial insemination does not violate Jewish law and does not constitute an act of adultery by the woman.

The second position, that of the Divrei Yoel [Rabbi Yoel Teitelbaum], is identical to that of Rabbi Feinstein's in acknowledging that the genetic relationship is of legal significance and the paternity is established solely through the genetic relationship. However, he also maintains that the genetic relationship predominates to establish illegitimacy and the legal propriety of these actions. Thus, heterologous artificial insemination is an act of adultery. . . .

Two other positions are also offered on this topic. The first is that of Rabbi Waldenberg. [See Text 8b.]

A fourth position is advocated by Rabbi [Mordecai] Breish, who maintains that heterologous insemination is not an act of adultery. . . . Nonetheless, he maintains that "from the point of view of our religion these ugly and disgusting things should not be done, for they are similar to the deeds of the land of Canaan and its abominations."[8]

QUESTIONS FOR INQUIRY

1. According to each of the four positions described here, is artificial insemination permitted under halakhah?
2. According to each of the four positions described here, who is the legal father of a child conceived by artificial insemination?
3. Which position do you find most convincing? Why?
4. How do these rabbis' conclusions reflect a variety of concerns aside from purely halakhic analysis?

COMMENTS

Unsurprisingly, various twentieth-century Orthodox ethicists confronting new forms of artificial insemination reached differing conclusions. Rabbi Moshe Feinstein, widely respected among American haredim, permitted AI and saw no violation of the law against adultery. He did, however, designate the sperm donor, not the husband, as the child's legal father. The longtime leader of Satmar Hasidism, Rabbi Yoel Teitelbaum, agreed with Feinstein about paternity, but parted in believing that because providing sperm makes a man the child's father, adultery has taken place when a woman conceives with sperm from anyone but her husband. (That is the meaning of *heterologous* in Rabbi Broyde's article.)

The third position is that of Rabbi Waldenberg (Text 8b): introducing semen into a woman's body amounts to an adulterous act of intercourse. Finally, Rabbi Mordecai Breish adopts parts of the other positions. He acknowledges that AI does not amount to adultery, which means children born from it are legitimate. However, he believes that AI practices reflect a lowering of the moral standards that Jews should adhere to. Apparently, married Jewish couples should only have children through intercourse, as the use of others' sperm—and perhaps other interventions—would be immoral.

This text serves as another reminder that close study of classical halakhic sources can lead to divergent conclusions. Interpreting the same sources, these four rabbis develop a range of opinions from approving artificial insemination to labeling it adultery. Rabbi Feinstein would disagree with the court ruling in Case Study #1 and declare William Marotta, the sperm donor, the child's legal father. Rabbi Teitelbaum's and Rabbi Waldenberg's concerns about adultery would not apply to the mothers in the case, who were not married at the time. Assuming the parties were Jewish, Rabbi Breish would disallow the arrangement they made on moral grounds, even apart from the question of their lesbian relationship.

Case Study #2 raises at least one issue not directly addressed by these thinkers. Sophia is unmarried; she cannot commit adultery, unless we define using donor sperm from a married man, should it occur, as such. But here, too, no Jewish consensus exists (again, even within a given movement) about the propriety of single women choosing to bear children. Rabbi David Golinkin, chair of the Va'ad Halakhah (law committee) of the Masorti movement, the Conservative movement in Israel, wrote a responsum about AI for an unmarried woman that four of his male colleagues voted to approve. (No women's names appear on the *teshuvah* [responsum], though women serve as Masorti rabbis.) The *teshuvah* forbids such insemination for five reasons:

1. Halakhah and tradition forbid destruction of sperm. Since a woman is not commanded to have children, any donor would waste sperm unnecessarily.
2. The fact that Israeli law forbids revealing the identity of a sperm donor raises concerns that the child will later form a forbidden marriage.
3. While using sperm from a non-Jewish donor would alleviate reason #2, donors to Israeli sperm banks are presumably Jews.
4. The sanctity of the Jewish family is of concern, as is the negative effect on children of growing up with only one parent.
5. Procreation is not the only purpose of Jewish marriage. It also includes loving companionship, which the woman in question lacks if she never marries.[9]

By contrast, Rabbi Susan Grossman of the North American Conservative Movement's Committee on Jewish Law and Standards wrote a *teshuvah* that reached a different conclusion.

FOR THE SINGLE INDIVIDUALS who want to turn to adoption or ART [alternative reproductive technologies] to become parents by choice, this teshuvah permits them to do so. Their decision to pursue adoption or ART is usually part of a painful and personal recognition that the chance of finding a marriage partner with whom to have children has become unlikely, particularly as individuals begin to age out of their optimal childbearing years. Rather than considering this desire for parenthood a rejection of marriage, this teshuvah embraces the desire for parenthood and the resulting decision to pursue adoption and/or ART as an affirmation of a commitment to raise Jewish children and build a Jewish family.

Nothing in rabbinic law technically prohibits adoption or the use of ART by a single.[10]

1. What kinds of reasons does this *teshuvah* offer in support of allowing single Jews to become parents?
2. How does it differ from the Israeli rabbis' approach?

COMMENTS

Rabbi Grossman opens her *teshuvah* with the story of a baby she named in her synagogue at the request of a single woman who used reproductive technology to become a mother. Several older congregants criticized Rabbi Grossman for "legitimizing" a child born "out of wedlock." As the rabbi well knew, halakhah does not impose any sanction on a child born to an unmarried mother. Only a child born from incest or adultery suffers the stigma of being a *mamzer*, who is not allowed to marry another Jew. Partly in response to that episode, she set out to explore whether Jewish tradition links the commandments to marry and to procreate, or whether it is permitted to fulfill one mitzvah without the other.

As this excerpt from near the end of her *teshuvah* makes clear, she concluded that marriage does not necessarily have to precede procreation. Acknowledging (as we learned in the discussion of Text 3) that women technically are not commanded to have children, Grossman argues that the exemption does not mean they may not choose to procreate if they so desire. Nothing in the halakhah forbids that choice.

The two divergent Conservative movement responses to the question of single parenthood illustrate ways that social concerns may influence legal rulings. The Israelis worry about the future of a child born to an unmarried woman. The American rabbi is concerned about contemporary social realities in which Jewish women either have not found husbands while they are still capable of childbearing or may never marry, even if they want to. In her view, these should not be reasons to deny such women the opportunity to become parents. She also expects no major difficulties for a dearly desired child growing up with one parent.

Our social outlooks may similarly influence our responses to Sophia in Case Study #2. Those who share the concerns of Rabbi Golinkin and his Israeli coauthors about the use of sperm from unknown donors and who share their understanding of the sanctity of Jewish marriage will likely be reluctant to sanction the formation of a single-parent household. Those who see the positive side of the wide variety of modern family structures, or simply accept them as reality, will likely not find reason to discourage single parenthood and will be more open to this request.

Text Study #3: Surrogate Motherhood

In situations where the prospective mother cannot conceive, or cannot carry a pregnancy to term, couples may turn to surrogacy. The Baby M case, Case Study #3, exemplifies one kind of surrogacy. In this method, the prospective father provides sperm to fertilize the surrogate's ovum. Doctors then implant the embryo in the surrogate mother's uterus, where it will develop until birth. By prior agreement, the woman who donates her ovum and carries the pregnancy relinquishes parental rights over the baby to the genetic father and his spouse.

This arrangement is called ovum surrogacy or traditional surrogacy: the baby's genetic parents are the husband (whose wife will adopt the baby) and the surrogate, whose ovum was fertilized. In a second type, called gestational surrogacy, the future parents' sperm and ovum are fertilized in a laboratory (in vitro) and the resulting embryo is implanted in the surrogate's womb to develop. A gestational surrogate has no genetic relationship to the child.

Here, too, halakhic literature provides scarce precedents for a method of creating children unimaginable before the late twentieth century. Some considering the ethics of surrogacy turn to two stories in the Torah involving the matriarchs Sarah and Rachel, in which the apparently infertile matriarchs use slaves to bear a child who will "belong" to their mistresses. (In Text 11a God has not yet changed the names of Sarah and Abraham; here they are still "Sarai" and "Abram.")

Text 11a — Gen. 16:1–4,15

SARAI, ABRAM'S WIFE, HAD borne him no children. She had an Egyptian maidservant whose name was Hagar. And Sarai said to Abram: "Look, the Lord has kept me from bearing. Consort with my maid; perhaps I shall have a child through her." And Abram heeded Sarai's request. So Sarai, Abram's wife, took her maid, Hagar the Egyptian . . . and gave her to her husband Abram as a concubine. He cohabited with Hagar and she conceived. . . . Hagar bore a son to Abram, and Abram gave the son that Hagar bore him the name Ishmael.

Text 11b — Gen. 30:1–6

WHEN RACHEL SAW THAT she had borne Jacob no children, she became envious of her sister; and Rachel said to Jacob, "Give me children, or I shall die." Jacob was incensed at Rachel, and said, "Can I take the place of God, who has denied you the fruit of the womb?" She said, "Here is my maid Bilhah. Consort with her, that she may bear on my knees and that through her I too may have children." So she gave him her maid Bilhah as concubine, and Jacob cohabited with her. Bilhah conceived and bore Jacob a son. And Rachel said, "God has vindicated me, and indeed, [God] has heeded my plea and given me a son." Therefore she named him Dan.

QUESTIONS FOR INQUIRY

1. How do Sarai and Rachel each respond to their experience of being unable to bear children?
2. In what ways do these stories parallel modern surrogate motherhood?
3. In what ways do these stories differ from modern surrogate motherhood?

COMMENTS

Difficulty in conceiving is a recurrent theme in the TANAKH. A number of significant figures suffer from infertility: not only the matriarchs Sarai and Rachel, but also Hannah, mother of the prophet Samuel; the unnamed mother of Samson; and others. That each of them eventually bears a son illustrates the theme of God's trustworthy nature. In God's own time, each of these women gives birth to a son who carries on God's covenant with the People Israel.

In the stories of Sarai and Rachel from Genesis, both women turn to a female slave to provide her with the child she cannot herself conceive. Notably, while the slave has intercourse with the mistress's husband, conceives, and carries the child to term, the child "belongs" to the mistress. Sarai and Rachel name the children and count as the official mothers. That fact suggests a parallel to ovum surrogacy, where the wife of the man providing the sperm officially adopts the child as mother, while the surrogate relinquishes parental rights.

There are other ways in which these stories resemble modern surrogacy. Writing for the Conservative movement's Committee on Jewish Law and Standards, Rabbi Elie Spitz enumerated these similarities:

DESPITE SOME DIFFERENCES BETWEEN the *shifchah* [maid servant] and the contemporary surrogate, there are significant shared values to glean from the Bible's acceptance of a third party to procreation. First, the use of a third party is a permitted last resort to assure genetic continuity for the husband. Although the patriarchs and matriarchs could have adopted a child, a legal category in the ancient world too, they chose the option of using a *shifchah*. Second, although children were born to the *shifchah*, the Torah recognized the maternal role of the "intended mother" and gave her rights. The offspring were adopted by the matriarchs and named by them. Third, although the *shifchah* was not recognized as a "wife," her offspring were treated as a descendant of the patriarch, which entailed full inheritance rights.[11]

QUESTIONS FOR INQUIRY

1. What similarities between the Torah's narratives and modern surrogacy does Rabbi Spitz discover?
2. What important differences do you notice between ancient and modern practices?

COMMENTS

Rabbi Spitz describes the maidservant stories in the Torah as precedents for using a third party to carry on the husband's genetic line when he and his wife cannot conceive a child together. He argues that the biblical characters chose this option over adoption — though whether the Torah is familiar with what moderns call adoption is an open question. Spitz considers the matriarchs the adoptive mothers of the maids' children. He notes that the children received the full rights of the patriarchs' children.

At the same time, significant differences exist between what the Torah portrays and what modern medicine allows. The Torah's stories assume a polygamous society in which a man could marry more than one woman simultaneously. The husband's relationship with the slave/concubine differs dramatically from his relationship with a modern surrogate mother. A consequential difference is that Hagar and Bilhah have no say in the matter. Neither could choose not to bear a child for her master and mistress. Today, a surrogacy agreement must be freely entered by all parties, including the surrogate.

Jewish ethicists confronting surrogacy have arrived at widely varying conclusions. Some have found the moral problems great enough to reject the idea. Others have suggested a number of reasons to permit couples to use surrogates, while disagreeing among themselves both about the bases for the permission and its wisdom. The next three texts (12a–c) are a sampling of opinions opposed to surrogate childbearing. Rabbi Marc Gellman (Reform) wrote his in the popular journal *Sh'ma*. Rabbi Barry Freundel (Orthodox) considered surrogacy in his book, *Contemporary Orthodox Judaism's Response to Modernity*. Rabbi Immanuel Jakobovits, an expert in Jewish ethics who served as chief rabbi of the United Kingdom, presented his arguments in his book, *Jewish Medical Ethics*. We will follow these excerpts with a sampling of three opinions in favor of surrogacy.

Text 12a—Gellman, "The Ethics of Surrogate Motherhood"

SURROGATE MOTHERHOOD EXPOSES THE contracted mother to the risks of pregnancy without justifying those risks. The Jewish prohibition against risk taking is derived from the fourth chapter of Deuteronomy, *v'nishmartem m'od l'nafshoteichem*, "guard your lives carefully." The rabbinic elaboration of this biblical law basically prohibits risking your health or life if there is no *mitzvah* which justifies the risk. . . . Pregnancy, no matter how routine, presents risks to the pregnant woman, risks which are justified if she is bearing her own child and thus helping her husband to fulfill the *mitzvah* of *p'ru ur'vu*, "be fruitful and multiply."[12]

Text 12b — Freundel, *Contemporary Orthodox Judaism's Response to Modernity*

THE TALMUD DESCRIBES THE parent-child relationship as based on responsibilities that the parent has to the child (the reverse is also true, but that is not relevant here). . . . In a surrogate situation, a biological relationship is created by the surrogate mother with a child, which is then legally severed through a contract entered into by the adoptive and biological parents. To me this smacks of the biological mother shirking her responsibilities. The surrogacy situation differs from the usual adoption case where, under the duress of difficult circumstances, a baby is given up to a better home. In the case of surrogacy the adoption transfer is premeditated and calculated. I find this reality troubling.[13]

Text 12c — Jakobovits, *Jewish Medical Ethics*

TO USE ANOTHER WOMAN as an incubator . . . for a fee . . . [is a] revolting degradation of maternity and an affront to human dignity.[14]

QUESTIONS FOR INQUIRY

1. What differing reasons does each author propose to explain why he believes surrogacy is not a morally sound Jewish choice?
2. In your view, do these writers respond appropriately to the new reality of surrogacy?

COMMENTS

These excerpts present several considerations the authors claim disqualify surrogacy as an appropriate choice for Jews. Marc Gellman relies on a well-known halakhah that we may not knowingly risk our safety if there is no mitzvah that justifies the risk. Fulfilling the commandment to procreate justifies the usual choice to conceive, but since the surrogate herself is not fulfilling the mitzvah—at best, she is helping the couple do so—she may not take on the risks pregnancy presents.

Barry Freundel's idea depends on an understanding of how halakhah establishes who is a child's legal mother. Along with many traditional writers, he believes that gestation determines maternity: whoever carries and births the baby is that child's legal mother. Thus Freundel suggests that entering into a contract to relinquish a child following gestation amounts to shirking parental responsibilities. (See chapter 1 for the halakhot he references.) While Freundel recognizes that this argument might also require rejecting adoption, since the birth mother also surrenders her parental rights to the baby, he holds that the cases are different. In adoption, unusual challenging circumstances justify finding a better home for the baby. Since the surrogate mother could presumably raise her own child safely and well, this justification is not available.

Immanuel Jakobovits presents a broader moral argument: surrogacy is an unethical use of a human body for others' benefit. Looked at from one angle, hiring a surrogate amounts to paying a woman to serve as an incubator for someone else's fertilized egg. Following the principle that we may not treat human beings as instruments for our benefit, then we may not use surrogates to bear children.

Each of these rabbis raises credible concerns about surrogacy. The surrogate undergoes risks while relinquishing (Freundel would say "shirking") responsibility for the future child. And certainly Jakobovits's concern about using human beings merely as tools to serve the adopting parents deserves strong consideration.

At the same time, each of these objections can be met with worthy counterarguments. Granted that the surrogate mother does not pursue the mitzvah of procreation with her own husband, we might see her as performing the mitzvah of contributing to others' desire to fulfill the commandment. While pregnancy carries risks even in the best of circumstances, surely adult women can make informed decisions about whether and when to become pregnant. These objections need not end the discussion.

Rabbi Freundel's concern matters only for those who agree with him that halakhah recognizes childbirth as the sole means of establishing maternity. Logically, that view would forbid a woman both from entering into a surrogacy agreement and from giving up her child for adoption. Those who believe that halakhic parenthood can be established by means other than childbirth will dismiss his concern, pointing out further that the child will have someone to carry out the halakhic duties of parents.

Meanwhile, inasmuch as Jewish thinkers opposed to surrogacy raise valuable objections, good arguments appear on the other side as well. The next three authors elucidate why they support surrogacy. Rabbi Walter Jacob led the Reform rabbinate's Responsa Committee for many years. Rabbi Elie Spitz wrote a *teshuvah* for the Conservative movement's Committee on Jewish Law and Standards. John Loike, a biologist and bioethicist at Touro College, and Rabbi Moshe Tendler, an Orthodox expert in halakhic medical ethics, published their opinion in *Hakirah*, an academic journal on Jewish law and thought.

Text 13a — Jacob, "Surrogate Mother"

WE WOULD . . . TREAT THE use of a surrogate mother as a new medical way of relieving the childlessness of a couple and enabling them to fulfill the *mitzvah* of procreation. It should cause us no more problems than modern adoptions which occur frequently. There, too, the arrangement to adopt is often made far in advance of birth, with the complete consent of one or both biological parents. Here we have the additional psychological advantage of the couple knowing that part of the genetic background of the child which they will raise as their own.[15]

Text 13b — Spitz, "On the Use of Birth Surrogates" (continued)

AT FIRST IMPRESSION THERE may be a visceral discomfort with these relatively new modes of reproduction, specifically the transfer of genetic material or the use of a womb for another couple. Yet, when we examine this new technology in the context of its outcome, we find the blessing of children to couples who want them very much. The bigger picture, which includes the intended result, makes surrogacy more acceptable upon reexamination. . . . It is permissible to employ a surrogate, whether gestational or ovum, to overcome infertility and to serve as a surrogate. A man fulfills the mandate of procreation in having a child with a surrogate.[16]

Text 13c — Loike and Tendler, "Gestational Surrogacy"

THE FACT THAT MATERNAL-FETAL cell exchange takes place in normal pregnancies is consistent with the few studies that it occurs in surrogacy as well. This information . . . indicates that the surrogate is more than merely an incubator for fetal development. Rather, she plays a critical role in fetal development and in the future behavioral and physiological health of the child.

We therefore propose the following scenario to avoid as many halakhic issues as possible and to allow surrogacy to become a viable therapeutic alternative for infertile couples. . . . We suggest that the gestational surrogate be non-Jewish and that the child should undergo conversion after birth. Anonymity of the surrogacy should be implemented in a computer-based registry. Finally, when the child born from the surrogate is ready to marry, he or she should undergo genetic testing with the prospective spouse to ensure that they are not genetically related. Adopting this paradigm may avoid potential halakhic problems and protects all parties involved in this therapeutic process and allows the dreams of the infertile couple to be fulfilled.[17]

QUESTIONS FOR INQUIRY

1. What reasons do these writers offer for approving surrogacy?
2. What concerns do they express, even as they approve surrogacy?

3. In your view, do these writers respond appropriately to the new reality of surrogacy?

4. Which side, pro or con, offers the more compelling arguments?

COMMENTS

These sources demonstrate, in order, that Reform, Conservative, and Orthodox rabbis all find support in the Jewish tradition for approving surrogate motherhood. Both Rabbi Jacob and Rabbi Spitz stress the infertile couple's desire for children above other factors. That serves as their trump card: whatever other concerns must be allayed, they want to do everything possible to help Jews fulfill the commandment to procreate. Both find it possible to overcome reservations about this method in order to serve that larger goal.

Rabbi Tendler, too, wishes to help fulfill "the dreams of the infertile couple." Supporting his views with medical information from Dr. Loike, he proposes allowing surrogacy agreements under specific conditions, given that the latest science shows that the gestating woman does not, in fact, merely "incubate" the fetus. Cell exchanges take place such that the pregnant woman influences fetal development. Gestating in a specific woman's body affects the child's future both physically and psychologically.

Given as well the aforementioned assumption that giving birth creates legal maternity, Tendler prefers that Jewish couples hire only non-Jewish surrogates. This way, there will be no issue with the child having a Jewish mother other than its adoptive one. This also necessitates that the infant undergo conversion to Judaism (based on the halakhah that Jewish identity passes only through the mother, a rule not adopted by all American Jewish communities today). Tendler also addresses the concern expressed by some sources (see Texts 6 and 8b) that the child might grow up to unknowingly marry a close relative, suggesting that such a scenario can be avoided through genetic testing before marriage.

This discussion exemplifies how strongly Judaism values the family. These rabbis work hard to find license in the tradition for couples to make use of a new means of overcoming infertility. Some would argue that they try too hard. Given the moral and legal considerations opponents of surrogacy emphasize, perhaps some means of procreation are simply not appropriate even for fulfilling the most important of mitzvot.

At the same time, Rabbi Spitz aptly points out, "At first impression there may be a visceral discomfort with these relatively new modes of reproduction." Often, new technologies make us uncomfortable. As time passes, however, we become acclimated to the new and more inclined to see the good in it. While still not an everyday experience as of this writing, surrogacy agreements have become more commonly accepted. Interestingly, one place where they operate under established law is the State of Israel.

Israeli law reflects the high value Jewish tradition places on procreation. A law enabling surrogacy arrangements, passed in 1996, requires Israeli couples to follow certain procedures.

Text 13d — State of Israel Ministry of
Health, "Surrogacy in Israel"

BY LAW, A MAN AND WOMAN who are partners are entitled to find a surrogate independently, or through a surrogacy agency, and to enter into a surrogacy agreement with her.

The surrogacy agreement is submitted to the Board for Approval of Surrogacy Agreements, which checks the compatibility of the parties to the process: a check that the surrogate is not entering the process out of (emotional or financial) distress, emotional and physical suitability of all those involved in the process, etc.[18]

QUESTIONS FOR INQUIRY

1. What underlying values does Israeli surrogacy practice, summarized here, reflect?
2. How does the Israeli law endeavor to address previously raised concerns about surrogacy?

Israeli society supports families raising children. The government provides tax rebates to couples with children and subsidizes large families. Additionally, public policy supports couples wishing to make use of reproductive technologies such as IVF. Israeli law treats surrogacy as one among several techniques certain couples and individuals who are infertile may choose in order to have children. In 2018, the Knesset amended the law to allow single women to pursue surrogacy arrangements and to forbid it to same-sex couples. (Some perceived the last rule as a concession to the *haredi* parties in the Knesset and the official Israeli Rabbinate.)

Notably, the procedure described in this source does not consider matters important to halakhah. It shows no concern for the legitimacy of the resulting child. Maternity and paternity are not in question. The law does evince care about the psychological welfare both of the surrogate and of the adopting parents. All of them must undergo an evaluation of their psychological readiness for the process. Everyone involved must have medical exams to assure that they will not endanger their health.

The Israeli law includes one other very important consideration: to avoid situations wherein a surrogate mother enters the contract out of desperation for money she believes she can only earn this way. Israel's vetting process aims to ensure that an infertile couple does not exploit the surrogate's financial struggles and thereby undermine her ability to freely choose to make this agreement.

Similarly, the board that approves the agreements is entrusted to make sure that the prospective surrogate is emotionally prepared for the rigors of surrogacy. If she is emotionally unstable, she may not make a free and informed decision. She may not have considered the discomfort she will experience during pregnancy and its potential dangers. She may not have thought clearly about the psychological impact of going through pregnancy and childbirth and then immediately surrendering the child to the adoptive parents. She must satisfy the board on all of these points. If all parties pass the evaluation by the board, they may proceed with their surrogacy arrangement.

Text Study #4: Parenthood through Cloning

We now turn our attention to a form of assisted reproduction that does not yet exist, but may in the near future. Our look at what Jewish tradition contributes to the debate over human cloning begins with a talmudic discussion about human beings creating new life out of nothing.

Text 14 — *Sanhedrin* 65b

RAVA SAID: IF THE righteous wanted, they could create a world, as it is said, "But your iniquities have been a barrier / Between you and your God" [Isa. 59:2].

Rava created a man and sent him to Rabbi Zeira. Rabbi Zeira spoke to him, but he did not reply. Rabbi Zeira said to him: "You were created by one of the Sages. Return to your dust!"

QUESTIONS FOR INQUIRY

1. On what condition does Rava claim certain people could "create a world," including human life?
2. Why did Rabbi Zeira destroy the man Rava created?
3. Does the text contribute usefully to the modern debate about human cloning?

COMMENTS

The Babylonian sage Rava asserts that the righteous could, like God, create a world from nothing. The verse from Isaiah he cites in support implies that this is true only of perfectly righteous individuals. Sinful people face a barrier that blocks them from achieving the godly powers available to the righteous.

As the story unfolds, Rava creates a man. Tradition labels this kind of being a *golem*, from a Hebrew root meaning "unformed"; in a sense, the golem is a mold that looks like a person but is not. Rava sends his creation to Rabbi Zeira, but once he finds the artificially created being unable to speak, R. Zeira orders it to return to its dust, to the material from which it was formed, ending its existence. Apparently R. Zeira considers the ability to speak the mark of humanity. What Rava created looked human, but it was not actually so. Perhaps to avoid confusion, R. Zeira destroys it.

Some interpreters of this text read it as prohibiting attempts to create human beings outside of the reproductive process. R. Zeira decides that Rava's creation is not human (some commentators point out that had it been human, R. Zeira would have been guilty of murder). It may follow that any being we create outside of the "natural" process of reproduction would not be fully human, and thus we should not undertake any such creation. But the discussion of reproductive cloning does not end here. In theory, if it became possible to produce babies by that means, they would grow up to share the power of speech with all other people. Such persons would not be subject to the stricture R. Zeira establishes.

Underlying the dispute is a basic disagreement about how far people should go in using capabilities created by new scientific discovery. We often must decide whether the fact that we can do something is enough to establish that we should. Already in medieval times, Jewish thinkers debated this question. We will study two contributions to the debate. The first appears in the Talmud commentary of Rabbi Menachem ben Shlomo HaMeiri, a leading scholar in thirteenth-century Provence. The second appears in a collection of responsa by Rabbi Tzvi Hirsch Ashkenazi, an important legal authority in seventeenth-century northern Europe.

Text 15a—Menachem HaMeiri on *Sanhedrin* 67b

ALL ACTIONS DONE NATURALLY are not considered [forbidden] witchcraft. Even if one knew how to create creatures by means other than sexual reproduction . . . it is permitted to do, because anything natural does not fall into the category of witchcraft. It is similar to medicine.

Text 15b—Ashkenazi, *Responsa Ḥakham Tzvi* 93

I AM SKEPTICAL WHETHER a person can be created . . . like that which Sanhedrin reports, "Rava created a man." . . . It appears to me that since R. Zeira said, "You were created by one of the Sages. Return to your dust!" . . . that there is no prohibition of murder. Because the verse [Gen. 9:6] says, "Whoever sheds human blood / By human [hands] shall that one's blood be shed"—that applies specifically to a person that was created inside another, i.e., a fetus that developed inside its mother's womb. That man that Rava created did not come from inside its mother's body.

QUESTIONS FOR INQUIRY

1. Do you find Meiri's comparison to medicine convincing?
2. Rabbi Ashkenazi expresses skepticism about the possibility of this kind of creation. What opinion about creation seems to undergird his distrust?
3. Which side has the more convincing argument?

COMMENTS

These premodern sources engage in a debate that feels contemporary. Unaware of the idea of cloning, they use the Talmud's description of a rabbi creating a "person" to argue about the ethics of humanity creating new life in a manner other than the one embedded in nature.

Meiri comments on a passage in the Talmud analyzing the Torah's prohibition of "witchcraft" (see Exod. 22:17 and Lev. 20:27). He proposes a negative definition: if something is done naturally it is not prohibited witchcraft. He compares such acts to medicine. Just as medical science transforms natural products and discoveries about the human body into means of healing, so, too, those who create new entities by means drawn from nature contribute positively to the world.

While the Meiri passage does not directly address the story of Rava's golem, it does imply that Rava's act might have been permissible. If we define the means Rava used as part of nature, then Meiri would say there is nothing wrong with his action. It follows that since cloning humans would make use of nature—in the form of new scientific understandings of genetics, cell biology, etc.—it would fit into the broad category of medicinal healing and merit ethical approval.

Rabbi Ashkenazi, who lived some four centuries later, draws the opposite conclusion. While doubting that such a creature could arise, he does not consider a golem a human being or a positive contribution to the world. He requires that a person be born directly of another person. The interpretation flows from two adjacent words in Genesis 9:6. First the text says "Whoever sheds the blood of *ha-adam*," meaning "man" or "human being"; then it continues, "*ba-adam*, By human [hands] his blood shall be shed." The phrase translated in context as "by man" literally means "in man." Therefore, Rabbi Ashkenazi reasons, only a person created "in" a person—that is, inside a woman's womb—is truly *adam*, a human being. This interpretation asserts that humans do not have the right to create beings by these "inhuman" means.

Modern thinkers recapitulate this debate. Rabbi Yosef Elyashiv, an important legal authority for *haredi* Orthodoxy in Israel in the late twentieth and early twenty-first centuries, forbids reproductive cloning (cloning to give "birth" to a new person) on the grounds that it brings a new creation into the world that is not part of God's plan. He allows cloning for medical research, however, including it in the well-established halakhic mandate that physicians do what is necessary to heal.[19]

By contrast, the American Orthodox ethicist Rabbi Michael Broyde denies that a cloned embryo would constitute a new "creation," writing:

> One could argue that the activity which defines the obligation to be fruitful and multiply solely involves a man giving genetic material to produce a child who lives. Such a child is produced in this case. There is at least one mother (gestational mother) and in most circumstances there will be a father/second parent. . . . This is particularly true when the fertilized egg is implanted in a woman, thus producing a child and a birthlike process that clearly resembles the natural birth process and motherhood.[20]

In short, a cloned infant would meet the criterion established by the Ḥakham Tzvi. Broyde sees it as fully human and not much different from a fetus created by IVF.

To make an ethical decision about human cloning, we need to decide which side has the better argument. Does cloning amount to playing God, which humans should avoid? Or is it the next step in human progress in helping infertile couples reproduce?

Before considering these questions in greater detail, let's look at some other issues that arise when we consider the possibility of cloning a human being. One of these has to do with a basic Rabbinic teaching about the nature of human beings.

Text 16 — *Mishnah Sanhedrin* 4:5

THAT IS WHY ONLY a single human was created... to teach us the greatness of the Holy Blessed One. When a human being makes coins with one mold, each looks exactly like the others. But the King of kings, the Holy Blessed One made all human beings in the mold of the first human, but not one of them looks just like their fellows. Therefore, each person is obliged to say, the world was created for my sake.

QUESTIONS FOR INQUIRY

1. What lesson does the metaphor of the coins teach?
2. What lesson does the Mishnah teach about the nature of humanity and its place in the world?
3. What does the Mishnah imply about the question of whether we ought to clone human beings?

COMMENTS

The Mishnah creates a metaphor about a manufacturing process familiar in its time and still in use today. Coins are minted by creating a mold from which each new coin can be struck. Each coin emerges exactly the same. That, of course, is the point: to create a uniform currency. Notice, the Mishnah's authors suggest, that each person born comes, in a sense, from the mold of the first human. Yet unlike coins, no two of them are alike. Each person has unique qualities. Even identical twins differ from each other in numerous ways.

That is the difference between what humans make and what God creates. If we make a mold, everything we use it for is identical. God, on the other hand, created a "mold" for humanity from which each of us emerges recognizably human, yet different. This, in turn, is a basic idea in Jewish ethics: The value of each person flows, in part, from his or her uniqueness. No one can replace any individual. Each individual matters equally to the world.

Weighing the Jewish ethics of cloning people involves considering the Mishnah's implications. What if the clone lacks the uniqueness essential to being human? The clone, who by the nature of cloning has the same genetic makeup as the original, might be like a coin struck from a mold: a precise replica of its progenitor.

Still, arguably a clone would not come out as a duplicate of the other person with the same genes. Since the clone would gestate in the uterus and be born like any infant, the exchange of cells between fetus and mother would likely make a difference. Furthermore, modern science instructs us that the nature/nurture debate is really nurture *and* nature: environmental factors combine with genetic ones to create each unique individual. Given that the clone would grow up with different parents than its progenitor, and in a different social milieu, it seems highly unlikely that humans could produce an exact replica of another person.

Reproductive cloning might, however, allow parents to predetermine the qualities they prefer their future child to have. The contemporary Jewish ethicists Rabbi Elliot Dorff and Laurie Zoloth, a professor of religion and ethics at the University of Chicago Divinity School, refer to this possibility as "rekindling our anxieties about designing our descendants."[21] Intuition tells us that designing babies to meet our preconceived preferences is an abuse of scientific capabilities. Moreover, from a Jewish point of view, doing so would deny the child who will be born the opportunity to develop into the unique individual carrying the seal of the Divine. Some thinkers, including the great rabbinic medical ethicist Eliezer Tzvi Waldenberg, have responded to these and other concerns by prohibiting human cloning before it becomes possible.

ABOUT THE IDEA TO bring forth a person through the astonishing procedure that is known as cloning. . . . This is what is called a complete biological creation of a human creature according to a predetermined plan, that will bring into reality traits its creators desire. Can one really call them offspring that are related to their parents? Besides the fact that their creation is distorted by being brought into the world in this manner, it is something that is likely to cause destruction and ruin to human creation. Chaos will reign and the problem of procreation will turn into a scientific procedure lacking humanity. Scientists have already protested against this and have expressed their fears about the expected future. Behold a generation will arise in which all who see it will say (Deut. 32:17), "New [gods] . . . whom your fathers did not know" — to see creations like this almost lacking free will and being artificial, lacking true familial relationships.[22]

QUESTIONS FOR INQUIRY

1. What specific concerns does Waldenberg express about cloning humans?
2. Does Waldenberg agree with those who see a clone as a person, or those who see it as a golem (see Texts 15a and 15b)?
3. Do you agree with his assessment that human cloning is likely to lead to chaos?

COMMENTS

Rabbi Waldenberg's tone in this *teshuvah* expresses revulsion at the prospect of reproductive cloning. To him, it represents the possibility of a dystopian world. His first objection is to "complete biological creation of a human creature according to a predetermined plan": ostensibly, making a human entirely through scientific manipulation, with no connection to the natural process of reproduction. More than that, the product of the process would have only "the traits its creators desire." This would deny the resulting persons the opportunity to develop what Judaism teaches is their God-given uniqueness. They would appear to have no choice but to become what their laboratory designers wanted them to be.

Waldenberg asks rhetorically if a clone can truly be related to the clone's parents. We saw earlier in the chapter that most Orthodox thinkers define maternity based on who gives birth, and paternity based on who provides the fertilizing sperm. Given that a human clone would still need to gestate in a uterus, Waldenberg's concern here is somewhat unclear. Possibly he has in mind a situation similar to surrogacy, where a man has his DNA inserted into a donor ovum and gestated either by the donor or by another surrogate. In such a case, the halakhic mother would be the surrogate and not the male donor's partner. In the absence of the usual process of fertilization, Rabbi Waldenberg may be at a loss to identify a halakhic father.

The next few sentences bring us to the heart of Waldenberg's unease about reproductive cloning. He fears that "procreation will turn into a scientific procedure lacking humanity." He takes literally the Torah's command that husband and wife come together to procreate. Disagreeing with other Jewish thinkers whose ideas we have encountered (for example, Texts 10, 13c), Waldenberg does not allow for ART (alternative reproductive technologies). Reducing the human interchange to a sterile procedure in a laboratory strikes him as engendering a world devoid of human qualities. As our study of *Mishnah Sanhedrin* 4:5 (Text 16) showed, Jewish tradition indeed cares for the unique qualities of each person. Yet not every rabbinic ethicist agrees with Waldenberg's conclusion that a clone by definition cannot meet the criterion of uniqueness in God's image.

Waldenberg correctly emphasizes that many scientists object to human cloning. In 2003 the American Medical Association approved physicians' participation in cloning stem cells solely for medical research to cure diseases. Laws in the United States, Canada, Great Britain, and France all make the same distinction, allowing research to help cure diseases but forbidding the creation of human life. The 2005 United Nations General Assembly Declaration on Human Cloning also forbids human cloning as a violation of the principle of human dignity.[23]

Thinking along similar lines, Waldenberg forcefully points to the unrecognizable world we would enter if we cloned human lives. The products of cloning strike him as "artificial," more golems than human beings. The presence of beings created in this manner would weaken family relationships forming the very basis of society. All social ties would be in danger.

On the other hand, perhaps the author of *Tzitz Eliezer* allows his imagination to run away with him. Perhaps a cloned person would be a human being in every respect. Like the products of IVF, clones would develop in a uterus and be born in the same manner as every baby. While defining parentage based on mitochondrial DNA represents a change from the past, it would hardly be the first significant change in the history of reproductive technology.

Indeed, other Jewish thinkers argue that we have no reason to fear adopting new technologies despite how bizarre they may strike us at first. The authors of a guide for Jewish couples facing infertility show that not all Orthodox halakhists agree with Waldenberg's restrictive view. In our concluding text study, Richard V. Grazi, a fertility doctor who studies Jewish ethics in his field, and Joel B. Wolowesky, an Orthodox rabbi and ethicist, discuss both points of view and how Jewish ethics may adapt to these new developments.

Text 18 — Grazi and Wolowesky, *Overcoming Infertility*

[CLONING] SHOULD PRESENT LESS ethical difficulty than, say, donor insemination. Transferring the husband's cell nucleus to the wife's egg and implanting it in her uterus seems more acceptable than involving a third person in the procedure. The "artificial" nature of it all will eventually fade as the procedure becomes more common — just as IVF did. . . .

According to [the] view [of Rabbi Yosef Elyashiv], the cloned individual is a new *beriah*, a new creation not intended by God's plan. Using cloning to achieve a pregnancy is impermissible. . . .

A completely opposite conclusion [permitting human cloning] is reached by Michael Broyde. . . . Regarding the viewpoint that the cloned individual is a new *beriah*, Broyde . . . points to the *prima facie* evidence that, by virtue of its gestation in utero and birth to a human mother, the child must be human. . . . It is unlikely that there will be a reconciliation of these opposing views, as it is not only differing halakhic analysis that divides them. Rather, they are basing themselves on radically different understandings of man's place in God's plan.[24]

QUESTIONS FOR INQUIRY

1. Why does Rabbi Elyashiv forbid human cloning, and how does Rabbi Broyde refute his concern?
2. Do you think cloning raises more problems than other forms of ART? Why or why not?

COMMENTS

These excerpts from an essay by an infertility specialist and a rabbi present two ways that Jewish ethicists might respond to human cloning. One, represented by the Israeli *haredi* rabbi Yosef Elyashiv, would forbid cloning because it would create a person in a manner not intended by God. (Review the discussion of Texts 15a–b to see that Elyashiv is consistent in this view.) In an opinion that may derive from Rabbi Zeira's reaction to the golem created by Rava (Text 14), humans may not create the way God did. Any manner of bringing a person into existence without uniting male and female gametes amounts to human beings usurping God's role. Rabbi Broyde, in contrast, argues that gestation in a uterus and birth through the natural process suffice to make a hypothetical cloned infant equivalent to every other human being. On this basis, he would permit Jews to use cloning to have children.

Grazi and Wolowesky note that these opposing views allow for no compromise. They are not different analyses of halakhic literature, but irreconcilable standpoints concerning human beings' roles in relation to God's creation. Ethicists differ irreparably on where to draw the line between the appropriate use of human scientific ingenuity, which tradition encourages, and playing God, which it forbids. Human cloning unavoidably confronts us with this problem. Deciding about its ethics requires deciding how far we are willing to go toward making new creations in God's world.

For their part, Grazi and Wolowesky distinguish between cloning as a medical solution to infertility, which they would permit, and cloning to make the child emerge exactly as the parents wish, which they would forbid. They write: "The use of such procedures on healthy . . . embryos in order to alter physical, mental or other characteristics that may render them more 'desirable' would be a frivolous intervention and therefore . . . prohibited."[25]

We may agree with these writers that a line is crossed when cloning goes from being a fertility technology to a means of selecting a child's characteristics. But the argument that such an intervention is "frivolous" does not complete the ethical case against such activity. Some might even see Jewish value in the possibility of bearing a Jewish child with certain desirable physical or psychological characteristics: perhaps a future Torah scholar of the caliber of Maimonides or Rashi, or super-strong Jews bred to defend the future State of Israel from violent attacks. If cloning and related technologies become practical, decisions about using them will require careful ethical analysis.

Dr. Grazi and Rabbi Wolowesky observe that no matter how strange and upsetting new technologies at first appear, in time we come to see them as normal. Imagine, they write elsewhere in their survey of future directions in reproductive technology, how it felt in 1909 to look up in the sky over New York City and see Wilbur Wright flying an airplane around the Statue of Liberty. No human then alive had ever seen such a sight. It must have been equal parts exhilarating and terrifying; indeed, many feared Wright would crash into the statue. In not too many years, however, people came to take flight for granted. Similarly, Dr. Grazi suggests, time will adjust us even to the cloning of human life.

Conclusion

The first mitzvah in the Torah is procreation. Generations of Jews considered having large families central to living a Jewish life and preserving the Jewish future (Texts 1–3). For these reasons, Jewish ethicists tend to sympathize with the desire to try any available means to help a couple have a child. While no one is required to try extraordinary methods, many rabbis and thinkers offer maximum flexibility to fulfill the dream of parenthood. While a few dismiss noncoital fertilization using donor semen as equivalent to adultery (Text 8b), many interpreters of the Rabbinic tradition consider IVF a permissible means of overcoming infertility (Text 7).

Jewish thinkers also express contesting views regarding surrogate motherhood. Our text study reveals that while some ethicists objected to surrogate motherhood, especially when it was new and unfamiliar (Texts 12a–c), many others came to see it as a legitimate means for Jews to achieve their dream of parenthood (Texts 13a–c). Concerns about exploitation of women and the shirking of parental responsibilities gave way to appreciation of this method of fulfilling the commandment to procreate. Elie Spitz (Text 13b) offers a poignant reminder of the joy and blessings surrogacy can bring to those who desperately desire children. It seems we can find good reasons to support the decisions the Sterns made in Case Study #3, and to agree with the court that they were Baby M's rightful parents.

In modern times more frequently than in the past, some adults prefer not to have children, or choose to become single parents. The Talmud frowns on those who abstain from procreation (Text 2), and some contemporary rabbis maintain that view (Text 5a). Others find ways to interpret the tradition to support the choice to remain childless (Text 5b). Similarly, some thinkers rely on the Talmud's decision that the commandment to procreate does not include women (Text 3) to deny them the choice to become single mothers.

Throughout this chapter, we confronted questions about the definition of parenthood. Does it derive from biology, or from the process of rearing children? As we've seen, most Jewish ethicists consider a child born through artificial insemination or surrogacy the child of the parents who raise it (Texts 6, 7, 9). Some Orthodox thinkers dissent (Texts 8b, 9) and argue that only genetic relationships establish parenthood. The majority opinion seems to favor Angela Bauer and Jennifer Schreiner in Case Study #1. Their written agreement with William Marotta, who donated sperm to them, that he would have no parental relationship to their child, finds support in halakhic ethics.

Sophia's desire to have a baby without a partner (Case Study #2) recalls our study of the Torah's command to procreate (Texts 1, 2). *Mishnah Yevamot* (Text 3) rules that the Torah obligates only men to procreate, though our discussion showed that talmudic authorities of later generations disagreed on this point. Susan Grossman's *teshuvah* (Text 10) demonstrates that no law forbids a single woman to bear or adopt a child. She encourages all Jews who so desire to build Jewish families. These considerations support Sophia if she chooses to conceive through ART.

Case Study #3 — the Baby M case, which brought issues of how ART establishes parenthood to public attention in the 1980s — raises dilemmas that remain current. A number of Jewish thinkers express discomfort with surrogacy as a method of fulfilling the commandment to have children. Those who share concerns about the potential dangers pregnancy poses to the surrogate (Text 12a), about women shirking the responsibilities of parenthood (Text 12b), or about surrogacy's inherent exploitation of the surrogate (Text 12c) would oppose its use and believe the court erred in finding for the Sterns over the Whiteheads. On the other hand, other Jewish ethicists who agree with Walter Jacob (Text 13a) that couples may hire surrogates as an alternate means of procreation compare surrogacy to adoption, allowing those who assume legal parenthood to be recognized as the child's halakhic parents. Still others may be swayed by Elie Spitz's sympathy for couples' profound desire to become parents (Text 13b) or agree with John Loike and Moshe Tendler that the surrogate serves as more than an incubator for the infant (Text 13c). Such thinkers would support the Sterns in their case against Mary Beth Whitehead.

It is hard to find a middle ground between these two positions. The writers we studied who expressed concern about the surrogate mother opposed this method of childbearing, while those whose analysis focused on the infertile parents permitted it. The decision one makes may depend on which of these parties one more naturally sympathizes with.

Regarding Case Study #4, Sonoma's desire to bear a cloned version of herself so as not to introduce an unknown donor's genetic material into her family line, various Jewish ethicists argue that only gestation in a womb creates human life (Texts 14, 15b), that cloning detracts from the required uniqueness of each person (Text 16), and that cloned babies have no genuine familial relationship to their parents (Text 17). Yosef Elyashiv goes further, contending that cloning impermissibly brings a new creation into the world (Text 18). Yet other ethicists like Menachem HaMeiri contend that Jewish tradition approves almost anything that human beings learn to do with their God-given intelligence (Text 15a). Since in practice human cloning would require a fertilized ovum to gestate in a uterus, Michael Broyde sees cloning as equally ethically acceptable to in vitro fertilization and surrogate motherhood (Text 18).

Additionally, we saw that cloning would also enable manipulation of the fetus's genes to allow parents to choose their child's characteristics. Relying on a precedent in the Talmud (Text 14), Jewish ethics might consider that an improper intervention in God's creation. Difficult problems of deciding when we are or are not playing God lie ahead.

Ultimately, then, Sonoma might find permission in Broyde's reasoning that even if fertilization happens through cloning, the child must gestate in her womb and be born in a natural manner. Our study leads to the conclusion that she could go forward if her only goal is to have a child, but not if she wants to predetermine her child's characteristics.

Hopefully this material has additionally offered us broader lessons surrounding ethical choices. Many difficult decisions are best made not in an intellectual vacuum, but when taking into account actual people and their experiences. There may also be divergent compassionate approaches to a complex matter: compassionate ethicists can reach opposite conclusions. And it is prudent to contemplate proactively scientific advances that may be on the horizon.

Two further examples come to mind. First, in 2019 scientists reported for the first time successfully editing genes in embryos to eliminate a mutation that causes serious heart disease. Not only would the editing prevent the heart condition in the embryo itself, should it develop until birth, but individuals benefiting from the editing would pass on the new genetic characteristic to their children. Gene editing thus promises the eventual possibility of preventing many diseases and disabilities before birth. At the same time, though, it opens the door to a new form of breeding technology — eugenics. Parents might be able to predetermine their children's attributes, selecting for height, athletic ability, certain kinds of intelligence, eventually even gender.

A second advance on the horizon is an artificial womb — an environment where a fetus could develop from fertilization to birth outside the human body. Such a device would offer a new path to parenthood for women whose wombs have been surgically removed, or who for medical reasons cannot safely carry a pregnancy. At the same time, we can imagine companies gestating infants for sale to couples wishing to adopt. It is hard to imagine a more dystopian example of playing God than creating a market in human lives. It seems we will need to continually wrestle to define the moral boundaries between helping nature and playing God.

In *Kiddushin* 30b the Talmud says, "There are three partners in a human being: the father, the mother, and the Holy One." (See chapter 1 for discussion of this text.) Advances in technology force us to think carefully about the precise roles played by each of the three partners in creating human life.

6

Abortion

Few topics arouse such divergence of views as abortion. Pro-life advocates consider all abortions acts of murder. Pro-choice advocates declare abortion a private decision for a woman to make, perhaps along with her partner and doctor.

The two sides defend radically different ideas about privacy and autonomy (one's right to make decisions on one's own behalf). Pro-choice supporters stress the privacy of the individual adult woman and her right to exercise autonomy over her own body. The state, they say, has no right to interfere in her private decisions about her body. Pro-life supporters argue that the fact that the fetus has a potential life sets a boundary on the mother's autonomy. Now she must take a second life into account. Her privacy ends when her pregnancy brings another potential person into being.

Can Jewish tradition contribute anything to this debate? Surprisingly, even ancient texts include discussions of the ethics of abortion. Furthermore, in the traditional sources we discover a different approach: halakhah considers the problems abortion raises in ways that do not easily fit into pro-life or pro-choice positions. Additionally, and unsurprisingly, contemporary Jews disagree amongst themselves about what the tradition teaches. The spectrum of Jewish voices raised in this chapter may well add new dimensions to public discussions of the issue.

Case Study #1: Fetal Reduction of Twins

A true story covered by the *New York Times*: Jenny and her (unnamed) husband had two children. As she entered her forties, they decided they wanted to add one more baby to their family. At her relatively advanced age, Jenny conceived only after fertility treatments. Following several years of effort and disappointment, she became pregnant with twins at age 45.

Both Jenny and her husband believed that caring for two newborns would be more of a burden than they could manage. They still wanted a third child, but not a third and fourth simultaneously as they reached middle age. They were also concerned about their financial ability to support four children. Jenny decided to ask her obstetrician to perform a fetal reduction, an operation to abort one fetus and leave the other to develop toward birth.

Jenny's doctor declined to perform the fetal reduction. He explained that the operation's purpose is to reduce medical risks to the pregnant woman and enable her to deliver a healthy baby. Originally, fertility specialists performed reductions when women carried three or more fetuses, situations that involve elevated risks both for the mother and the potential babies. Since Jenny did not face a medical risk from carrying the twins, ethically he did not feel comfortable proceeding with the operation. He acknowledged that other doctors would agree to the request.[1]

Would Judaism approve of Jenny and her husband's wish to abort one of the two fetuses?

Case Study #2: Abortion of a Fetus with a Deficit

At eleven weeks' gestation, a blood test and sonogram show that Amy and her husband Bruce's fetus will likely be born with Down syndrome. Resulting from "trisomy" in chromosome 21—all or a portion of that chromosome appears three times, rather than twice, in the body's cells—individuals with Down syndrome usually exhibit low muscle tone, a tendency to keep the mouth open with the tongue protruding, a head shape typical of the syndrome, poor coordination, mild to severe mental impairment, and damaged hearing. Amy and Bruce are now considering aborting the fetus rather than subjecting their child to this condition. Candidly, they discuss among themselves, they are also concerned about their commitment and ability to raise a special needs child. Neither of them wants to give up their professional ambitions, and they do not live near any family who could help. What does Judaism say about taking into account illness or disability and the effect of raising a special needs child on prospective parents who don't feel prepared for that when deciding whether or not to carry a fetus to term?

Case Study #3: When Contraception Fails

Candice and her husband Ari discover to their shock that she is pregnant. The birth control they were diligently using has failed. They do not believe this is the right time for them to have a baby, as they planned to wait until she finished graduate school and they could afford to buy a house. From a Jewish perspective, is it appropriate for Candice to abort this pregnancy?

Thinking about the ethics of abortion forces us to tackle difficult questions. First, we need to decide what defines a human life. A living person generally has a right to go on living; is a fetus a living person in the same way as a pregnant woman?

Our study begins with what halakhah says about fetal status.

Text Study #1: Halakhic Status of the Fetus

Text 1a — Exod. 21:12

HE WHO FATALLY STRIKES a man shall be put to death.

QUESTION FOR INQUIRY

1. What conclusions could you draw from this verse about the value of human life?

Text 1b — Exod. 21:22–23

WHEN MEN FIGHT, AND one of them pushes a pregnant woman and her child goes out, but no other damage ensues, the one responsible shall be fined according as the woman's husband may exact from him, the payment to be based on reckoning.

But if other damage ensues, the penalty shall be life for life.

QUESTIONS FOR INQUIRY

1. What could the Torah mean by "no other damage ensues"?

2. Is the situation described in these verses a good analogy to abortion? What strengths and weaknesses do you find in that analogy?
3. Based on this information, what conclusion can you draw about the status of the mother?
4. What conclusion can you draw about the status of the fetus?

COMMENTS

The first inference we can draw from the Torah is that ending the development of a fetus does not amount to murder. Exodus 21:12 teaches that anyone "who fatally strikes a man shall be put to death." Yet in the case of the men who accidentally cause a woman to miscarry, the Torah rules that if the woman survives the blow, the penalty is a fine to compensate the woman and her husband for the loss of the fetus. Analogously, if causing a miscarriage amounted to murder, the Torah would impose capital punishment on the person responsible. Exodus 21:23 demonstrates that the pregnant woman herself is a person (in the language of 21:12, Hebrew *ish*); killing her earns the death penalty. The fetus, then, is not a living human being in the same sense as the mother.

It makes sense to ask if that distinction between mother and fetus remains true throughout pregnancy. A normal pregnancy lasts about forty weeks. Even without today's imaging of fetuses in the womb, people long felt that the closer to term the fetus comes, the closer it comes to deserving the treatment it would receive after birth. Some of the modern thinkers we will discuss later in this chapter point out that for the first forty days of pregnancy, the Rabbis considered the embryo merely fluid in the mother's body; after that, it gains ethical status. The question remains: When does a fetus reach the status called in Rabbinic Hebrew a *nefesh*—a life?

Key to answering this question is *Mishnah Ohalot* 7:6.

Text 2 — Mishnah Ohalot 7:6

A WOMAN WHO IS having trouble giving birth, they cut up the fetus inside her and take it out limb by limb, because her life comes before its life. If most of it had come out already they do not touch it, because we do not push off one life for another.

___

1. In the first half of the Mishnah, why does the mother's life take precedence over the fetus's life?
2. What changes in the second half of the Mishnah, so that the mother's life does not take precedence?
3. What does this Mishnah suggest about when life begins?
4. What should happen if the woman giving birth asks those attending her to do all they can to save her fetus, not her?

COMMENTS

The Mishnah discusses a woman whose labor endangers her life. It rules about two situations. In the first, where the fetus has not yet emerged from the birth canal, the Mishnah rules that we abort because the mother's life takes precedence over the fetus's. Only one factor changes in the second situation. Now, the majority of the fetus—or, in the version quoted in the Talmud and accepted by Rashi and Maimonides (see Texts 4 and 5a–b), the fetus's head—has emerged from the mother's body. Then, the Mishnah rules, we may not abort. The rationale: "We do not push aside one life [*nefesh*, a critical term throughout this chapter] for another."

That reason informs us that, with the emergence of the majority (or head) of the fetus from the birth canal, we now confront two lives. In the hypothetical situation, if we abort the fetus, the mother will live; if we do not abort, she may well not survive. The Mishnah rules that we may not choose which life to save. That implies letting labor take its course. Possibly both baby and mother will survive; possibly one of them will die. Either way, those attending the mother must leave that result to nature, or to God. It further implies that we may not choose to save the baby over the mother even at her request.

Most important, all of this implies that the fetus reaches equal status with the mother when the head (or majority) leaves the mother's body. At that moment, the fetus too becomes a *nefesh*. While some readers may recognize this word in its meaning of "soul," in these texts the word consistently means "a life." *Nefesh* indicates full status as a living human being.

In modern terms, a fetus considered a *nefesh* is now a person. Philosophers define a *person* as someone who has an intrinsic right to life, meaning that this someone does not have to justify that right; all persons are simply entitled to live. In principle, Jewish tradition does not allow human beings to choose one *nefesh* or person over another, as our Mishnah states. It reserves that privilege for God.

The Mishnah, it emerges, teaches a fundamental concept for thinking about all of our case studies. In none of them has the majority—or any portion—of the fetus emerged from the womb. That means that none of these fetuses holds the halakhic status of *nefesh*. That provides some support for the side that favors abortion in any of these cases.

At the same time, the mere fact that the fetus is not a *nefesh* does not by itself end the debate. The fetus will attain this status if allowed to continue developing. Those who want to permit any of the women in the case studies to abort must still show that the fetuses in question do not have any legal or moral status that would protect them from having their natural development abruptly cut off.

The next set of texts (3a–c) introduces a related concept in classical halakhah. Because *Mishnah Ohalot* 7:6 focuses on a birth that threatens the mother's life, the sources wonder if the fetus fits the category called *din rodef*, "the law of the pursuer." To understand this law, we begin with its background in the Torah (Exod. 22:1–2), as explained by Rashi. These verses introduce the law governing the *ba-mahteret* (literally "one who comes in from underground"), a thief who tunnels into a house to steal valuables.

The Torah differentiates between a thief who breaks in under cover of darkness and one who attempts a burglary in daylight. As we will see, while the sources do not accuse the fetus in a woman's body of being like a "thief breaking in," this material nonetheless serves as background for the discussion of whether or not the fetus can fall into the legal category of a *rodef*. Text 3c, Sanhedrin 73b, details the law of the pursuer.

Text 3a—Exod. 22:1-2

IF THE THIEF IS seized while tunneling, and he is beaten to death, there is no bloodguilt in his case. If the sun has risen on him, there is bloodguilt in that case.—He [the thief] must make restitution; if he lacks the means, he shall be sold for his theft.

Text 3b—Rashi on Exod. 22:1-2

1 IF . . . WHILE TUNNELING. While he was in the act of breaking in.

There is no bloodguilt in his case. This is not considered murder, because he (the thief) is considered already dead. Here the Torah teaches: if someone comes to kill you, kill him first. This [thief] came with every intention of killing you; for he knows that a person cannot hold himself back while seeing his property taken from him and remain silent. Therefore, it is with that purpose that he came—that if the owner of the property will resist him, he will kill him.

2 *If the sun has risen on him.*

This is nothing but an allegory: If the matter is clear to you that his intentions toward you are peaceful—like the sun represents peace in the world—so, too, if it is obvious to you that he has not come with the intention of killing, even should the property owner resist.

For example: a father who breaks in to steal the property of his son, where it is known that a father has pity for his child and he does not come with any intention of taking a life—*there is bloodguilt for him*—he is considered alive and it would be murder if the property owner killed him.

QUESTIONS FOR INQUIRY

1. How does Rashi explain why the homeowner is not guilty of murder if he kills the thief at night?

2. Does it seem reasonable to assume we understand the thief's motivations and intentions in this way?
3. How does Rashi explain the significance of the phrase, "if the sun shone on him"?
4. In what sense is the thief at night "already dead"?

COMMENTS

The Torah rules that a homeowner has the right to kill a thief who breaks into his house to steal property under cover of night. Rashi explains the law based on the Talmud. Because the thief relies on darkness to hide him, the law presumes he will kill anyone who gets in his way. In that sense, the thief is already guilty of the capital crime of murder. That is what Rashi means when he writes, "This [thief] came with every intention of killing you."

The homeowner may justifiably kill the thief to save his own life. Rashi quotes a talmudic injunction from *Sanhedrin* 72a that justifies self-defense: "If someone comes to kill you, kill him first." One may save one's own life by preemptively taking the life of the intended murderer.

According to *Sanhedrin* 72a, breaking in during daylight hours does not create a presumption that the thief intends to kill. While the Torah appears to speak literally of daytime and nighttime, Rashi otherwise explains the reference to "the sun rising." It is a metaphor: the "light" represents the clarity of the thief's intentions. If he has no murderous intent, killing him is not justified.

Notice that for the first time, we confront the reality that we cannot imagine a fetus intending to kill the mother. That fact will become important as we continue studying texts related to abortion ethics.

With this background, we can explore the law of the pursuer (*din rodef*) introduced in the Talmud.

Text 3c — *Sanhedrin* 73a

Mishnah

THESE ARE THE ONES we save at the expense of their lives:
One who pursues another person to kill him. . . .

Gemara

OUR RABBIS TAUGHT IN a *baraita*:

How do we know that one who pursues another person to kill him may be saved [from sinning] at the expense of his life?

Because the Torah says, "Do not stand by the blood of your neighbor" [Lev. 19:16].

QUESTIONS FOR INQUIRY

1. What biblical source does the Talmud evidence for the law of *rodef* (the pursuer)?
2. What justifies killing the *rodef*?
3. Can you imagine a circumstance in which a fetus might act as a *rodef* toward the pregnant woman?

COMMENTS

The Mishnah includes the *rodef* as one of three categories of criminals who may be saved from committing their sin at the cost of their lives. In short, one who chases another person with intent to kill the pursued may be killed by a bystander. As Rashi commented on Exodus (Text 3b), it is as if the *rodef* has already earned the death penalty, because he will murder the innocent person he pursues if no one stops him.

The Gemara implicitly asks this question: What justifies a private individual's killing of the *rodef*? Only the Sanhedrin (the high court in the time of the *tannaim*) has the right to execute a murderer, and that execution can only proceed after a careful and extensive legal process. Further, since the *rodef* is not killed by the person he pursues, this is not homicide justified by self-defense.

The Talmud derives its answer from Leviticus 19:16, "Do not stand by the blood of your neighbor." We must not stand idly by and watch an innocent person's blood being shed. Instead, anyone who has the opportunity must save the intended victim by killing the *rodef*.

The Talmud excerpt that follows tries to connect the law of the *rodef* with the issue of the fetus whose birth threatens the mother's life.

RAV HUNA SAID: A minor pursuer (*rodef*) — it is permitted to save him at the expense of his life.

He holds the opinion: A pursuer (*rodef*) does not require a warning. It makes no difference if he is a minor or an adult.

Rav Hisda objected to Rav Huna: "'If its head had come out already they do not touch it, because we do not push off one life for another.' But why? It is a pursuer (*rodef*)!"

It is different in that case, for she is pursued from Heaven.

QUESTIONS FOR INQUIRY

1. How does Rav Hisda use a quotation from the Mishnah in attempting to refute Rav Huna's statement?
2. How does the anonymous voice of the Talmud resolve the apparent contradiction between Rav Huna's statement and the Mishnah?
3. What difference do you notice between the way Rav Hisda quotes the Mishnah and the text of the Mishnah (see Text 2)?
4. At this point in our text study, what might we learn from this talmudic discussion about the relative status of a fetus and the mother?

COMMENTS

This brief passage reports a debate between two Babylonian *amoraim*, Rav Huna and Rav Hisda. As is common in Babylonian Talmud style, parts of the text — specifically, the sentences beginning, "He holds the opinion" and "It is different" — speak in the "voice" of its anonymous editors.

Rav Huna's claim at the outset relies on the Rabbinic development of the halakhah of murder. According to the Torah, a murderer is subject to the death penalty (see Text 1a). Yet the Talmud forbids the court to sentence the murderer to death unless he received a warning (*hatra'ah*) before committing the murder. Furthermore, two lawful witnesses must warn the individual that the act he is about to commit carries the death penalty, and the criminal must declare that he is aware of the punishment and does not care (*Sanhedrin* 40b). If these conditions are not met, the court cannot execute the criminal (Sanhedrin 41a).

Rav Huna suggests that the *din rodef* (law of the pursuer) applies to minors. This is a significant extension of the law's application, because normally halakhah (like U.S. law) does not hold minors responsible for their actions in the same way as adults. Jewish law holds that a minor cannot form the intention to commit a crime, or understand that a certain act would be a crime. *Mishnah Niddah* 5:4–5, for example, exempts both male and female minors from the capital punishment otherwise due for incest.

Nevertheless, the Gemara deduces that Rav Huna believes that no *rodef*, adult or minor, requires a warning before being put to death. His statement, "It is permitted to save him [the victim] at the expense of his [the *rodef*'s] life" would logically imply that one can kill the *rodef* before he can commit the murder he intends. There is no time to warn him of the consequences.

Rav Hisda now attacks the core of Rav Huna's statement. Rav Huna may think a minor can fall into the category of *rodef*, but what about the contradictory Mishnah: when the head of the fetus whose mother is in danger emerges from the vagina, we may not touch it? (see Text 2). If Rav Huna is correct, that makes no sense. We should kill the fetus, which is a *rodef* against the woman in labor! If Rav Hisda understands the Mishnah correctly, Rav Huna must be wrong; as we saw in the introduction to Rabbinic literature, an *amora* cannot directly contradict a Mishnah.

At this point, the anonymous voice of the Gemara comes to Rav Huna's rescue. It identifies a difference between the circumstances Rav Huna had in mind and the circumstances in the Mishnah. The Mishnah is different because the potential mother is "is pursued from Heaven." That is, "Heaven"—not the fetus—is directly threatening her life.

The Gemara may mean that God puts the woman's life in danger, though a more likely interpretation is that childbirth is inherently dangerous. The process of labor, not the fetus, is the threat. (A similar implication emerges from the *Mishneh Torah*, Text 5b.)

As we will now see, this understanding that when labor threatens a woman's life, halakhic tradition does not treat fetuses as if they fell under the law of the pursuer influences two Jewish stances on abortion.

Text Study #2: Two Approaches to Abortion Ethics

We now turn to Rashi's comment aimed at explaining the context of the ruling in *Mishnah Ohalot* 7:6 that once the majority of the fetus emerges, we cannot choose between the fetus and the mother (Text 2; also cited in the debate in Text 4). Rashi's explanation of the second half of the Mishnah becomes the foundation of one Jewish approach to abortion ethics.

Text 5a—Rashi on *Sanhedrin* 72b, s.v. "If its head came out"

IF ITS HEAD CAME OUT—

The Talmud refers to a woman having a difficult labor that endangers her. The beginning of the Mishnah teaches: "The midwife stretches out her hand and cuts up the fetus and takes it out by limbs," for the whole time it has not come out into the air of the world it is not a living being [*nefesh*], so it is permitted to kill it and save its mother.

But "once its head came out, we do not touch it" to kill it; for it is as if it is born, and "we do not push off one life for another."

QUESTIONS FOR INQUIRY

1. How does Rashi explain the situation presented in the Mishnah in which we give preference to the mother's life over the fetus's?
2. How does Rashi explain the situation in which we do *not* give preference to the mother's life over the fetus's?
3. What conclusion might we draw from the assertion, "the whole time it has not come out into the air of the world it is not a living being"?
4. How might Rashi's words here support a relatively permissive attitude toward abortion?

Rashi reminds us of the context of *Mishnah Ohalot* 7:6 (Text 2): a woman whose labor endangers her life. In Rashi's language, the first half of the Mishnah instructs the midwife to cut up the fetus limb by limb. As long as the fetus remains inside the mother's body, the fetus is not a *nefesh*. As long as the fetus does not have the status of a *nefesh*, he adds, it is permitted to kill the fetus in order to save the mother.

Turning to the second half of the Mishnah, Rashi explains the version that appears in the Gemara, which reads "if the fetus's head came out." By contrast, in the Mishnah itself, in tractate *Ohalot*, we read "if the majority of [the fetus] came out." Why the discrepancy? Possibly this version is an explanation of the Mishnah's meaning: the emergence of the head represents most of the baby. It could also be an attempt to simplify the Mishnah, since a "majority" of a fetus is difficult to define. A third possible explanation refers to the Mishnah's origins as traditions taught orally. Confusing "its head," *rosho*, and "its majority," *rubo*, would not be difficult—especially for someone trying to memorize large amounts of *tannaitic* material.

Regardless of the reason, Rashi's comment influenced later debates over abortion ethics. Rashi explains that once the head emerges, "it is as if [the fetus] is born." At that point the fetus is considered a living person with equal status to the mother and may not be killed. Rashi reiterates the Mishnah's explanation: "We do not push aside one life [note the use, again, of the Hebrew word *nefesh*] for another."

Perhaps the most interesting phrase in Rashi's comment is the assertion that "the whole time it has not come out into the air of the world it is not a living being [*nefesh*]." A number of modern Jewish thinkers use this phrase to justify permitting abortion in many circumstances. They reason that Rashi's words mean what they say. As long as the fetus remains inside the mother's body, it is not a living being. It does not have the natural right to the life of a human person. Therefore, the mother has the right to save herself, a person, by aborting the fetus, which has lesser status.

Yet this interpretation of Rashi's comment on the Talmud does not settle the argument. The next selection, Maimonides' interpretation of *Mishnah Ohalot* 7:6, published in 1180 in his *Mishneh Torah*, became the supporting text for modern Jewish thinkers who wish to restrict abortion to limited circumstances.

Text 5b — *Mishneh Torah*, Laws of Murder and Preservation of Life 1:9

THIS, INDEED, IS ONE of the negative mitzvot — not to take pity on the life of a *rodef*.

On this basis, our Sages ruled that when a woman has difficulty in giving birth, it is permitted to abort the fetus in her womb, whether by hand or with drugs. For the fetus is considered like a *rodef* of its mother.

If the head of the fetus emerges, it should not be touched, because we do not push off one life for another. [Although the mother may die], this is the nature of the world.[2]

QUESTIONS FOR INQUIRY

1. What three details does Maimonides add to the discussion of *Mishnah Ohalot* 7:6 that we have not seen before?
2. What implications does the phrase, "For the fetus is considered like a *rodef* of its mother" have for understanding Jewish abortion ethics?
3. How might Rambam's words here support a relatively restrictive attitude toward abortion?

COMMENTS

Rambam's summary of the halakhah returns our thoughts to the law of the *rodef*. We may not "take pity" on the life of a *rodef* — that is, we must kill the *rodef* to save his intended victim. Rambam describes that rule as the basis for the permission *Mishnah Ohalot* 7:6 gives to kill the fetus whose birth threatens the mother's life. Adding to Rashi's description in his commentary on *Sanhedrin* 72b (Text 5a), Rambam says that the abortion may be done "by hand or with drugs." In our terms, this means surgically or medically.

It is important to notice the precise phrasing Rambam uses. He says that we may abort this fetus because "it is considered like a *rodef* of its mother." Rambam does not claim that the fetus *is* a *rodef*; all the *Mishneh Torah* asserts is that, in this specific circumstance, we treat the fetus *as if it were* a *rodef*. That allows us to put the fetus to death to save the mother's life.

Like all our sources, Rambam follows the Mishnah's ruling that if the fetus's head has already emerged, we may not harm the fetus. In that situation, we may not choose one life over the other. In adding the phrase "This is the nature of the world," Rambam seems to be saying that childbirth is inherently dangerous: some women die giving birth.

The *Mishneh Torah*'s authority lends support to modern ethicists who take a stringent (*mahmir*) line on abortion, specifically by limiting the situations in which abortion is permitted. Certain ethicists understand the phrase "for [the fetus] is considered like a *rodef* of its mother" to mean: We may abort *only* when the fetus can be considered as if it were a *rodef* trying to kill the woman in labor. If the birth does not directly threaten her survival, we may not abort. That said, as we will see, not every modern thinker who propounds a position on abortion deriving from the *Mishneh Torah* forbids every abortion where the mother's life is not endangered. Jewish ethicists differ over how severe and how immediate the threat must be.

We now turn to another passage from the Babylonian Talmud that complicates the debate over whether the fetus is a separate being or a part of the pregnant woman's body. In the Gemara of Text 6, the words in italics translate the Talmud's words directly, while those in regular type add phrases that help readers understand the passage's logic.

Text Study #3: Fetal Personhood

Text 6—Arakhin 7a

Mishnah

A WOMAN GOING OUT to be executed, we do not wait for her to give birth.

If she sat on the birth stool [that is, she is already in labor], we do wait for her to give birth.

IT IS OBVIOUS THAT we do not wait for a woman who is going out to be executed to give birth, for *the fetus is* part of *her body*— not an independent entity! Why did the Mishnah find it at all necessary to relate this ruling?

The Gemara answers:

It is necessary to teach this ruling, for *you might have thought to say* that *since it is written: "as the husband of the woman shall cause to be assessed against him,"* this indicates that the fetus *is the property of the husband. Therefore, we may not cause him to lose* the fetus. The Mishnah therefore *informs us* that we do not wait, and we execute her before the child is born.

. . . .

The Mishnah states:

If she sat on the birthstool [that is, she is already in labor].

The Gemara asks:

What is the reason that we wait here for the child to be born?

The Gemara answers:

Since the fetus *has moved* from its original position to exit the womb, *it is* deemed *a different body*, and it is no longer considered part of the mother's body. Thus, it may not be killed.[3]

QUESTIONS FOR INQUIRY

1. In what cases does the Talmud consider the fetus merely a part of the mother, and in what cases is the fetus considered a separate being?

2. What are the implications for abortion if the fetus is part of the mother's body?

3. What are the implications for abortion if the fetus is separate from the mother's body?

4. Does it make more sense to think of the fetus as part of the mother's body, or as a separate body?

Arakhin 7a complicates the discussion of when the fetus becomes a person in an interesting way. The Mishnah discusses a pregnant woman sentenced to death. In light of Rabbinic law requiring capital punishment to proceed immediately after sentencing, out of a desire to spare the condemned person the mental anguish of anticipating death, *Mishnah Arakhin* rules that a condemned pregnant woman is to be executed before giving birth. Given this ruling, the Mishnah must consider the fetus part of the woman's body. If the fetus were a separate being, the execution would have to be postponed until after the fetus's birth, since the fetus has not committed a capital crime.

Confirming this intuition, we read in the second half of the Mishnah that if the condemned woman "sat on the birth stool," indicating that labor began, we do postpone her execution. This rule implies that labor marks the moment when the fetus becomes a separate being. At this point the fetus would seem to have an intrinsic right to life, with the status of *nefesh* equal to the mother.

Directly addressing this situation in the second part of the Mishnah, the Gemara queries "why do we wait for her to give birth if labor has begun?" and answers that since the fetus has "uprooted" or moved position inside the uterus, the fetus is a different body. Once the fetus begins passage from the uterus to birth, the fetus legally counts as separate from the mother's body. Notably, *Arakhin* 7a thus defines the fetus as a separate being from the mother at an earlier moment than identified in *Mishnah Ohalot* 7:6, which labels the fetus a *nefesh* only when the head or the majority emerges from the mother's body.

With this in mind, we turn to another passage from the Gemara that debates the possibility that the fetus counts as a human person.

Text 7 — *Sanhedrin* 84b

IT WAS NECESSARY [FOR the Torah] to write, "He who fatally strikes a man [*ish*]," and it was necessary [for the Torah] to write, "Anyone who kills a person [*nefesh*]."

For if the Torah had written only "He who fatally strikes a man" — I would have said, a man, who is of the age of *mitzvot* — yes [the death penalty applies], but a minor, no [it does not apply].

And if the Torah had written only "Anyone who kills a person [*nefesh*]" — I would have said, [this rule includes] even miscarriages, even a fetus of eight months' development —

Therefore, both verses are necessary [to show us who does and does not count as a person whose murder is a capital crime].

QUESTIONS FOR INQUIRY

1. What does this text add to our understanding of the status of the fetus?
2. From what we have seen so far, does halakhah treat the fetus as a person [*nefesh*]?

COMMENTS

The Gemara here analyzes two verses from the Torah in which one person kills another. The killing is intentional in Exodus 21:12 (Text 1a:) — "He who fatally strikes a man shall be put to death" — but accidental in Numbers 35:15, which reads: "These six cities shall serve the Israelites and the resident aliens among them for refuge, so that anyone who kills a person unintentionally may flee there."

The Gemara focuses on the exact phrasing of each verse. Whereas Exodus reads *makkeh ish*, "one who kills a man," Numbers reads *kol makkeh nefesh*, "anyone who kills a person." Since a basic talmudic interpretive principle holds that each word in the Bible is meaningful, the Rabbis understand the discrepancies in word choice as significant.

The Talmud begins by declaring that the Torah had good reasons for including each of these phrases about killing. In each case, if we read only one of the phrases, we would misunderstand something important about the law.

First, had the Torah written only "He who fatally strikes a man [*ish*]," we would conclude that the death penalty applies only to one who kills an adult. A person who kills a minor (in the Talmud's language, one not yet responsible for the mitzvot) would not be guilty of capital murder. Since the death penalty does apply in case of such a murder, the Torah needed to also include the phrase *kol makkeh nefesh*, "anyone who kills a person."

Now the Talmud turns to the other side. It needs to prove that we would be misled if the Torah only mentioned *kol makkeh nefesh*, "anyone who kills a person." In that case, the Talmud argues, we would mistakenly think that the law of homicide applies even to one who causes a miscarriage, or to a person who kills a fetus of eight months' development. Since those are not, in fact, capital crimes in halakhah, the Torah needed to add "*makkeh ish*, one who kills a man." That lets us know that the death penalty applies solely to killing someone in the category of "man": a viable human being.

This discussion, too, implies that a fetus lacks the same status we accord to a human being after birth. From what we have seen so far, rabbinic tradition does not consider ending fetal development in the same legal category as ending a human life. That, of course, does not necessarily mean that abortion is desirable, or that it is always acceptable. But it does imply that abortion is not always forbidden.

We now turn to more contemporary views on abortion. After the U.S. Supreme Court made abortion in America legal in 1973, religious groups of all stripes issued public statements of their views on its morality. What follows are two very different Jewish responses from the Reform and Orthodox movements. We begin with an excerpt from a 1975 resolution adopted by the Reform rabbinic organization, the Central Conference of American Rabbis.

Text 8a—Central Conference of American Rabbis, Resolution on Abortion

WHEREAS IN OUR EFFORTS to restore the world to sanity we affirm the following position which we take knowing full well the complexity of such an issue but knowing also that we cannot be silent,

Be it therefore resolved that as inheritors of and participants in a religious tradition that encompasses all human experience in its scope, we recognize that Jewish tradition has addressed itself to the question of the termination of pregnancy. We believe that in any decision whether or not to terminate a pregnancy, the individual family or woman must weigh the tradition as they struggle to formulate their own religious and moral criteria to reach their own personal decision. We direct the attention of individuals and families involved in such decisions to the sentiments expressed in Jewish legal literature looking favorably on therapeutic abortion. We believe that the proper locus for formulating these religious and moral criteria and for making this decision must be the individual family or woman and not the state or other external agency.[4]

QUESTIONS FOR INQUIRY

1. Why does the Central Conference of American Rabbis find it necessary to express a view about abortion?
2. What understanding of the halakhic tradition about abortion does this resolution imply?
3. Does the resolution fairly describe Jewish law (as stipulated by the classical halakhah, Texts 1a–7) as favoring therapeutic abortion?

COMMENTS

Notice first the reason the Central Conference of American Rabbis (CCAR) gives to explain why the Reform rabbinate is speaking publicly about abortion: to "restore the world to sanity." Apparently, the Reform rabbinic body felt that arguments over abortion had exceeded rational disagreement.

The resolution itself takes the view that decisions about ending a pregnancy belong to "the individual family or woman and not the state or other external agency." In describing how individuals or families should make these decisions, the resolution calls on them to "weigh the tradition as they struggle to formulate their own religious and moral criteria to reach their own personal decision." This process makes sense given the Reform ideology of "informed choice" in which individual Jews decide moral matters for themselves by engaging with and interpreting Jewish law and tradition. That does not mean that these Jews will necessarily choose to follow the tradition's advice.

Finally, the resolution directs Jews thinking about the problem of abortion to an understanding of what the halakhic literature says. According to the CCAR, the halakhah "look[s] favorably" on "therapeutic abortion." The inclusion of the word "therapeutic" implies the rabbis' approval of abortion solely *when it has a therapeutic purpose* — that is, when it serves a healing purpose for the pregnant woman.

The next entirely different position paper was promulgated by Agudath Israel, representing *haredi* Orthodox American Jews, in 1999.

Text 8b — Agudath Israel of America, National Public Policy Position Paper

GOVERNMENT IS NOT A neutral actor in the field of social morality. The law is a teacher. It conveys certain basic societal attitudes. As such, it is important that the law embody positive values, promote both the ideals and the interests of the traditional American family, exhibit compassion to the needy, and encourage good citizenship. . . .

In the context of abortion . . . Jewish tradition teaches that a human fetus has status and dignity; and that termination of pregnancy raises profound moral concerns. Agudath Israel accordingly has urged the Supreme Court to reconsider its holding in Roe v. Wade, and supports legislation that restricts abortion on demand. At the same time, in line with its support for religious freedom, Agudath Israel opposes initiatives that would make abortion unlawful even in situations where termination of pregnancy is mandated by religious law as it is, for example, under Sinaitic Jewish law when the pregnancy endangers the life of the mother.[5]

QUESTIONS FOR INQUIRY

1. Why does Agudath Israel find it necessary to express a view about abortion?

2. What understanding of the halakhic tradition about abortion
   does this statement imply?

Agudath Israel asserts that all laws, by their very nature, express values that matter to the society that passes them. American law ought to
teach "positive values," including what Agudath Israel understands to
be appropriate family values.

Interestingly, the *haredi* rabbis state that Jewish tradition gives the
human fetus "status and dignity." On that basis, they urge the Supreme
Court to overturn *Roe v. Wade*, which they understand as allowing abortion
"on demand." While that phrase is hard to define precisely, here it seems
to imply that a woman may have an abortion at any time she chooses,
for any reason.

While it is certainly in line with the more restrictive view of Jewish
tradition, the position paper does not take the maximalist pro-life position that abortion is always an act of murder. Despite the fetus's "status
and dignity," Agudath Israel recognizes that Jewish tradition requires
abortion when necessary to save the mother's life.

Individual scholars also responded to the new controversy on abortion
based on their various understandings of halakhah. First we examine one
of the first *teshuvot* about abortion following *Roe v. Wade*. After extensively
reviewing the textual tradition, Rabbi David Feldman, who published
widely about bioethics for the Conservative movement, turns to the
contemporary context to elucidate reasons for permitting or forbidding
abortion in specific circumstances.

Text 9 — Feldman, "Abortion: The Jewish View"

THE PRINCIPLE IN JEWISH LAW is *tza'ar gufah kadim,* that [the
mother's] welfare is primary. Rabbinic rulings on abortion are
thus amenable to the following generalization: If a possibility
or probability exists that a child may be born defective, and the
mother seeks abortion on the grounds of pity for a child whose life
would be less than normal, the rabbi would decline permission.

Since we do not know for sure that it will be born defective, and since we do not know how bad such a defective life will be for the child, and since no permission exists in Jewish law to kill born defectives, permission on those grounds would be denied. If, however, an abortion for the same potentially deformed child were sought on the grounds that the possibility is causing severe anguish to the mother, permission would be granted. . . .

Implicit in the Mishnah above [*Mishnah Ohalot* 7:6, Text 2] is the teaching that the rights of the fetus are secondary to the rights of the mother all the way up until the moment of birth. This principle is obscured by the current phrase, "right to life." In the context of abortion questions, the issue is not the right to life, which is very clear in Jewish law, but the right to be born, which is not as clear. The right to be born is relative; the right to life for existing persons is absolute. "Life" may begin before birth, but it is not the life of a human person; animal life, plant life or even pre-human life are not the same as human life. Rabbinic law has determined that human life begins with birth. This is neither a medical nor a court judgment, but a metaphysical one. In the Jewish system, human life in this sense begins with birth. Of course, potential life already partakes of the potential sacredness of actual life, since the latter can have its inception only through the former.

Another slogan-like phrase is dealt with in the same Mishnah, wherein it is ruled that "once the fetus has emerged from the womb, it cannot be touched" even to save the life of the mother, "for we cannot set aside one life for another." The "quality of life" slogan or concept is thus inadmissible. The life of the mother has more "quality"; she is adult, has a husband, children, associations, while the newborn has none of these yet. Still, the sanctity of life principle means that life is sacred regardless of differences in quality; mother and newborn babe are equal from the moment of birth. . . .

Procreation is a positive mitzvah, and he who fails to fulfill this mitzvah is called "guilty of bloodshed." And much of the pro-natalist attitude of Judaism helps account for its abhorrence of casual abortion. There may be legal sanction for abortion where necessary, but the attitude remains one of hesitation before the sanctity of life and a pro-natalist respect for potential life.

Accordingly, abortion for "population control" is repugnant to the Jewish system. Abortion for economic reasons is also not admissible. Taking precaution by abortion or birth control against physical threat remains a mitzvah, but never to forestall financial difficulty. Material considerations are improper in this connection.[6]

QUESTIONS FOR INQUIRY

1. What Jewish principle does Rabbi Feldman assert for making decisions about abortion? Do you think the texts support his claim?
2. How does he differentiate Jewish and American approaches to abortion?
3. When does he say Jewish tradition permits abortion?
4. When does he say Jewish tradition prohibits abortion?

COMMENTS

Rabbi Feldman argues that common American phrases like "right to life" and "quality of life" are not relevant to an abortion analysis based on Jewish sources. Instead, such an approach must grapple with the way the sources balance the mother's status and the fetus's status against each other.

Feldman points out that medieval and modern authorities read *Mishnah Ohalot* 7:6 (Text 2) in two ways: one more permissive or *maikeel*, the other more restrictive or *machmir*. The permissive approach, which begins with Rashi's comment on *Sanhedrin* 72b (Text 5a), focuses on the phrase, "The whole time it has not come out into the air of the world it is not a living being [*nefesh*], so it is permitted to kill it and save its mother." Jewish ethicists who adopt this approach argue that throughout the pregnancy, the fetus essentially lacks a right to life; therefore, abortion is almost always acceptable. Most thinkers, however, are uncomfortable with the implication that a woman may abort at any time for any reason. Therefore, as Rabbi Feldman shows, they build some restrictions around the general permission to prefer the mother's life over the fetus's.

Another, less permissive approach reads the Mishnah as Maimonides does in the *Mishneh Torah* (Text 5b): suggesting that, when the mother's life is endangered in labor, we treat the fetus *as if it were a rodef*, a "pursuer." Since halakhah rules that the *rodef* must die to save the innocent person he pursues (Texts 3a–c and 4), treating the fetus as if it were a *rodef* allows us to abort the fetus. Here, permission to "kill" the fetus is only granted when giving birth endangers the mother's life. Yet, according to Feldman, some contemporary ethicists, too, back away from the full implications of this analysis. They interpret "danger to her life" more broadly; for example, they might allow an abortion if giving birth will leave the mother's health permanently damaged.

Feldman introduces the classical Jewish principle of the sanctity of life: human life transcends other values. On that basis, while permitting therapeutic abortion both for the mother's physical and psychological health, he expresses hesitation about allowing abortion under many circumstances. The mitzvah of procreation overrides other considerations. Jews must seek to increase, not control, the Jewish population.

Feldman seeks a middle ground. He asserts that if the abortion is therapeutic for the mother, meaning it contributes to her physical or psychological health, Jewish tradition not only approves, but may even require it. At the same time, he worries that women will resort to abortion "casually," without a reason for which he finds validation in tradition. Additionally, Feldman does not want abortion to become an obstacle to fulfilling the commandment to be fruitful and multiply.

Feldman's approach offers interesting perspectives on our case studies. He would support Jenny's request for a fetal reduction in Case Study #1, because she frames it in terms of the deleterious effects bearing twins would have on her, not the children. He might permit abortion in Case Study #2, in which Amy seems likely to birth a child with Down syndrome, but it would depend on how Amy described her fears about her ability to handle raising a child with special needs. If Amy and Bruce presented a "maternal criterion"—the mother cannot bear the pressures of raising the disabled child—he might grant permission on the grounds that "the mother's welfare is primary" and overrides that of the fetus.

Feldman's response to Candice in Case Study #3 would similarly depend on how she presented her concerns to him. If she says only that now is not the right time to have a child, he would likely tell her that is not an acceptable therapeutic reason. On the other hand, if she describes ways in which she would suffer emotional distress if required to carry the pregnancy to term, Feldman likely would approve the abortion.

Other contemporary rabbis emphasize different ideas from the Oral Torah sources, allowing us to explore the contemporary debate in more depth. We turn next to the thinking of Rabbi J. David Bleich, a leading Orthodox expert in halakhic medical ethics who serves as a Rosh Yeshiva at Yeshiva University. In his book *Judaism and Healing*, published in 1981, a few years after the *Roe v. Wade* decision, he adopts a restrictive view of Judaism's approach to abortion.

Text 10—Bleich, *Judaism and Healing*

JUDAISM REGARDS THE KILLING of an unborn child to be a serious moral offense. An abortion may be performed only for the gravest of reasons, and even then, only subsequent to consultation with a competent rabbinic authority.

In some circles confusion has arisen with regard to the status of the fetus by virtue of the fact that feticide on the part of a Jew is not considered to be a capital crime. It must be stressed that the lessened severity of the statutory punishment imposed upon the malefactor in no way mitigates the odious nature of the act. . . .

Both the argument that a prospective mother may seek an abortion for any reason because denial of this right would interfere with her "right to privacy" as well as the argument that a decision to abort is entirely a matter between a woman and her physician must be rejected as incompatible with Jewish teaching. . . . Judaism teaches that man does not enjoy unrestricted . . . rights with regard to his own body, much less so with regard to an unborn child. . . .

It is instructive to note that, historically speaking, societies which condoned abortion invariably practiced infanticide as well. Prior to the advent of Judaism, the ancient societies of the West practiced abortion to a greater or lesser degree. ... Judaism, of course, opposes abortion on intrinsic grounds, and not simply because it may lead to infanticide. The erosion of sensitivity to the sanctity of human life does, however, magnify the odium associated with abortion.

The net effect of the ban against feticide, on whatever grounds it is based, is to endow the unborn fetus with a "right to life." Whether the unborn child is a "person in the full sense" or simply a "fetus" is irrelevant insofar as the fetus' title to life is concerned. It is only when respect for the fetal right to life poses a threat to the mother that a question arises.[7]

QUESTIONS FOR INQUIRY

1. In what way, according to Rabbi Bleich, have some Jews misinterpreted the Jewish tradition in regard to abortion?
2. What argument does Rabbi Bleich offer against the suggestion that a woman may do as she pleases with her own body?
3. What fears does he express about a society that allows abortions?
4. How does he address the problem of determining when a fetus acquires the status of a person? How convincing is his argument?

COMMENTS

Rabbi Bleich's ideas present an interesting contrast to Rabbi Feldman's approach. He starts from the presumption that "killing an unborn child" is "a serious moral offense." Unimpressed by the conclusions others draw from Exodus 21:22–23, Rabbi Bleich asserts that the passage does not condone abortion. All it establishes is that the legal punishment for feticide (killing a fetus) is less severe than the punishment for killing a person.

Bleich also refutes certain contemporary Jewish arguments. He denies that Jewish tradition allows a right to privacy in regard to one's body.

Rather, he asserts, the tradition describes the body as God's property, which humans use only with divine permission (so to speak). Thus a woman does not have the right to do whatever she pleases with her body. And, he argues, this restriction applies even more when a fetus (which he notably refers to as an "unborn child") is developing inside her body. The ban on feticide he finds in Judaism effectively endows the fetus with a right to life. All considerations of personhood are thereby irrelevant to this basic norm.

Furthermore, Bleich makes what amounts to a slippery slope argument. Historically, he asserts, there is a societal connection between the sanctioning of abortion and the practice of infanticide: "Societies which condoned abortion invariably practiced infanticide as well." For him, the lack of respect for developing human life implied by ready access to abortion is likely to lead to a lack of respect for infant life after birth. Condoning abortion may set our society on a slippery slope toward infanticide.

Thus, unlike Rabbi Feldman, Rabbi Bleich appears to refuse the women in our case studies permission to abort. He would endow both of Jenny's fetuses with a right to life; since neither threatens her life, she cannot end either of theirs. He would not consider the challenges of raising a child with Down syndrome sufficient reason for Amy and Bruce to terminate the pregnancy. Nor would he consider Candice's desire not to have a child at this time a valid reason in Jewish tradition.

Next we delve further into contemporary Orthodox views on abortion. In her entry on abortion in the *Encyclopedia of Jewish Women*, Tirzah Meacham (leBeit Yoreh), an Orthodox professor with feminist commitments who teaches philosophy and Rabbinics at the University of Toronto, presents trends in Orthodox halakhah about abortion since World War II. While reviewing some of the halakhic literature we studied above, Meacham identifies social factors that have influenced how Orthodox rabbis applied those sources in recent times.

Text 11 — Meacham (leBeit Yoreh), *Encyclopedia of Jewish Women*

AT NO POINT IN the Responsa literature up to the twentieth century is abortion considered murder. There are definitely positions which allow abortion even when the mother's life is not at stake and lenient positions outnumber the more stringent positions....

In the twentieth century ... the militant pro-life position of the Catholic Church and various fundamentalist Christian groups became the model for modern rabbinic positions on abortion. Pro-choice was considered ... morally reprehensible on the basis of "whatever is forbidden to Gentiles should certainly be forbidden to Jews." ... That the mother's life took precedence over the fetus's life was the major distinguishing factor between most Orthodox positions published in English and the pro-life positions. Rabbis responded to changes in sexual norms with repugnance and sought to prevent licentiousness by forbidding abortion.... To remain consistent, rabbis and Orthodox writers would sometimes espouse positions which had no basis in traditional Jewish sources and use language such as "appurtenance to murder" (Unterman), "crime" (Jacobovits) and "moral murder" (Rosner). Even rabbis and authors who wrote more comprehensively on abortion would de-emphasize, dismiss or denigrate lenient positions....

Ohalot 7:6 [see Text 2] has led all *poskim* [halakhic decision-makers] to agree that if the birth (and, they extrapolate ... the pregnancy itself) endangers a woman's life, abortion is acceptable even at the moment of birth. The disagreements among the *poskim* reflect the level of damage to the woman ... they considered acceptable in order not to abort or cause the death of the fetus at birth....

One area of leniency ... involves IVF ... Another area is multi-fetal pregnancy reduction ... seen as a life-saving technique for the remaining fetuses.... Doctors are allowed to decide which fetuses to save....

Women's voices still remain absent in the halakhic discussion on abortion. Those rabbis who preach the most stringent positions do not carry the pregnancies with all the physical stress and danger, bear unwanted or defective children, or bear the major burden of caring for them. Their stringencies, couched in moralistic terms, are played out on women's bodies.[8]

1. What changes beginning in the twentieth century affected the way Orthodox rabbis think about the ethics of abortion?
2. What does the author's view about a halakhic approach to the problem of fetal reduction contribute to thinking about Jenny in Case Study #1?
3. What voice does Meacham seek to add that is otherwise missing from the abortion debate?

COMMENTS

Writing not as a rabbi responding to halakhic questions but as a scholar surveying the Orthodox response to abortion, Meacham points out that as abortion became both legal and socially acceptable in North America, Orthodox rabbis joined other conservative religious groups in opposing it. While Rabbinic and medieval texts never label abortion as murder (as our text studies show), many Orthodox authorities adopted such rhetoric after the legalization of abortion in many Western countries. Meacham implies that Jewish tradition was lenient about permitting abortions until recent times, when Orthodox leaders became concerned about sexual morality in general. She argues that their strident opposition to abortion except in case of dire threats to the mother's survival derives from their desire to regulate sexual behavior.

Related to this is Meacham's trenchant point that Orthodox halakhists, by definition all men, impose their stringent views on the bodies of women. The voices of those who experience pregnancy and undergo its risks are absent from these discussions.

Even without these voices, Meacham points out that the tradition puts the mother's welfare ahead of the fetus's (she cites the Mishnah that is our Text 2; see also Texts 5a–b and 7), and she proposes that halakhah allows fetal reduction as a life-saving measure. That assertion does not resolve all issues in Jenny's desire (in Case Study #1) to reduce her twin pregnancy. As Meacham writes, Jewish ethicists differ over what constitutes a serious enough threat to the mother's welfare to justify an abortion. Those who would want to allow Jenny to go forward must still determine that her concerns about her age and economic situation are significant enough to sanction aborting one of her fetuses.

Our next two passages illustrate the divide Meacham mentions between Orthodox rabbis who define danger to the mother broadly and those who define it narrowly. First is a responsum from Rabbi Eliezer Tzvi Waldenberg, the twentieth-century medical ethicist whose approach we encountered in the last chapter.

Text 12 — Waldenberg, *Responsa Tzitz Eliezer*

ONE SHOULD PERMIT . . . ABORTION as soon as it becomes evident without doubt from the test that, indeed, such a baby [with Tay-Sachs disease] shall be born, even until the seventh month of her pregnancy. . . . If, indeed, we may permit an abortion according to the halakhah because of "great need" and because of pain and suffering, it seems that this is the classic case for such permission. And it is irrelevant in what way the pain and suffering is expressed, whether it is physical or psychological. Indeed, psychological suffering is in many ways much greater than the suffering of the flesh.⁹

QUESTIONS FOR INQUIRY

1. How does this responsum by an Orthodox rabbi fit into the description of Orthodox approaches Meacham gives in Text 11?
2. What approach does Waldenberg take to the issue of the mother's pain and suffering?
3. How would you apply this responsum to the case studies?

COMMENTS

Rabbi Waldenberg permits abortion of a fetus with Tay-Sachs disease, even up to the seventh month of pregnancy. In striking contrast to the North American Orthodox authorities referenced by Tirzah Meacham, he expresses leniency to alleviate the mother's pain and suffering. Notice that he uses the same standard identified by the Conservative rabbi David

Feldman: the so-called maternal criterion. Furthermore, Waldenberg extends permission for abortion from physical suffering to psychological suffering, noting that psychological suffering may be harder to bear than bodily suffering. He does not label abortion as murder.

His reasoning in this excerpt suggests that Waldenberg might permit an abortion in Amy's situation (Case Study #2). That permission would depend on what exactly Waldenberg means by "great need." While a child with Down syndrome is disabled, the disability is not comparable to the physical suffering and shortened life span of a child with Tay-Sachs disease. Leniently inclined ethicists, including some Orthodox rabbis (as Meacham notes), might extend the principle of "great need" to alleviate the future suffering of a child with Down syndrome, or to the future suffering such a child's parents might experience in raising this child.

By contrast, our next text, by Rabbi Moshe Feinstein (1895–1986), a leading American *haredi* halakhic authority, takes the opposite approach. Text 13 is from one of many volumes of Feinstein's responsa appearing under the title *Iggrot Moshe*, literally, "Moshe's letters," reflecting their origins in his correspondence with questioners and other rabbis.

Text 13 — Feinstein, *Responsa Iggrot Moshe*

IT IS CLEAR . . . THAT there is . . . no difference between new-borns. Even in the case of those newborns who in the view of the doctors, are of the type who will not live for many years, like those children who are born with a disease called Tay-Sachs — even if it is known by means of fetal testing . . . that the newborn will be in this category — [abortion is] prohibited. Since there is no danger to the mother, and the fetus is not a *rodef*, one may not permit [an abortion] even though the pain will be very great and the mother and father will suffer from this.[10]

QUESTIONS FOR INQUIRY

1. What does Feinstein mean by "there is . . . no difference between newborns"?

2. What approach does he take to maternal pain and suffering?

COMMENTS

Rabbi Feinstein, who represents the stringent approach to abortion, allows only danger to the mother's life (only if the fetus acts as a *rodef* against the mother's life) to justify abortion. He denies abortion to spare the parents or the child from suffering through the short, difficult life of Tay-Sachs disease. In Feinstein's view, all newborns are the same: created in God's image, with a right to life.

Furthermore, rabbis such as Feinstein do not recognize what in American politics is sometimes called the "rape exception," the idea that abortion is generally immoral but may be permitted if the pregnancy resulted from rape. They do not fully adopt the idea of a maternal criterion that gives weight to the mother's pain and suffering, because they accord the fetus a higher status. As the feminist scholar Ronit Irshai writes about the Orthodox responsa literature on abortion: "The picture that emerges is that the strict position allows no room for leniency when the fetus is a *mamzer* [the product of incest or adultery] or in cases of extramarital relations or even of rape, for the law is grounded in the status of the fetus and not at all in factors related to the woman."[11]

We turn now to a discussion of abortion based on the Reform movement's very different philosophy of halakhah. In 1985, Rabbi Walter Jacob, who led the movement's Responsa Committee for many years, wrote a responsum addressing a question arising from the rule in *Roe v. Wade* that the law of abortion varies according to how far the pregnancy has progressed.

Text 14—Jacob, "When Is Abortion Permitted?"

QUESTION: ASSUMING THAT ABORTION is *halakhically* permitted, is there a time span in which abortion may take place according to tradition? (Rabbi A. Klausner, Yonkers, New York)

Answer: The fetus is not considered to be a person (*nefesh*) until it is born. Up to that time it is considered a part of the mother's body, although it does possess certain characteristics of a person and some status. During the first forty days after conception, it is considered "mere fluid." . . .

We feel that the pattern of tradition, until the most recent generation, has demonstrated a liberal approach to abortion and has definitely permitted it in case of any danger to the life of the mother. That danger may be physical or psychological. When this occurs at any time during the pregnancy, we would not hesitate to permit an abortion. This would also include cases of incest and rape if the mother wishes to have an abortion. . . .

Traditional authorities would be most lenient with abortions within the first forty days. After that time, there is a difference of opinion. Those who are within the broadest range of permissibility permit abortion at any time before birth, if there is a serious danger to the health of the mother or the child. We would be in agreement with that liberal stance. We do not encourage abortion, nor favor it for trivial reasons, or sanction it "on demand."[12]

QUESTIONS FOR INQUIRY

1. Under what circumstances does Rabbi Jacob sanction abortion?
2. Under what circumstances does he disapprove of abortion?
3. From our text study to date do you agree with his assertion that prior to the current generation, "danger to the mother's life" always included physical or psychological harm? Consider Texts 2 and 5a–b.
4. What additional factor does Rabbi Jacob consider that other writers in this chapter do not mention?

COMMENTS

Rabbi Jacob builds his argument on the claim that prior to the current generation, the "danger to the mother's life" that halakhically permits abortion always included physical or psychological harm; it never solely meant that the mother would otherwise die.

This claim is hard to support from the early textual tradition we have studied. The Mishnah in *Ohalot* (Text 2) calls for an abortion when the mother will otherwise die; it does not refer directly to psychological danger, or even to a physical danger other than a fatal one. The *Mishneh Torah* (Text 5b) explicitly limits abortion to situations that endanger a woman's life. Only an expansive reading of Rashi on *Sanhedrin* 72b (Text 5a) might support Rabbi Jacob's assertion. We must consider the possibility that an aspiration to expand the realm of permissible abortions leads Rabbi Jacob to interpret the tradition more broadly than strictly warranted. After all, as he writes in the responsum excerpted above, "The Reform Movement has had a long history of liberalism on many social and family matters," as we also saw in the 1975 CCAR resolution (Text 8a).

Still, Rabbi Jacob does not allow all abortions. He explicitly rejects "abortion on demand," that is, abortion available at the woman's request, no reason necessary. He establishes limits at later stages of pregnancy. He does not "favor [abortion] for trivial reasons" (though he does not define "trivial" in this context).

Rare among Jewish ethicists ruling on abortion, Jacob explicitly considers stages of fetal development. A talmudic passage that refers to a fetus during the first forty days of pregnancy as "mere fluid" leads him to take the most lenient approach until forty days have passed. After that, while acknowledging differences of opinion among Jewish thinkers, Jacob sides with those who allow abortion at any time during the rest of the pregnancy, in case of a "serious threat" to the health of either mother or child.

How Jacob would respond to our case studies is uncertain. He might agree that Jenny identifies enough of a threat to her welfare, and the welfare of her young family, to permit the fetal reduction. In Amy's case, he would likely want to know more about the stage of her pregnancy and how she and Bruce expect having a disabled child will affect their lives. How he would view Candice's rationale is unclear.

Comparing Rabbi Jacob's Reform responsum to the Reform rabbinate's earlier resolution on abortion (Text 8a) allows us a deeper look into the movement's thinking on the subject. The CCAR resolution vividly demonstrates the point made by Meacham (Text 11) that in the twentieth century, ideas and language from American and European political debates entered Jewish discussions. While encouraging women and their families to pay attention to "Jewish legal literature," the resolution stresses that abortion is a "personal decision." It supports the pro-choice position that women (and not "the state") must be able to make that choice. In short, the Reform rabbis' resolution allows pregnant women substantially more leeway to consider their personal situations than does their responsum featuring Jacob's halakhic analysis. A woman might consult the responsum, but then assert her right to make a personal decision to override its conclusions.

Next we turn to how the State of Israel treats abortion, as explained in a Library of Congress report summarizing Israeli abortion law.

Text 15 — "Israel: Reproduction and Abortion: Law and Policy"

THE [ISRAELI] LAWS GOVERNING abortion generally prohibit what the law codes refer to as the "interruption of pregnancy." However, they provide a number of exceptions. A physician may perform an abortion to save the woman's life or to "prevent her from incurring a serious uncorrectable harm." A doctor may also "interrupt" pregnancy if the abortion happened in the course of providing a necessary medical intervention, when the doctor did not previously know about the pregnancy.

Israel's Public Health Ordinance allows each hospital to appoint a Committee for the Interruption of Pregnancy. The committee must include at least one woman, as well as a specialist in obstetrics and gynecology; another medical practitioner; and a social worker. The committee may approve an abortion if: the woman is under seventeen or over forty years old; the pregnancy derives from a relationship prohibited by law, is incestuous, or out of wedlock; the fetus may have a physical or mental disability; or continuation of the pregnancy may endanger the woman's life or cause her physical or mental harm. If the committee approves, the woman must also give her informed consent to the abortion. That means that the pregnant woman must agree to the abortion after being informed of how the procedure will take place and of its physical and psychological risks.[13]

1. Which aspects of Israeli abortion law derive from halakhah?
2. Which derive from other sources?
3. How do the stipulations in Israeli law compare to halakhah (consider Texts 5a, 7, 9, and 14)? to American law?

COMMENTS

Israeli abortion laws allow us to see the interaction of halakhic traditions with modern ideas in both law and medicine. Significantly, when deciding to approve or disapprove an abortion, the law does not direct the hospital committee to consider the stage of a woman's pregnancy or fetal development. Only if the fetus is likely to have a physical or mental disability does the committee evaluate the fetus.

In keeping with what we have seen in the halakhic literature, the hospital committee primarily considers the mother. If the pregnancy threatens her life, or will cause her physical or mental harm, abortion may be approved. Essentially the Knesset agrees with those who extend the idea of harm to the mother to include damage to her psychological state.

The hospital committees established under the Public Health Ordinance also weigh factors not derived from the halakhic tradition but from modern Western society: the age of the pregnant woman and the nature of the relationship in which she conceived her pregnancy. Daniel Schiff, a student of the history of abortion in Judaism, elucidates that except for the provision about women under seventeen and over forty years of age, "Israel's abortion amendment . . . provides an approximate legislative reflection of the halakhic grounds sufficient to allow for an abortion to be permitted, viewed from a lenient perspective."[14]

Meanwhile, the established Orthodox rabbinate and many Orthodox and *haredi* Israelis object to these laws. In their stringent view of the halakhah derived from the *Mishneh Torah* (Text 5b), abortion may take place only in face of a direct threat to the mother's survival. However, as of this writing the Orthodox and *haredi* parties have not succeeded in lobbying the Knesset to change the law to accord with their views. Israeli law remains a fusion of ideas from halakhah and other legal traditions.

Israeli feminists had brought their views to the Knesset's attention in ways that influenced the final law. Feminists would have preferred a bill that gave the state no say in a woman's decision about abortion, on the grounds that she should have complete autonomy over her body. Recognizing, however, that such a law would arouse fierce opposition from the Orthodox parties in the Knesset, potentially leading to the loss of abortion rights, advocates agreed to the establishment of the Committees for the Interruption of Pregnancy, which take into account both physical and emotional considerations that may justify a woman's wish to end a pregnancy.[15] Still, women's voices have largely been absent from the Jewish debate over abortion, even though, as Meacham points out (Text 11), women undergo the hazards of pregnancy and, at times, abortions.

More recently, in North America women have begun to demand a hearing in Jewish discussions of abortion morality. In our final text, from the article "Sometimes the Law Is Cruel" published in the *Journal of Feminist Studies in Religion* in 1995, the Reconstructionist rabbi and scholar Rebecca Alpert insists that women be treated as "moral agents" in the conversation.

Text 16 — Alpert, "Sometimes the Law Is Cruel"

A JEWISH CONVERSATION ABOUT abortion . . . must treat women as moral agents. It must not speak a glib language about the use of abortion as a sexual deterrent nor avoid a more complex discussion of sexuality. It must not fail to examine the complexities of the need for abortion in a society with many unwanted children . . . and with little concern for how those children . . . are cared for. And it must not ignore the fact that children are still cared for predominantly by women, often for low wages or at the cost of their own individual and collective development and growth.[16]

QUESTIONS FOR INQUIRY

1. What does Rabbi Alpert say is missing from the Jewish conversation about abortion?
2. What social concerns does she raise that male authors ignore?

In urging contemporary Jews to discuss abortion in ways that acknowledge women as moral agents, Rabbi Alpert charges that Jewish ethical claims about abortion have long been made in a vacuum, without taking into account that women think and make moral choices just as men do. Women, in effect, may look at the moral ramifications surrounding abortion more broadly than the male rabbis issuing the rulings. She adds to the moral agenda the question of whether or not the prospective parent wants the child. Many children in our society suffer from inadequate care because in one way or another they were unwanted. Men—who even today rarely shoulder the major share of caretaking responsibilities—must consider the significant emotional, financial, and spiritual toll on the lives of women raising unwanted children: the cost to their individual and collective development and growth. It might be said that the rabbinic scholars we have encountered, all men, treat pregnancy and abortion as abstractions. They show more interest in the moral status of the fetus than in the moral and lived experience of the woman carrying the fetus in her body.

Treating women as moral agents requires granting them more autonomy than traditional halakhah does. Even the stances we studied that consider the woman's welfare the primary consideration in evaluating a given request for abortion require that she consult a (usually male) rabbi. A feminist Judaism that treats women equally to men would instead ask rabbis to discuss with women their concerns and experiences in light of their particular pregnancies.

Alpert also objects to those traditionally minded rabbis who claim that knowing that abortion will not be available will deter women from engaging in sex outside of marriage. She calls for a more nuanced discussion of sexuality, presumably one that recognizes the fact that most adults today do not consider consensual sex between unmarried partners immoral (see chapter 4, "Sex and Intimacy").

Given the paucity of women serving as *poskim*, even in the liberal branches of Judaism, Alpert's voice stands as a call for contemporary Jews to see that women exercise autonomy equal to men when making decisions about their own bodies. Men who respond to this area of halakhah are to listen to the voices of those who actually experience pregnancy and face decisions about abortion. Further, Alpert usefully calls for a conversation among people of all genders to ensure that all children grow up in settings where they are wanted, loved, and cared for.

Conclusion

There is no such thing as "the Jewish view" on abortion: Jews remain divided on the issue. Some Jews consider abortion morally deplorable, while others believe abortion can be the best moral choice depending on the individual circumstance.

That said, as Rabbi Danya Ruttenberg wrote in 2018, "The latest Pew data [from 2018] estimated that a whopping 83% of Jews believe that in all or most cases, abortion should be legal, putting us at the fourth most pro-choice group surveyed (behind only atheists, agnostics, and Unitarians)." In her view, the reasons for the strong Jewish pro-choice standpoint include but go beyond the fact that Jewish law allows for abortion in select circumstances:

> This body of literature . . . comes in stark and striking contrast to arguments that life—and personhood—begins at conception. . . .
>
> Another reason . . . I suspect . . . is connected to the fact that we [Jews] have historically been among the strongest supporters of the separation of church and state, and have long been wary of legal maneuvers that appear to be coming from a place of Christian religious conviction. . . . Even among Jews who may be personally against abortion for themselves or think that it's morally wrong, there may be a reticence to impose their individual thinking on other people, and certainly the country as a whole. Cynthia Ozick put it once thusly: "What our faith communities would be wise to choose is religious responsibility undertaken autonomously, independently, and on cherished private ground, turning their backs on anyone, however estimable or prudential, who proposes that the church steeple ought to begin to lean on the town hall roof."
>
> I also wonder if our long-standing tradition of embracing *machloket*, divergent opinions, makes a Jew who feels personally against abortion more able to see the possibility that someone else

might legitimately understand the world in a different way, and to value that perspective.[17]

Our first case study presented a new variation on the old abortion dilemmas. Reducing a fetus in a multiple pregnancy, as Jenny wishes to do, essentially amounts to abortion by another name. Interestingly, Professor Meacham (Text 11) points out that the usually strict Orthodox rabbinic authorities allow "multi-fetal pregnancy reduction," viewing it "as a life-saving technique for the remaining fetuses even though each fetus is equally a *rodef* of the others." While ostensibly that might imply that even some of the most restrictive contemporary rabbis would give Jenny permission to go ahead, nothing in Jenny's situation implies that either fetus threatens the other—neither is even a metaphorical *rodef* of its twin (see Texts 3c and 5b). Since Jenny can safely carry both fetuses to term, the abortion she seeks cannot be justified on the grounds of saving either the fetus's life or her own.

This fact returns us to the basic disagreement about abortion in Jewish ethics: What kind of harm to the mother, and what degree of harm, justify ending fetal development? We must examine the reasons Jenny gives for seeking a reduction.

She cites her age—forty-five years is an advanced age for new motherhood. Israeli law identifies maternal age over forty as a legitimate basis for an abortion (Text 15). Jenny also expresses economic concerns. She and her husband doubt their ability to provide as they would like to for an "extra" child beyond the ones they planned on having. Some of our texts rule out financial considerations as an appropriate factor in deciding to end a pregnancy. (Texts 9 and 14) In this case they would claim that the second fetus's potential life matters more than economic concerns (Text 10); but at least one Jewish ethicist, Rabbi Rebecca Alpert, would support this couple's wish to decide how to raise their children (Text 16).

I sought insight into this and our other case studies from Rabbi Analia Bortz, the first woman ordained in Latin America by the Seminario Rabbinico Latinoamericano, who also holds a medical degree from Universidad Buenos Aires, did postdoctoral studies in bioethics, and founded Hope for Seeds to help couples struggling with infertility. Rabbi Bortz's perspective on Jenny's situation is different from Rabbi Alpert's. She finds Jenny's reasons insufficient to overcome Jewish tradition's preference for life as the highest value. She points out that Jenny had desired this pregnancy without strings attached:

> Jenny had decided to become pregnant at 45 years old without mentioning any deep anguish, nor physical health restriction regarding her body or the fetus health conditions. The fetus does not enter the Maimonidean category of *rodef*. . . .
> I consider this . . . a baseless reason for fetal reduction. During my personal experience as a bioethicist, a Rabbi-counselor and a founder of a group for couples struggling with infertility, this kind of decision, based on convenience, takes an emotional toll and leaves behind an open wound, that is not pre-sighted by the couple . . . at the moment of the decision but emerges later in life.[18]

The sources we have studied leave equal room for debate over the chapter's other case studies. Amy and Bruce's case illustrates how prenatal testing will raise new ethical issues as it improves. Some would argue that Amy may abort if her concern is for her own emotional welfare and not the welfare of her child (Text 9). Some would allow the abortion simply because the child will be disabled (Texts 12 and 14). Others would deny permission entirely, because all potential human life equally reflects the divine image (Texts 10 and 13). Concurring with this, Rabbi Bortz notes that individuals with Down syndrome now have the ability to live full lives, adding: "We should . . . invest in creating frameworks of inclusivity in our society to embrace people with special needs and different abilities," rather than aborting such fetuses.[19]

As for Case Study #3, only those who advocate unlimited personal choice would accept without question the right to abort in Candice and Ari's common situation of unplanned pregnancy. Even though Jewish tradition may not consider the conceptus a *nefesh* (Texts 1b, 2, 5a), many ethicists hesitate to grant women an unconditional right to abort. This includes Analia Bortz, who holds that nothing in Jewish ethics considers "a convenient time for a woman with certain aspirations" as a legitimate reason to permit abortion.[20] Like other thinkers we studied, like J. David Bleich (Text 10), she denies that we have complete rights over our own bodies.

Exceptionally in our review, Rebecca Alpert (Text 16) would suggest that Candice's personal autonomy entitles her to make this decision, especially since her husband agrees and Alpert believes that children should be born only in situations where their parents definitely want them. In her view, Candice and Ari may proceed to terminate this unexpected pregnancy.

Abortion ethics of the future will also have to take into account new developments. Women now have the ability to terminate pregnancy via a regimen of pills taken in the privacy of their home. What are the implications of this new form of abortion intended to help women who live far from an abortion provider or who want to terminate a pregnancy without the potential complications of a surgical procedure?

Another advance in medical technology presenting new questions is the ability to save premature infants. In earlier times, those born before full term usually had severe medical problems and little chance of survival. Today, neonatal intensive care has advanced to the point that even some fetuses at twenty-four weeks' gestation—just a few weeks past the midpoint of pregnancy—can survive to adulthood. For those who argue that abortion may be ethically acceptable because those in the womb are not "living" in the same sense as those already born, these new technologies that enable a fetus at twenty-four weeks (or earlier, as medicine advances) to survive outside the womb affect the question of when a fetus becomes a person with a right to life.

How does the centuries-long Jewish discussion of the morality of abortion contribute to the whole issue? Rabbi Daniel Gordis puts it well:

We ought not confuse Judaism's compromise or ambivalence with apathy. A tradition that both commands abortion in certain cases but that forbids it in many others is not a tradition predicated on a lack of interest; it is a tradition committed to recognizing complexity. Judaism insists that the value of religion ought not be in providing pithy theological positions that make intricate questions facile. Its real value is in sensitizing human beings and society to the profound intricacies raised by issues such as abortion.[21]

Studying this issue through a Jewish lens requires thinking about complexity. Good decisions about abortion will never depend on a single factor. Respect for life and respect for choice matter; but, as Judaism shows, they do not tell us all we need to know to reach morally defensible conclusions.

7

Medical Ethics at the End of Life

A medical treatment may promise a human being more time in this world, but sometimes that time comes at the cost of pain, or awareness. Are the benefits worth the cost? Who has the right to decide when the person cannot?

Halakhic tradition teaches a number of basic values about human life and healing the sick. Applying them in the unprecedented context of modern medicine will challenge some assumptions about Jewish ethics we have made throughout our study.

Case Study #1: Defining Death

A true story: Jahi McMath, thirteen, of Oakland, California, had an operation to remove her tonsils. Afterwards, she developed severe bleeding. Three days later, while a ventilator kept Jahi breathing, doctors determined there was no electrical activity in her brain. California law, like that of almost every U.S. state, defines the absence of brain activity as death. The hospital declared Jahi dead and encouraged her family to remove the life-support machinery as soon as possible.

Jahi's family could not accept that she was dead as long as she breathed. They fought the hospital in court, winning the right to move their daughter elsewhere despite expert testimony that keeping her on a breathing machine amounted to desecration of a corpse. A hospital in New Jersey agreed to continue ventilating Jahi, though she still showed every sign of brain death. In the new hospital, therapists played music in her room; her family spent long hours caring for her and talking to her. Within months, Jahi began to respond to simple commands, such as moving a finger when asked. Seven months later, she had her first menstrual period. A new doctor performed further scans and found that parts of Jahi's brain were intact and functioned more than would be expected, given her medical history. The family felt vindicated for their insistence that their child remained alive. Jahi lived five more years, until liver failure caused fatal bleeding.[1]

What does Judaism say about how we ought to define death in cases like Jahi's?

Case Study #2: Extending Life at What Cost?

Robert, eighty, has advanced dementia. He needs others to assist him with basic tasks of daily living like eating and toileting. He no longer speaks or recognizes his children. The children feel that while Robert's body remains in bed, what made him their father is no longer present. A few days ago, Robert had a serious heart attack and doctors placed him on a ventilator to help him breathe. Now that he is a bit stronger, the doctors recommend heart bypass surgery. Without the operation, Robert's heart will never recover enough strength to keep him alive and he will quickly die.

Robert's children must make decisions for him, since he is not competent to decide for himself. They doubt the value of a long, risky surgery to restore their father to a state in which he still will not recognize them or enjoy any of life's pleasures. They also know that Judaism places human life above all other values. Is it ethically appropriate for them to refuse the surgery and allow their father to die?

Case Study #3: Physician-Assisted Dying

About three months ago, Eleanor, sixty-five, received a diagnosis of stage 4 liver cancer. Doctors informed her that no treatment exists to cure her cancer and she could expect to live for no more than six to nine months.

After careful thought and discussion with loved ones, Eleanor decides she wants to end her life on her own terms, before suffering the debilitating pain and loss of independence the final stages of her illness typically bring. As a California resident, Eleanor has the right to invoke the state's End of Life Option Act, which went into effect in 2016. She meets the law's criteria: she is over age eighteen, exhibits appropriate decision-making ability, and can take medicine by herself. Under state law, Eleanor can request a prescription for drugs she can take when she decides the time has come to end her life. Her family agrees in principle with her decision. They also agree that before going forward, Eleanor will ask the family's rabbi for guidance. Does Jewish tradition support her decision to end her life to minimize her suffering?

These cases raise just a few of many complex issues surrounding death and dying.

Case Study #1 addresses the reality that we cannot always say with certainty who is alive and who is dead. Until late in the twentieth century, death meant the end of respiration (breathing). After 1968, medical science adopted a new criterion: the cessation of measurable electrical activity in the brain, which gave rise to the misleading phrase "brain death." Yet the description of "no brain activity" proves more complicated than it sounds, giving rise to cases like Jahi McMath's.

Case Study #2 looks at the ethics of euthanasia. If Robert's children decide not to allow doctors to operate on him, they will in effect choose passive euthanasia, withholding treatment to allow his natural dying process to unfold.

Case Study #3 raises issues of physician-assisted dying enabled by state law. Assisted dying occurs when a mentally aware and competent patient in the last phase of a painful terminal illness requests doses of medicines that will result in death. The patient decides when to die and takes the drugs independently. The physician assists only by diagnosing the condition and writing the necessary prescriptions. Assisted dying became an option in recent years in parts of the United States; it is also practiced in Canada and more extensively in the Netherlands.

Is it ever appropriate to end one's own life, which Judaism defines as a gift from God? May a physician ethically participate in such a choice? How should possible unintended consequences — family members subtly pressuring terminally ill relatives to end their lives to save the costs of medical treatment and pain relief, the imaginable devaluing of life by a society that allows assisted dying — factor into ethical decision-making?

Adding to these challenges is the difficulty of using centuries-old texts in discussions of brand-new technologies and possibilities. How can we best use traditional Jewish teachings whose analogies to our own times are less than clear-cut? We begin our inquiry with two texts, from Psalms and Maimonides' *Mishneh Torah*, often cited as setting forth basic principles underlying Jewish medical ethics.

Text Study #1: Basic Principles of Jewish Medical Ethics

Text 1a — Ps. 24:1

THE EARTH IS THE Lord's and all that it holds, the world and its inhabitants.

Text 1b — *Mishneh Torah*,
Laws of Proper Conduct 3:3 and 4:1

PEOPLE MUST TAKE CARE that their bodies be well and strong so that their souls will be tranquil to seek knowledge of God. For it is not possible to understand and appreciate and to grow in wisdom when one is hungry or sick, or one of one's limbs hurts.

It follows that having a healthy, strong body is one of God's ways. For it is not possible to understand or to know anything of the Creator when one is ill. Therefore, one should distance oneself from anything that damages the body.

QUESTIONS FOR INQUIRY

1. What implications does the verse from Psalms have? What does it imply specifically about our lives and bodies?
2. Why does Rambam frame our physical welfare as a spiritual matter?
3. What ideals are articulated in these texts?
4. How might these ideals help us to think about medical dilemmas near the end of life?

COMMENTS

Psalm 24:1 provides the biblical basis for a Rabbinic idea central to our discussion: everything in the world ultimately belongs to God, its Creator. This generalization includes the human body. We do not own our bodies. Just as we must return any property another person allows us to use in good shape, we are to keep our bodies in the best possible condition for as long as God allows us to inhabit them.

In Text 1b, Rambam codifies this advice. We must seek the necessary care to maintain our health and avoid doing anything that harms it. Further, the Mishneh Torah explains the need to stay healthy not simply as a way of caring for God's property but as part of a higher duty. The purpose of human life is "to understand and appreciate and to grow in wisdom," wisdom understood as the cultivation of a deeper knowledge of the Creator. We are to do all we can to stay healthy—not, as we might imagine, to enjoy life more, but to serve God better. Since illness keeps a person from both intellectual and spiritual pursuits, in the interest of these higher callings, so that we may come to know the Divine in our lives, we must take responsibility for caring for our bodies.

As we will see, the basic principle that our lives and bodies ultimately belong not to us but to God will influence Jewish perspectives on the ethical issues raised by this chapter's case studies. The next principle, articulated in a talmudic discussion about how far we should go to save a life, follows naturally from the idea that our lives are God's gift to us.

Text 2a—*Mishnah Yoma* 8:6–7

RABBI MATYA BEN CHERESH further says: One who has a severe sore throat, it is permitted to pour medicine into his mouth on Shabbat because it represents possible danger to his life; and any possible danger to life sets aside Shabbat.

If debris falls and it is not certain whether a person is buried under it or not; or if it is not certain whether the person is alive or dead, or whether the person is a Jew or a Gentile, we remove the debris from him on Shabbat.

If he is found alive, we remove all the debris from him; but if he is dead, we leave him.

Text 2b — *Yoma 85b*

RABBI SHIMON BEN MENASYA says: "The Israelite people shall keep the Sabbath" [Exod. 31:16]. The Torah means: Desecrate one Shabbat for him so that he can observe many Shabbatot.

Rav Yehudah said that Shmuel said: If I had been there, I would have offered a better proof: "You shall keep My laws and My rules, by the pursuit of which human beings shall live" [Lev. 18:5]. Meaning: shall live and not shall die.

Text 2c — *Yoma 85a*

"IF HE IS FOUND alive, we remove all the debris from him."

But that is obvious! [We don't need a Mishnah to explain that!]

We need the Mishnah to explain that we remove all the debris even if the person will have only a moment of life.

QUESTIONS FOR INQUIRY

1. What principle do the laws in the Mishnah teach?
2. What idea do Rabbi Shimon ben Menasya and Rav Yehudah in the name of Shmuel both try to prove?
3. What do the values in these texts contribute to thinking about the case studies?

COMMENTS

Traditional Shabbat observance requires refraining from many activities. The Talmud identifies thirty-nine basic categories of forbidden labor, each of which has multiple derivatives. Several of the primary categories involve preparing food. In ancient times, ingredients for each dose of medicine had to be ground by hand. Since grinding is prohibited labor on Shabbat, the law generally forbids medicine on Shabbat.

Thus R. Matya b. Cheresh teaches that saving someone whose life is endangered overrides the laws of Shabbat. What is more, we are to violate a Shabbat prohibition to save a life even if death without such intervention is not certain.

Mishnah Yoma 8:7 builds on this idea. When a building collapses, or debris otherwise falls in a way that may hide a person underneath it, we are to violate Shabbat to possibly save a life. Notice that we are to go no further than the mission of life-saving requires. If the digging reveals that the person is already dead, the permission to desecrate Shabbat ends. We may not remove the body for burial until after Shabbat.

These *mishnayyot* are the primary source for the halakhah of *piku'aḥ nefesh*, saving a life. While translated as "saving" a life, the verb in the phrase literally refers to the act of digging through or removing debris, as used in *Mishnah Yoma* 8:7. *Piku'aḥ nefesh* supersedes all other mitzvot. (The Talmud identifies three exceptions to that rule, but they do not matter for our purposes.) God's commandments give way to save human life.

In the Gemara (Text 2b), sages debate why this should be so. Rabbi Shimon ben Menasya offers a sort of cost-benefit analysis. We desecrate Shabbat once—by compounding medicine or digging through rubble—to enable the endangered individual to observe many future Shabbatot. Rav Yehudah quotes his teacher Shmuel as offering a more general answer: Leviticus exhorts us to observe God's laws and rules by which "human beings shall live." Emphasizing the final word, Shmuel makes the point that God gave us commandments to live by, not to die by. We need not insist on rigid adherence to a mitzvah at the cost of a human life.

Piku'aḥ nefesh demonstrates the high regard Judaism holds for each human life. Every Jew is mandated to violate Shabbat (or other mitzvot) to save another human being.

Text 2c underscores that the tradition values life regardless of how long it lasts. The Mishnah stresses that we must set aside Shabbat to free a living person even if that person will die shortly thereafter. Length of life does not matter; life itself is the highest value. Later halakhic tradition uses the

Hebrew phrase in this passage, *ḥayyei sha'ah*, a moment's life, as a guiding principle: Any moment of life is a precious gift from God. We do not distinguish between long life and short life, or between a moment of joy and a moment of suffering. All of these are life, and life, as we saw, belongs to God.

Some Jewish ethicists use the principle of *ḥayyei sha'ah* as the basis for judging hard cases. Such thinkers would agree with Jahi McMath's family that Jahi should receive everything that extends her life even briefly. Similarly, they would urge operating on Robert in Case Study #2, reasoning that neither the medical team nor the family may decide that Robert's life should end before God makes that choice. They would tell Eleanor in Case Study #3 not to relinquish any time that she might continue living, regardless of pain or loss of consciousness.

Before looking at factors that might complicate these analyses, we will establish one more relevant principle from Jewish tradition. Speaking not to patients but to healers, the Talmud quotes a teaching from the school of the *tanna* Rabbi Ishmael that derives this rule from a verse in Exodus through *midrash halakhah*, the ancient technique for deriving laws from the Torah's words. The *Mishneh Torah* later develops the other side of this rule, directed to patients.

Text 3a — Exod. 21:18–19

WHEN INDIVIDUALS QUARREL AND one strikes the other with stone or fist, and the victim does not die but has to take to bed — if that victim then gets up and walks about outdoors upon a staff, the assailant shall go unpunished — except for paying for the idleness and the cure.

Text 3b — *Bava Kamma 85a*

IT WAS TAUGHT IN the school of Rabbi Ishmael: "and the cure" [*ve-rappo yerappe*, literally: "heal, he will heal"] — from here we learn that the physician has permission to heal.

IT IS A POSITIVE commandment to remove and protect oneself from any potential hazard that might threaten life. One must be extremely careful about such matters, as it is said (Deut. 4:9), "Take utmost care and watch yourselves scrupulously."

QUESTIONS FOR INQUIRY

1. What law does the verse in Exodus teach?
2. What additional rule does the school of Rabbi Ishmael derive from Exodus 21:19?
3. Why would anyone doubt that the Torah allows physicians to heal the sick or injured?
4. What does the *Mishneh Torah* here add to our understanding of the ethics of medical care?

COMMENTS

Exodus 21 contains a number of laws governing damage and injury. Here we learn that an assailant who strikes another person who does not die, but suffers an injury severe enough to become bedridden, does not suffer a legal penalty, but he must compensate the victim for the future remuneration the victim would have received by working (since he no longer can work) and the costs of his cure.

In the Talmud, the school of R. Ishmael finds further meaning in these verses. In Hebrew, the phrase translated as "pay . . . for his cure" repeats the same verbal root, *r-p-'*, which means "heal," so that the Torah is saying "heal, he will heal." R. Ishmael's students query: why the repetition, when one "heal" alone would have been enough? The repetition, they claim, teaches us that doctors have permission to do what they can to heal their patients.

While that lesson might seem obvious at first glance, in fact the school of R. Ishmael presents an important theological idea. We might imagine that since our bodies belong to God, so does their health. If God wants an individual to become sick, perhaps we humans have no right to interfere. If God wants the injury the person in Exod. 21:18–19 suffered to heal, it will heal; if not, that too is God's will. Or perhaps we may heal injuries one person inflicts on another, but not illnesses that humans do not cause.

The Talmud here teaches us *not* to think this way. Because the Torah emphasizes healing with the double verb, "heal, he will heal," we understand that the physician *always* has permission to heal, to the extent medical knowledge allows.

The *Mishneh Torah* (Text 3c) points out that the Torah requires us to "take utmost care" of ourselves. While the context in the Torah warns against the temptations of worshiping false gods, Rambam alludes to rabbinic *midrash* that reinterprets the verse to mean caring for our physical welfare. We must remove any hazards in our physical environments, and we must seek expert care for our bodies when we fall ill. Just as Texts 3a and 3b show that physicians may, and must, use their skills to heal, Text 3c rejects the thought, "If God wants me to get better, I will." Judaism teaches that God uses human beings as the means to heal God's creations. Doctors must heal, and patients must seek care.

Still, complications arise when medical treatment no longer works — when either no treatment exists, or available treatments neither cure the underlying illness nor meaningfully improve quality of life. We turn first to that issue in *Massekhet Semahot,* one of the so-called small tractates (work of the *tannaim* contemporary with the Mishnah, covering halakhah not included in the Mishnah itself).

Text Study #2: When Death Is Inevitable

Text 4a — *Semaḥot* 1:1–1:4

A *GOSES* IS CONSIDERED a living person for every purpose in the world. . . .

We may not move him or place him on sand or on salt until the moment he dies.

We may not close the eyes of a *goses*. Anyone who touches him to move him sheds blood. Rabbi Meir used to compare it to a flickering candle: Anyone who touches it, extinguishes it. So, too, anyone who closes the eyes of a *goses* is considered as if he took the *goses*'s life.

Text 4b — Shulḥan Arukh, *Yoreh De'ah* 339:2

IF THEY TELL SOMEONE: We saw your relative as a *goses* for three days, he must mourn for the relative, for [the *goses*] has certainly already died.

QUESTIONS FOR INQUIRY

1. Based on the information in these excerpts, what does it mean to be a *goses*?
2. Does Rabbi Meir's metaphor add to our understanding of the law?
3. What does the law in the Shulḥan Arukh add to our understanding of the status of a *goses*?
4. What is the modern equivalent of a *goses*?

COMMENTS

The halakhic category of *goses* describes a terminally ill patient close to death. Patients who have no chance of recovery from their underlying ailment fall into this category. The Shulḥan Arukh source demonstrates the classic understanding that a person becomes a *goses* when the expected survival is no longer than three days.

Given the Jewish principle of the sanctity of life, we can understand the first rule in *Massekhet Semaḥot*. As long as a person lives, we treat that individual with the respect owed to the living. We do nothing to prepare for death. We do not move the patient, out of fear of hastening death from the shock of the move. In earlier times, corpses were preserved on sand or salt before burial. Placing patients on those surfaces amounts to treating them as already dead, while a *goses* by definition still lives.

Semaḥot 1:4 demonstrates how seriously Rabbinic tradition takes the requirement to treat the dying patient as fully alive. It compares closing the eyes of the *goses*—apparently, hastening the death or encouraging it—to homicide. Rabbi Meir's parable vividly expresses the idea. It compares the life of the *goses* to the flickering flame of a candle. We know that if a candle begins to flicker, anything that disturbs it will extinguish the light. Undisturbed, the flame may go out, or it may continue to burn. So, too, the human soul: the life force may remain with the body, or it may flicker out. Any direct interference may extinguish it sooner. Since the decision about when life ends properly belongs to God, anyone taking any action that may hasten the *goses*'s death effectively takes the patient's life.

Many Jewish ethicists use the laws of *goses* to analyze hopeless cases in modern medicine. A patient with no hope of recovery and no expectation of survival beyond a brief period counts as a *goses*. We must treat this patient as fully alive. Not only are we forbidden to take any action that would hasten the moment of death; we must do everything for this patient we would do for any other person. As we would medicate any living person, we continue providing medicine and other treatments to the *goses*. Neither the hopelessness of the case nor the imminence of death excuse us from these duties.

Such an analysis has significant implications for this chapter's case studies, especially Case Study #2. Robert seems at least to be on the verge of becoming a *goses*. No one can say whether his life will end within three days, but he meets the criteria of having an untreatable, terminal condition that will lead to death if his family does not authorize further treatment. It follows that we must treat him as "alive for every purpose," meaning that just as we would continue providing treatment to any other person, we must provide the same to Robert. His family must allow the surgery to go forward.

It isn't possible to apply this principle to Eleanor's situation (Case Study #3) because her death does not seem imminent enough to meet the strict definition of a *goses*. But if Eleanor did meet the criteria for a *goses*, she would be viewed as akin to any living Jew and prohibited from taking her own life. And, of course, Jahi's case (Case Study #1) is further complicated by the fact that her doctors in Oakland, her family, and New Jersey caretakers do not agree on her status.

To shed more light on these cases, we begin with a talmudic passage that most Jewish ethicists understand as teaching about what we may and may not do when a person's suffering causes them to long for death.

Text 5 — Avodah Zarah 18a

[AFTER THE ROMANS PUT down the Bar Kochba revolt, they forbade teaching Torah.] They found Rabbi Ḥanina ben Teradion sitting and engaging in Torah study and gathering groups of people in public; and a Torah scroll was resting against his breast. They brought him and wrapped him in a Torah scroll, and they surrounded him in bundles of branches and they kindled the fire with them, and brought bunches of wool and soaked them in water and wrapped them around his heart, so that his soul would not depart quickly.

His daughter said to him: "Father, must I see you like this?" He said to her: "If I were burned by myself, that would be a hard thing for me. Now that I am burning and the Torah scroll is with me, the One Who cares about the disgrace of the Torah scroll will care about my disgrace."

His students said to him: "Rabbi, what do you see?" He said to them: "The parchment is burning but the letters fly off."

"Open your mouth and the fire will enter you." He said to them: "Better the One that gave it should take it, but one should not injure oneself."

The executioner said to him, "Rabbi, if I increase the flame and lift the bunches of wool from your heart, will you bring me to the life in the world to come?"

He said to him: "Yes." "Swear to me!"

He swore to him.

Immediately he increased the flame and lifted the bunches of wool from his heart; his soul departed quickly.

He jumped and fell into the fire.

A heavenly voice came out and said: "R. Ḥanina ben Teradion and the executioner are invited to the life of the world to come."

1. Why did R. Ḥanina refuse to open his mouth and end his suffering immediately?
2. Why did R. Ḥanina allow the executioner to remove the tufts of wool and increase the flame? What is the difference between doing that and R. Ḥanina's opening his mouth to allow the fire to enter his body?
3. Does the Talmud approve of what the executioner did?
4. In modern medical situations, what parallels might there be to the Rabbi opening his mouth to the flames?
5. In modern medical situations, what parallels might there be to the executioner removing the bunches of wool?
6. In modern medical situations, what parallels might there be to the executioner increasing the flame?
7. In what ways does the story fail to provide useful analogies to modern situations?

COMMENTS

R. Ḥanina ben Teradion is one of the ten rabbis martyred by the Romans commemorated in the Yom Kippur liturgy. For many thinkers concerned with medical ethics, R. Ḥanina stands for those who suffer a painful, drawn-out process of dying.

To some ethicists, the Romans' use of wet wool to torture R. Ḥanina by slowing down his dying resembles certain interventions that can prolong death from terminal illness. For example, a patient who cannot breathe independently would die far more quickly without the oxygen provided by a ventilator that pushes air into the airways. If the patient lingers only because of the machine, loved ones may wonder if the support prolongs suffering more than it relieves it. Perhaps its removal is more compassionate than keeping the patient alive in such a state.

Some readers understand such compassion to motivate R. Ḥanina's students' proposal. If the rabbi opens his mouth, he will swallow flames and die immediately. His suffering will end. Ḥanina refuses on the grounds that human life belongs to God: "the One who gave" life must take it, and no person may choose to intervene otherwise. R. Ḥanina interprets ingesting the fire as an act of suicide.

If that ideal controls our decisions about life and death, we must wonder about the story's final scenes. Now the executioner offers to hasten the end of the rabbi's suffering by not only removing the wool, but also by increasing the flame. R. Ḥanina agrees, swearing that in return the executioner will receive the reward of eternal life in the world to come. When the executioner takes the two promised steps, the rabbi dies quickly. The executioner ends his own life by jumping into the flames, and a voice from heaven confirms divine approval of his actions by welcoming the executioner along with R. Ḥanina to the world to come.

The Talmud apparently endorses some actions to speed the death of the suffering. What analogies in modern medical practice can we find to removing the soaked wool and increasing the fire? As the wool slows the progress of the flames, perhaps we may remove something that stands between the patient and the disease process that would otherwise quickly result in death. In some circumstances, that factor might be the ventilator. If the ventilator mechanically inflates the lungs long past the point when they would function on their own while the patient suffers pain without any hope of recovery, we might argue that the machine functions like the wet wool in the Talmud: it serves no therapeutic purpose, and furthermore artificially prolongs the process of dying. If so, the Talmud appears to justify removing it to end the patient's suffering.

Parallels may also exist to the executioner's increasing the intensity of the fire. Medical caregivers could take certain steps to allow a suffering patient's soul to depart quickly. The most extreme would be administering a drug that would stop the patient's heart or otherwise cause death directly. Less drastic might be administering an increasing dosage of pain relief medicine to the point that it reduces the patient's respiration, quickly leading to death.

Such actions amount to active euthanasia and are illegal in many locales. Still, the evidence in the Talmud indicates approval. As we will see below (Texts 8a–c), the majority of traditional sources prohibit steps that directly shorten a life. This talmudic story takes a more lenient view of ending a terminal patient's suffering.

That said, when considering Case Study #3, the rabbi's refusal to take death into his own hands might imply that Eleanor should not receive the option of physician-assisted death. While R. Ḥanina does allow another person, the executioner, to remove impediments and hasten his dying, he rejects the possibility of taking action himself. Perhaps Eleanor, too, should follow the principle that "the One Who gave life should take it, but a person should not injure herself."

Be that as it may, these analogies to modern medical challenges may have limited utility. First, context demonstrates that the Talmud tells this story not so much to teach ethical lessons about suffering and dying as to offer R. Ḥanina's willing martyrdom as a model of devotion to Torah. Some halakhic authorities argue that such *aggadot* do not carry legal authority. Second, R. Ḥanina dies from execution by burning, not from illness. Third, comparing wet tufts of wool, a torture device, to modern medicines and devices that seek to heal, seems dubious.

Now we turn to a medieval text that became the basis for the notion that we may remove obstacles that delay the death of a terminally ill patient.

Text 6 — Shulḥan Arukh, *Yoreh De'ah* 339:1

A *GOSES* IS CONSIDERED a living person for every purpose in the world. . . . We may not remove the pillow or blanket from under him or place him on sand, clay or the ground . . . and we may not close his eyes until his soul departs. Anyone who closes the eyes of a *goses* sheds blood. . . .

Note: . . . So, too, it is forbidden to cause the dying to die quickly. For instance, someone who is goses a long time and cannot separate [from life], it is forbidden to remove the pillow or blanket from underneath him on the grounds that they say there are certain bird feathers that cause this. Similarly, we may not move him from his place. It is also forbidden to place the keys of the synagogue under his head in order that he may separate. But if there is something present that causes a delay in the soul's departure, such as if near the house there is a banging sound, as of someone chopping wood, or there is salt on his [the goses's] tongue, and these prevent the soul's departure, it is permitted to remove it, for there is no direct action at all in this; it simply removes the impediment.

QUESTIONS FOR INQUIRY

1. What situation does R. Moshe Isserles discuss in his note?
2. What distinction does Isserles make between actions we may perform and those we may not?
3. In modern medical situations, what parallels might exist to Isserles' idea? When would he suggest we can help a patient die? When would he suggest we must not intervene?

COMMENTS

The Shulḥan Arukh here codifies the law we first encountered in *Massekhet Semaḥot* (Text 4a): a person at death's door remains a live human being, and must be treated as such. Moving or manipulating the person's body in a way that hastens death amounts to homicide.

The note by Isserles adds details that have become central to traditional Jewish medical ethics. Starting from the established rule that we may not directly hasten a person's death, Isserles describes a familiar situation when a terminally ill person lingers, unable to recover but also unable to die. His use of the phrase "someone who is *goses* a long time" is interesting in itself. We saw in the Shulḥan Arukh (Text 4b) that by definition a *goses* is not expected to live more than three days. Presumably even in medieval times some terminal patients outlived their prognosis. Isserles rules consistently with other halakhic sources that we may not take any steps to precipitate the patient's death, no matter how long they linger. Even if we suspect that something in the pillow or bed linens keeps the individual alive, we may not remove them. Even an indirect approach, like placing the keys of the synagogue under the pillow (apparently a belief existed that the synagogue keys could release the ill person from suffering), is forbidden on the same grounds. Such acts would lead to death immediately, or nearly so, violating the principle of treating a *goses* as we would any living person.

However, Isserles goes on to describe another principle that exists in tension with the first. While we may not hasten death, we may remove anything that impedes dying. Offering as examples the loud, repetitive noise of chopping wood and the strong taste of salt on the tongue as phenomena that may draw patients' attention too vigorously for them to let go of the world, he rules we may stop the sound or remove the salt to allow the patient's soul to leave the body. Isserles writes explicitly that these do not amount to "direct action," which is prohibited; all they accomplish is "removing the impediment."

Isserles' distinction that prohibits hastening death but sanctions removing anything that impedes it seems to depend on an understanding that a given illness will naturally lead to death within a certain amount of time. We may not take steps that would cause someone to die before that time. But if an external factor is causing the patient to linger beyond the expected time, we may remove that factor. While the removal causes the patient to die sooner than otherwise, nothing we do actually hastens death before that person's time has come. We have simply dismantled a barrier to the natural process of dying.

Modern medical ethicists distinguish between active euthanasia, when someone causes a patient to die through an act like administering an overdose of medicine, and passive euthanasia, when someone causes a patient to die through an omission, like withholding a life-sustaining treatment. In effect, the halakhah forbids active euthanasia: we may not directly cause death. It allows a form of passive euthanasia: as long as we do not touch the patient, we may remove anything that impedes death. Perhaps this analysis can solve some ethical problems we encounter near the end of life.

The passage also speaks to another issue not directly addressed by our case studies: whether or not we should be providing nutrition and hydration intravenously (through tubes inserted directly into the veins) or enterally (directly into the intestines) to terminally ill patients who cannot take food or water orally. After a loved one loses all hope of recovery, must families allow the provision of nutrition and hydration, which does not improve a patient's condition but may prolong life?

One way of framing the question uses one of Isserles' categories from the Shulḥan Arukh: since nutrition and hydration do not serve a healing function, perhaps they are impediments to the natural process of dying. If so, we could remove them, or at least never hook up the tubes in the first place. On the other hand, we might argue that we owe food and water that sustain life to all people. Jewish tradition certainly commands us to feed the hungry who cannot obtain food on their own. Denying food to terminal patients, on this view, is an act of cruelly hastening their deaths.

Seeking to adapt Isserles to modern realities, Rabbi Elliot Dorff points out that the way we administer nutrition and hydration to such patients has more in common with the way we administer medicines than the way we offer food. Just as we evaluate whether or not a given medicine will contribute to healing before giving it to a patient, he suggests we can consider whether artificial nutrition and hydration will contribute to healing. If not, he says, while we may begin nutrition and hydration if we choose, we are not obligated to do so.[2]

Isserles' distinction is also key when considering the case of a patient who is beyond any hope of recovery and remains on a ventilator to support breathing. How should we understand the ventilator's role? Is it like the pillow, because if we remove it we cause the patient's immediate death? If so, Jewish ethics would forbid us to turn the ventilator off. Perhaps, though, at some point the ventilator becomes like the noise of chopping wood: it only serves to keep the patient in the world far beyond the expected time of death. If that is so, Isserles would sanction shutting off the ventilator on the grounds that doing so merely removes an impediment to the dying process God initiated.

The choice of how to characterize the respirator under this halakhah becomes even more difficult when we consider the definition of the *goses*. The three-day standard does not work well in the contemporary medical setting. In some circumstances, medicines and machinery can sustain the body for extended periods of time. Does a terminally ill patient on modern medicine or machinery qualify as a *goses*, even if we cannot say this person is within a few days of death? Or might we argue that this is precisely what Isserles describes as "*goses* for a long time"? If we adopt this understanding, we return to the question of whether to label the ventilator an impediment to death or an essential part of life that we may not tamper with lest we be guilty of killing the patient.

Modern Jewish ethicists take both sides in this debate. Two Israeli rabbis offer typical arguments. Haim David HaLevi was Sephardic rabbi of Tel Aviv from 1973 to 1978. We again meet the *haredi* halakhist Rabbi Eliezer Tzvi Waldenberg, who wrote widely in Jewish law and medical ethics.

Text 7a — HaLevi, Natural and Artificial Life

THE PERMISSION TO REMOVE a grain of salt is undisputed and clear. . . . Now a respirator is exactly the same. For this patient, upon being delivered to the hospital in a critical condition, was immediately attached to the respirator and was revived with *artificial life* in order to try and treat him and to cure him. So when the physicians come to the conclusion that there is no cure for his condition, it is clearly permitted to disconnect the patient from the machine to which he was attached.[3]

Text 7b — Waldenberg, *Responsa Tzitz Eliezer*

[THE ARUKH HASHULḤAN WRITES]: "And although we see him suffering greatly in dying and that death is good for him, nevertheless we are forbidden to do anything to hasten his death, as the universe and all within it belongs to the Holy One . . . and such is His exalted will."

For no creature in the world owns a person's life; that includes also that person himself, who has no license at all regarding his own life, nor is it his property. His granting permission is in vain concerning something which does not belong to him, but rather is the property of God, Who alone bestows it and takes it away.[4]

QUESTIONS FOR INQUIRY

1. One rabbi allows disconnecting a respirator in hopeless cases; the other forbids it. How does each thinker justify his conclusion?
2. Which view do you find more convincing? Why?

3. What do these texts suggest about using premodern Jewish sources and values to solve contemporary problems in medical ethics?

COMMENTS

Both of the halakhic experts presented here (now deceased) answered questions in medical ethics for Israeli hospitals. According to Rabbi HaLevi, the respirator is best compared to the salt on the tongue of the *goses*. No one disputes that we may remove the salt when it prolongs the patient's suffering. So too, if a respirator extends life, that life should be considered "artificial." Therefore, once physicians conclude that the machine contributes nothing further to healing an incurable patient, they may disconnect the respirator. In effect, R. HaLevi considers disconnecting it as removing an impediment to natural dying.

By contrast, according to Rabbi Waldenberg, even if people were to beg us to help end their suffering with death, we may not do so. Their bodies are not their (or our) property to dispose of: human life belongs to God. Further, Waldenberg makes no distinction between life with or without mechanical support. He does not consider life on a ventilator artificial; he considers it life. Moreover, the machine is not a mere impediment to dying, but part of the actual life of the patient. Therefore, we may never turn off a life-support machine until the patient irrevocably dies. We may never do anything to shorten an individual's life.

These two responsa illuminate a fundamental debate in Jewish medical ethics. One side asserts that the value of human life, controlled by God, determines everything that follows. It denies us the right to make any decision, no matter how seemingly compassionate, that shortens a person's life. The other side, while not denying the value of life, seeks to limit unnecessary suffering. This approach considers many of the interventions modern medicine makes possible not as supporting life, but as impeding death. Such a view would allow us to adhere to the rules of the Shulḥan Arukh (Text 6), ending the patient's misery without impermissibly taking a life.

Other recent thinkers point out that cases of terminal patients lingering on life support, like the ones presented in Texts 7a and 7b, demonstrate the limits of the category of *goses* in modern times. Since medical science can sustain a form of life for far longer than three days, we can no longer assume that a terminally ill person will die within that time frame.

But if describing a patient as a *goses* (see Texts 4a–b) no longer helps, where in Jewish halakhic or ethical traditions might we turn for guidance? Avram Reisner, a Conservative rabbi and member of the movement's Law Committee, believes the category can still work, if we redefine it. Daniel Sinclair, a philosopher, proposes different halakhic concepts that might replace the idea of *goses*.

Text 8a — Reisner, "A Halakhic Ethic of
Care for the Terminally Ill"

SHARP AS THIS CONUNDRUM [of using *goses* in modern settings] appears, we firmly believe that it can be . . . resolved in a way which responds to our moral and psychological needs and remains true to the intent of the sources before us, while addressing as well the medical knowledge and technologies of our day. The first key to this resolution is to recognize that whatever *goses* may have meant specifically to our rabbinic sources, it refers in our day to all those who have been diagnosed as imminently dying.[5]

Text 8b — Sinclair, *Tradition and the Biological Revolution*

IN THE HUMAN CONTEXT . . . the meaning of the term *terefah* is much less precise [than for animals]. . . . Maimonides's definition runs as follows: "it is known for certain that he had a fatal organic disease and physicians say that his disease is incurable by human agency." . . .

The *terefah* category applies to internal disease, and not necessarily to an injury sustained as a result of an external blow. . . . On this basis, therefore, any person suffering from a fatal internal disease may be classified as a *terefah*, and his killer will be exempt from the death penalty provided that there is sufficient medical evidence of the fatal nature of his victim's condition.... The fundamental concept in the definition of human *tarfut* is, therefore, the inevitability of death....

The outstanding feature of the category of human *tarfut* for the current debate concerning the treatment of the critically ill is the exemption of the killer of a *terefah* from the death penalty. This feature focuses attention upon the fact that a fatal disease does not detract from the legal status of a person, and also introduces a measure of flexibility into the issue of terminating such a life. This is in direct contrast to the category of *goses*, which is based on the premise that the *goses* is like a living person in all respects.[6]

QUESTIONS FOR INQUIRY

1. How does Rabbi Reisner redefine the category of *goses* to adapt it to modern medical realities?
2. How is a *terefah* different from a *goses*?
3. What implications do the differences have for ethical decision-making?
4. According to Sinclair, what are the advantages of using the *terefah* instead of *goses* category in contemporary decision-making?
5. Which of these views is more convincing? Why?

COMMENTS

Rabbi Reisner speaks for those who prefer to retain the category of *goses* and continue to treat dying patients as living in every respect. Acknowledging the uncertainty of modern medical prognosis—we cannot predict when an individual will die to the point when a patient may be a *"goses"* for weeks and even months—he offers a subtle redefinition. The term "refers in our day to all those who have been diagnosed as imminently dying."

Reisner proposes that adopting this definition of *goses* helps solve ethical dilemmas by extending our ability to distinguish treatments of illness from impediments to death. He would retain the tradition's requirement that we treat illness and extend life as far as medical science allows. But if we understand that a patient can become a *goses* and still survive far longer than three days, we recognize that many interventions do not in fact treat the underlying illness. They only impede the patient's natural process of dying.

This line of thinking allows us to remove mechanical ventilation, for example, under more circumstances than would the traditional definition of *goses*. A respirator can still be curative, for example in helping a patient recover from surgery, but in the last stage of terminal illness, the machine does not perform any therapeutic function. As Isserles taught in the sixteenth century, we may ethically remove an impediment to a death that would otherwise come far sooner—such as, in our day, a machine that forces oxygen into the bloodstream—to allow the sufferer to die.

Reisner's proposal might help Robert's family (Case Study #2), since Robert received a diagnosis of imminent death and would fit this adjusted definition of a *goses*. His family could consequently define the ventilator as an impediment without therapeutic purpose, remove it, and allow Robert to die more quickly.

Going further than Reisner, Sinclair proposes a different halakhic category for ethical analysis: *terefah* in place of *goses*. When *terefah* refers to human beings, the term means a person with an incurable, fatal disease.[7]

An advantage of the *terefah* category is that unlike the *goses* category, it has no built-in time limit. A person can remain a *terefah* indefinitely. That allows us to decide how a person's life should end as soon as the diagnosis becomes clear. We no longer need to wait to the last moment, when doctors expect the patient to survive no more than three days. A further benefit is that while we must treat a *goses* as alive, a *terefah* is a kind of "dead man walking." As Sinclair notes, the Talmud exempts the killer of a *terefah* from the usual penalties for homicide. One cannot be convicted of murder without killing a living person, which the *terefah* technically is not.

This fact allows us to treat anyone known to be suffering from a fatal illness differently than we would treat a living human. The *terefah* category provides flexibility, because we do not have to fear that anything we do to end the patient's suffering amounts to shedding blood (see the warning in *Semaḥot*, Text 4a). If we describe end-stage patients as *terefot*, we may remove ventilators and other life support. We have no obligation to support life for those who are halakhically dead.

Rabbi Amy Eilberg, the first woman ordained a Conservative rabbi, who worked for much of her career as a healthcare chaplain, agrees that we should adopt the *terefah* standard proposed by Sinclair. In a responsum for the Conservative movement's Committee on Jewish Law and Standards, Eilberg writes, "The question is not: are we being rigorous enough, in every case, about the prolongation of life? Rather, the question for the contemporary halakhist . . . is: what is the intent of a life-affirming, life-sanctifying tradition in the world of the hopelessly ill patient?" She therefore supports using *terefah* as "the operative category for the terminally ill patient."[8]

Sinclair's proposal also sheds interesting light on each of our case studies. Jahi McMath may not meet the definition of a human *terefah*, because the evidence that she suffers from a fatal condition is not clear. Since her body continued to develop and she became more responsive over time, it seems possible that her body could recover even more of its normal functioning. Thus, her family correctly insisted on continuing to provide her with life support.

Robert's family might find Sinclair's idea helpful. Because he has an irreversible, terminal illness, he meets the halakhic requirements to be declared a *terefah*. The family's decision to forego heart surgery then becomes easier to make than if they think of Robert as a *goses*, who must be treated as fully alive. He need not undergo heart surgery after death, as it were. The family could allow the final end to come as soon as possible.

Eleanor has an argument that she is already a *terefah*. All evidence indicates that her underlying condition is fatal and irreversible. She need not do anything that prolongs her dying. But we must also ask if the status of *tarfut* overrides the rule that we do not control the beginning and ending of our own lives. Being a *terefah* does not necessarily mean that Eleanor may abandon what remains of her time on earth. Sinclair's proposal makes it easier to justify forgoing life-extending treatment, as in Case Study #2, without necessarily justifying suicide or physician-assisted dying, as in Case Study #3.

Of course, introducing the category of *terefah* to consideration of end-of-life problems has its own weaknesses. Some, including Rabbi Reisner, who argues for maintaining the category of *goses* (Text 8a), suggest that invoking the category of *terefah* debases the God-given life of the patient. As we saw earlier in this chapter, Judaism holds human life in the highest regard. When we declare people effectively dead while they remain alive, we set aside the ultimate responsibility of preserving life gifted to us by the Divine. Others point out an important distinction: the fact that a person is a *terefah* does not mean we have permission to end that life; it only means that the act is not subject to the same penalties as unlawful killing. While we may not have to do for a *terefah* everything we would do for a *goses*, nothing in halakhah permits us to decide to end the *terefah*'s existence at a moment we choose.

Cases like Robert's and Eleanor's confront us with the question of whether life is always preferable to death. Should Robert's family subject him to an operation that will not restore his ability to interact with those he loves? Should Eleanor have to accept a long period of physical suffering? A few modern ethicists claim that Jewish tradition can support using a person's quality of life to justify removal of medical interventions. Instead of insisting on maintaining the principle of *ḥayyei sha'ah*, keeping moribund patients alive as long as possible by any means necessary, they would allow forms of passive euthanasia to end the agony of a suffering, terminal patient. One such argument was made by Rabbi Byron Sherwin, a professor at Spertus College of Judaica who published extensively in the field of Jewish ethics.

Text 8c — Sherwin, *Jewish Ethics for the Twenty-First Century*

[I]N VIEW OF CONTEMPORARY realities, I have felt it necessary to defend a position within the framework of classical Jewish sources that would justify active euthanasia in at least certain circumstances. I believe that [those] . . . who deal with the death and dying of individuals — whose last days are overwhelmed with unbearable agony, who have no hope of recovery, . . . and who have exhausted all medical remedies — should be able to advocate and to practice active euthanasia . . . without feeling that they have rejected the teachings of Jewish tradition. To be sure, Judaism instructs us to "choose life" (Deut. 30:19), but Judaism also recognizes that "there is a time to die" (Eccles. 3:2). . . . Scripture says, "You should love your neighbor as yourself" (Lev. 19:18), which the Talmud takes in certain circumstances to mean, "Therefore, choose an easy death for him" (Talmud Pesahim 75a).[9]

QUESTIONS FOR INQUIRY

1. What contemporary realities does Rabbi Sherwin have in mind?
2. What basis does he find in Jewish tradition for considering the patient's suffering to sometimes allow active euthanasia?

COMMENTS

Rabbi Sherwin wants Jewish ethics to respond to the real challenges we face in the twenty-first century, in which modern medical capabilities render the traditional notions of *ḥayyei sha'ah* and *goses* difficult if not impossible to sustain. Someone can remain a *goses* for "a long time," and with new technologies that person can remain alive almost indefinitely.

Sherwin suggests that we balance the Torah's command to "choose life" with Ecclesiastes' philosophical recognition that "there is a time to die." The Talmud's exhortation to help someone whose death is inevitable to seek an easy death ("Therefore, choose an easy death for him") grounds his argument that we may justifiably take steps to end a terminally ill patient's suffering. The time that comes for everyone has arrived for the patient; we should ease that necessary experience, allowing the individual to suffer less by dying sooner.

Sherwin goes further than Sinclair and others who advocate considering the terminally ill in the category of *terefah* instead of *goses*. He would approve active euthanasia, direct steps to end the life of the patient, much more readily. In the case of Robert (Case Study #2), they would agree that the family need not take further measures to prolong his life, but after that decision, Sherwin would be more willing to approve of removing Robert from a ventilator so he can die without a prolonged period of suffering.

Sherwin's proposal arises out of concern for the patient's agony. Those who believe that showing compassion for those who suffer is a central ethical principle will be most willing to adopt his idea. Others may believe that other values explored in this chapter make it impossible to favor active euthanasia as Sherwin advocates.

The technological advances we have been discussing also give rise to another difficult question: what do we mean by "death"? Case Study #1 asks how we as a society should define death. We saw in the discussion of Texts 8a and 8b that a person with a fatal organic condition can be halakhically dead while medically alive. What criteria should physicians use to declare a patient dead? We turn next to efforts to define death among bioethicists in general and Jewish medical ethicists in particular.

Text 9a—Uniform Determination of Death Act (1980)

AN INDIVIDUAL WHO HAS sustained either (1) irreversible cessation of circulatory and respiratory functions, or (2) irreversible cessation of all functions of the entire brain, including the brain stem, is dead. A determination of death must be made in accordance with accepted medical standards.[10]

Text 9b—*Mishneh Torah*, Laws of Shabbat 2:19

[WHEN A PERSON IS found under debris on Shabbat], we search up to the individual's nose. If we find no breath, we leave him, as he is already dead.

Text 9c—*Mishnah Ohalot* 1:6

DOMESTIC AND WILD ANIMALS also do not impart ritual impurity until they die. If their heads were cut off, they impart ritual impurity even though they move convulsively, like a lizard's tail that twitches after being severed from the body.

Text 9d—Rosner, *Biomedical Ethics and Jewish Law*

JEWISH WRITINGS PROVIDE CONSIDERABLE evidence for the thesis that the brain and the brain stem control all bodily functions, including respiration and cardiac activity. It therefore follows that if there is irreversible total cessation of all brain function including that of the brain stem, the person is dead, even though there may still be some transient spontaneous cardiac activity. Brain function is divided into higher cerebral activities and the vegetative functions of the vital centers of the brain stem. A criterion of death based on higher cerebral death alone is ethically and morally unacceptable. . . . If one can medically establish that there is total cessation of all brain function including the brain stem, the patient is as if "physiologically decapitated."[11]

Text 9e—Waldenberg, *Responsa Tzitz Eliezer*

THERE ARE THOSE WHO err in thinking that examination of the nose is indicative of cessation of brain activity and, on this basis, want to establish that life is contingent on the brain. . . . In truth this is an absolute error and contradicts that which our Sages, of blessed memory, have established.[12]

Text 9f—Veatch, "The Evolution of Death and Dying Controversies"

ONE COULD BE DECLARED dead by cardiac, whole-brain, or higher-brain criteria. . . . Critics showed that standard, accepted criteria for measuring whole-brain death in fact were compatible with the presence of certain brain functions remaining intact, such as the secretion of hormones. Thoughtful scholars challenged the presumption that the brain was the sole organ responsible for . . . orchestrating the body's varied activities to operate as part of a whole.[13]

QUESTIONS FOR INQUIRY

1. What criteria does the Uniform Determination of Death Act (UDDA) use to determine death? What does this definition imply for Case Study #1?
2. Why does the UDDA provide multiple means of determining death?
3. What does Rambam in the *Mishneh Torah* add to our understanding of the law of *piku'aḥ nefesh* in Text 2a?
4. What does *Mishnah Ohalot* 1:6 imply for the determination of death? How does that differ from the *Mishneh Torah*, Laws of Shabbat?
5. On what basis does Dr. Rosner argue that Judaism accommodates the cessation of brain activity as a definition of death?
6. On what grounds does Rabbi Waldenberg reject the cessation of brain activity as a definition of death?
7. What problem does Veatch point out with the standard of whole-brain death?
8. What implications do these definitions have for our case studies?

COMMENTS

Common euphemisms such as "breathed her last" demonstrate the close association we typically make between respiration and life. To live is to breathe; life ends when breathing stops. Until the late 1960s, that was also the medical standard. "Irreversible cessation of circulatory and respiratory functions," as the Uniform Definition of Death Act (UDDA), drafted by the National Conference of Commissioners on Uniform State Laws, puts it, had constituted death.

Beginning around 1968, medical experts identified problems with using respiration as the exclusive standard for determining death. One issue was the possibility of using machines to oxygenate a person's blood. A patient might continue to "breathe" mechanically even if other bodily functions had ceased. Another factor was medical science's new ability to transplant human organs. Organs for transplantation must have oxygen flowing through them when removed from the donor in order to benefit their recipients. But doctors cannot remove healthy organs, especially hearts, from living patients: that would constitute abuse, or even murder. These developments raised the question of whether it would be possible to declare a patient dead on grounds other than the end of blood circulation and respiration.

A committee at Harvard developed the idea that came to be known as "brain death." Under this standard, doctors declare a patient dead when the entire brain ceases to function. That kind of death can occur even while breathing continues through mechanical ventilation. If a person dies when the brains stops functioning, doctors can remove organs, including the heart, while the tissues are still oxygenated and thereby save other lives.

The Harvard committee's work proved so influential that a model law based on it was adopted throughout most of the United States (only Arizona, North Carolina, Texas, and Virginia do not accept its understanding of brain death).[14] The UDDA uses the standard known as "whole-brain" death. That means that both the "higher" parts of the brain, the centers of thinking and personality, and the "lower" parts including the brain stem, which control the body's autonomic functions, must stop working for the patient to be declared dead. The whole-brain standard helps differentiate the dead from those in a persistent vegetative state (PVS), where the cerebral hemispheres sustain severe, permanent damage while the brain stem continues to function.

Interestingly, the law allows doctors to use the irreversible cessation of either respiration or brain function as the crucial indicator of death. Apparently not every situation requires resorting to the brain definition to declare death; sometimes, the end of breathing is enough. Defining the exact point separating life from death proves more difficult than we might imagine.

For the most part, the medical profession considers a patient whose cerebral hemispheres and brainstem stop functioning to be dead. That explains the actions of Jahi McMath's original doctors in Case Study #1. When they no longer detected activity in Jahi's brain, they considered ventilating her body a waste of precious resources. Further treatment would cruelly deceive the girl's family into thinking that her life might continue.

Can halakhah accept the modern definition of death? Traditionally it upheld a standard based on respiration. The *Mishneh Torah* (Text 9b) clarifies how we decide if a victim is alive (if the searchers can detect breathing through the victim's nose) or dead (if they cannot). Before changes in medical practice led to promulgation of the whole-brain standard of death, Jewish ethicists discussed dying only in these terms. For that reason, some opposed the UDDA. Important Orthodox halakhists wrote to the New York State legislature when it debated the bill and convinced it to include a religious exception to the brain-death rule. Others, however, found reasons in classical halakhah to support the move to a whole-brain standard for death.

Some Jewish ethicists argue that *Mishnah Ohalot* 1:6 presents a model for recognizing the brain, which controls breathing and all bodily functions, as the center of life and death. This Mishnah presents a law concerning the ritual purity standards of the ancient Temple. The main source of ritual impurity (*tumah*) is contact with a dead body. Both human and animal corpses impart *tumah*. The Mishnah rules that animals' bodies do not cause impurity while they live. To clarify how we know that a given animal is definitively dead, it discusses the movements that some animals continue to make after decapitation. Those spasmodic movements are not signs of life. Without its head, the animal cannot live; despite appearances, it is dead.

By analogy, a human whose brain stops functioning may continue for a short while to breathe or display other reflexive movements, but such a person cannot be alive. That is the argument made by Dr. Fred Rosner (Text 9d), professor of medicine at Mt. Sinai School of Medicine, who chaired the New York State Medical Ethics Committee and published extensively in Jewish medical ethics. Since the brain actually controls breathing, determining that all brain function has ceased means, by definition, that breathing has as well. Complete cessation of all functions of the brain amounts to decapitation. It must be accepted as an indicator of death.

Text 9e shows that Rosner's view remains controversial, especially among Orthodox thinkers. Rabbi Waldenberg forcefully rejects efforts to interpret halakhic literature to allow the brain-death standard. He insists that the halakhah established respiration alone as the criterion for deciding when a person dies.

Bioethicists from outside Jewish tradition, such as Robert M. Veatch, emeritus professor of medical ethics at Georgetown University and senior research scholar at its Kennedy Institute of Ethics, also take issue with the whole-brain standard of death, as Text 9f illustrates. Clinical experience has shown that some bodies meeting the criteria for whole-brain death continue to display certain functions, among them hormone secretion, as seen when Jahi McMath experienced the onset of menstruation (Case Study #1). Professor Veatch writes that "Now no reasonable person can accept a literal whole-brain definition [of death] in which every last function of the brain, but no bodily functions outside the brain, counts in defining death."[15] And so, while the UDDA remains the law and generally guides mainstream medical practice, the science and the philosophical understanding of the meaning of death remain in dispute.

Even the ancient technique of checking breathing as a method for determining if a person is alive may prove unreliable. In August 2020, a twenty-year-old Michigan woman, Timesha Beauchamp, was declared dead when paramedics reported that despite thirty minutes of effort, they found no signs of respiration in her — but two hours later, a funeral home employee opened a body bag and found her breathing with her eyes open. In reporting this story, the *New York Times* added, "It is not unheard of for people to be declared dead only to be found alive hours later. In 2018, a South African woman was pronounced dead at the scene of a car wreck but hours later was found breathing in a mortuary. And in 2014, a Mississippi man who had been pronounced dead was found alive inside a body bag at a funeral home."[16] No matter which definition of death we adopt, we cannot always distinguish with certainty between the living and the dead.

These debates over understandings of death shed important light on two of this chapter's case studies. In Jahi's case, the Oakland doctors made reasonable decisions in light of modern medical practice and the law, yet her state proved part of Veatch's critique of the whole-brain death standard. Her brain continued to secrete hormones, as demonstrated by her beginning to menstruate. If Jahi truly moved her hand in response to her family's instructions and not as mere reflex, her hearing remained intact and she retained some understanding of language. The standard tests produced a misleading result: Jahi remained alive.

Robert (Case Study #2) continues to have most of his brainstem functions, though doctors believe he requires a respirator to support his breathing before the proposed surgery. One might make an argument for testing his state. By turning off the machine for a few minutes, physicians could see whether or not Robert's brain can control his respiration. If not, he might meet the criteria for brain death.

The scenario represented by Eleanor in Case Study #3, who wishes to remain alive only while she can experience what she considers a reasonable quality of life, pits against one another two divergent approaches to medical ethics. The "curing" approach, which holds that medicine's goal is to heal and assumes the patient's right to life, forbids any medical professional to end a life or to help a patient end her life. The "caring" approach, drawn from the utilitarian tradition in philosophy, which argues that the goal of ethics is to maximize happiness and minimize suffering, holds that the healthcare professional's role is to minimize pain, even when the only available relief involves ending the patient's life. A physician holding this view could enter into partnership with a patient like Eleanor, fulfilling her request for a fatal prescription to relieve her suffering.

Readers will recognize the difficulty in applying the caring approach in a Jewish context. We saw that the first principle of halakhic medical ethics is that our lives belong not to us but to God. Many Jewish ethicists would discourage fulfilling Eleanor's request for that reason alone.

Furthermore, as we saw in the story of R. Ḥanina b. Teradion (Text 5), halakhah forbids suicide. History shows that rabbis granted narrow exceptions to those who feared religious persecution in the Middle Ages. One rabbi during the Holocaust allowed a questioner to die by suicide rather than undergo torture by the Nazis that would have caused him to reveal the locations of Jews in hiding, but directed that his decision not be published.[17] While we may be moved by compassion for her future suffering, it is hard to argue that Eleanor's situation rises to the level of these rare examples.

First, let us take a closer look at the halakhah of suicide.

Text Study #3: Suicide

Text 10a — *Semaḥot* 2:1

WE DO NOT ATTEND to one who commits suicide in any way. . . . Mourners do not tear their clothing, . . . nor do we eulogize the person.

QUESTIONS FOR INQUIRY

1. What rules does *Semaḥot* teach about how to respond to a suicide?
2. What general understandings about the tradition's attitude toward suicide can we derive from these rules?

COMMENTS

The halakhot recorded in *Semaḥot* 2:1 deny traditional Jewish mourning rites to the family of the person who takes their own life: the tearing of a piece of clothing as an inarticulate expression of grief, as well as a eulogy describing how the person lived and the lessons this life offers to those of us left behind. What is more, later legal sources add that the deceased may not be buried within the sanctified grounds of a Jewish cemetery, but must be interred outside the fence.

The halakhah demonstrates the tradition's strong disapproval of suicide. Human beings do not have the right to decline God's gift of life. Decisions about when to take life away must be left to God.

Despite the strength of this halakhic disapproval, Jewish tradition records some instances of suicide without adverse comment. The most famous case is that of Saul, the first king of Israel. He found himself facing military defeat and capture by the enemy Philistines.

Text 10b — 1 Sam. 31:3–4

THE BATTLE RAGED AROUND Saul, and some of the archers hit him, and he was severely wounded by the archers. Saul said to his arms-bearer, "Draw your sword and run me through, so that the uncircumcised may not run me through and make sport of me." But his arms-bearer in his great awe, refused; whereupon Saul grasped the sword and fell upon it.

QUESTIONS FOR INQUIRY

1. Why does Saul die by suicide?
2. Can Saul's situation be compared to modern circumstances? What are the commonalities and differences in relation to Eleanor in Case Study #3?

COMMENTS

When King Saul sees that defeat in the battle against the Philistine army is inevitable, he decides that his life must end before the enemy can capture him, torture him, and mutilate his body. When his arms-bearer refuses to run him through with his sword, Saul falls on the sword, killing himself.

Why doesn't the TANAKH express disapproval of Saul's choice? Perhaps because Saul was the divinely chosen king of Israel, any possible measure had to be taken to prevent him from falling into the hands of Israel's bitter enemies. Some traditional commentators justify his suicide on the grounds that one may take one's own life to avoid a *ḥillul ha-shem*, a public desecration of God's divinity: Saul feared that under torture, he would agree to the Philistines' demands to worship their idols. Others propose that Saul ended his life when the Philistines surrounded his army so that other Israelites would not lose their lives in a futile attempt to rescue him.

Any of these interpretations allows us to see that Saul's situation does not provide a helpful analogy to a terminal patient seeking to end her life. Nothing in Saul's story justifies taking one's life to avoid one's own potential suffering.

Halakhic tradition includes other values relevant to Eleanor's case. Texts 11a through 13 help us understand them.

Text 11a — Lev. 19:14

YOU SHALL NOT INSULT the deaf, or place a stumbling block before the blind. You shall fear your God: I am YHVH.

Text 11b — *Sifra Kedoshim* 2:14

"OR PLACE A STUMBLING block before the blind" — [meaning], before someone blind about a matter. . . . If someone asks advice, do not give unsuitable advice. Don't tell him, "Leave early" so that bandits will attack him, or "leave at midday" so that he will get heatstroke.

Don't tell someone, "Sell your field and buy a donkey" because you're plotting to take that field away from him.

QUESTIONS FOR INQUIRY

1. What is the *pshat* (contextual) meaning of Leviticus 19:14?
2. How does the midrash in the *Sifra* extend the meaning of the word *blind*? What moral rule does it read into the verse?
3. What relevance does this rule have to the problem of assisted dying?

COMMENTS

Chapter 19 of Leviticus contains the Holiness Code, giving rules by which Israelites will build a holy community. Verse 14 warns us not to insult someone who is deaf or put something in a place where someone who is blind will trip over it. The midrash halakhah from *Sifra Kedoshim* takes *blind* as a metaphor. We may not take unfair advantage of information that someone else is blind to. We are not to benefit from someone else's ignorance.

This law became known by part of the phrase from the Torah, *lifnei iveir*, "before the blind." Many thinkers suggest that the person who provides a terminally ill patient with the means of ending their own life violates this law. The assistance misleads the patient into thinking that doing so is permissible. That help abuses the patient's blindness to the tradition's prohibition of such acts.

Some suggest that anyone helping a patient choose suicide violates another halakhah.

Text 12 — *Mishnah Gittin* 5:9

THE WIFE OF A *haver* (who is meticulous about laws of ritual purity) may lend the wife of an *am ha-aretz* (one who is not meticulous about these laws) a winnowing tool or a sieve, and may select, grind and sift grain alongside her. But once the wife of the *am ha-aretz* pours water into the flour, rendering it susceptible to ritual impurity, the wife of the *haver* may not touch it; for we do not assist those who sin.

QUESTIONS FOR INQUIRY

1. Why may the wife of a *haver* risk sharing her kitchen equipment with a woman who does not meticulously keep ritual purity laws?
2. What limit does the Mishnah place on sharing in the preparation of flour with those who do not observe a high standard of ritual purity?
3. What general principle do we learn? What application might it have to assisted dying?

COMMENTS

The earliest creators of what became Rabbinic Judaism distinguished themselves from other Jews by their observance of Temple rules of ritual purity outside the Temple, including not sharing food with other Jews who did not adhere to that standard. In this Mishnah, which is explaining one of a series of laws that fall under the category of *mipnei darkei shalom*, meaning they are done for the sake of peace, the wife of a *haver*, who does observe purity laws, may share her utensils for preparing bread flour with a friend who does not, for the sake of neighborly peace. The Mishnah draws a line, however, at the point at which the other woman adds water to the flour to begin making dough. Since foods can become ritually impure only after getting wet, at that point the dough becomes subject to the complex laws of purity. Then the focus shifts away from neighborly peace. The Mishnah now invokes a different principle: "We do not assist those who sin." We may not be able to stop others from doing what we consider wrong, but we must not take any step that helps them in that activity.

Some suggest that the individual who helps the suffering patient die by suicide becomes guilty of "assisting those who sin." Given the halakhic prohibition on taking one's own life, providing the individual with the means to do so would be like helping the neighbor knead her ritually impure dough. A Jew may not contribute to another Jew's sin. Hence, no one may offer assistance in dying.

Even thinkers from more liberal wings of the Jewish community agree on this conclusion. Michael Cahana, a pulpit rabbi who did advanced studies in medical ethics, chaired a commission of Reform rabbis appointed in 2003 to respond to proposed legislation in several states allowing doctors to assist in suicides upon request. In its June 11, 2003, report the CCAR Task Force on Physician-Assisted Suicide decided that six reasons weigh more heavily than the patient's autonomy and self-assessed quality of life.

Text 13 — Cahana, "'Who Shall Live . . .'"

1. The respect for life and the universal rejection in halakhic text of suicide;
2. The recognition that disabled people . . . are full human beings and deserving of the full protections of life;
3. The concern that . . . a "right to die" could become a "duty to die," especially as the costs of long-term healthcare increase;

4. The belief . . . that when pain and suffering is appropriately managed, the desire to end one's life diminishes;
5. Organizations such as hospice provide palliative care as well as aid to families of terminally ill patients;
6. Physician-assisted suicide breaks down the very nature of the doctor-patient relationship.

QUESTIONS FOR INQUIRY

1. Which of these reasons draw on the halakhic tradition?
2. Which reasons reflect values from sources outside of halakhic tradition?
3. Does this list make a convincing case that assisted dying should be forbidden?

COMMENTS

The Reform rabbinate's commission report combines values derived from Jewish and general ethics, beginning with the classical Jewish respect for human life—including diminished life.

The report expresses fears heard in many discussions of assisted dying. Perhaps if we allow people to end their lives in the face of severe illness, thereby sparing themselves and their families long periods of suffering as well as exorbitant health-care costs, they will come to feel obliged to die. Meanwhile, insurers might pressure patients to choose physician-assisted death rather than pay the high costs of end-of-life care, and family members might subtly encourage patients to end their lives to avoid depleting their expected inheritance. In similar vein, the commission also feared that some would try to extend the permission to choose death from terminally ill patients to people who are permanently disabled, to save the time and associated expenses of caring for them, too.

The commission further stated that new methods in pain control mean that doctors can keep any patient comfortable throughout the final stages of disease. That level of palliation eliminates the need for anyone to choose earlier death over unbearable pain.

Finally, the commission agreed with those medical professionals who believe that a doctor's exclusive duty is to heal, and the physician who undertakes to adjudicate when someone's life will end violates that duty.

Assisted dying presents a rare instance of unity among Jewish ethicists. All agree that Judaism, with very limited exceptions, forbids suicide; that helping someone end life violates the prohibitions of putting a stumbling block before the blind and helping those who sin; and that a physician's job is curing, not to be undercut by motives, however well intentioned, of caring.

Conclusion

Our study in this chapter showed that while laws govern the matter, we lack a clear definition of when life ends (Texts 9a–9e). If scans of brain activity can show the difference between life and death, then, medically speaking, Jahi McMath's doctors in Oakland were right to insist that she had died (Case Study #1). If, however, the presence of brain functions like hormone secretion and some voluntary responses indicate the presence of life, then, clinically, Jahi's family was right to move her to a facility that agreed to continue caring for her. The Jewish moral perspective prioritizes human life and encourages us to do everything possible to preserve and extend life, even if we must violate other commandments in the process (Texts 2a–b). Building on this understanding, the Talmud introduces the notion of *ḥayyei sha'ah*, the need to sustain even the shortest span of life (Text 2c), which would mean that all efforts to preserve Jahi McMath's life must continue without stint. If so, her family was right to insist on moving Jahi to a facility that would maintain her on life support as long as it was effective.

Ḥayyei sha'ah also suggests that Robert's children must allow him to undergo open-heart surgery, even if the procedure only briefly extends his life (Case Study #2). Finally, it implies that Eleanor (Case Study #3) must not take her own life before the natural process of her disease ends it. Eleanor's request also violates a separate set of values that declares God the ultimate owner of human life (Texts 1a–b and 5) and forbids suicide in most circumstances (Texts 10a–b and 13).

And yet analyses that end with *ḥayyei sha'ah* oversimplify Jewish bioethics. True, halakhah requires us to treat imminently dying patients as fully living persons (Texts 4a–b and 8a). At the same time, a well-established law articulated by Isserles in the Shulḥan Arukh (Text 6) allows removing an impediment that prevents a suffering person from dying quickly. We remove a loud noise or other external factor so that the patient need not linger unnecessarily. Since Robert's underlying illness cannot be cured, this halakhah supports an argument in favor of allowing him to undergo a shorter period of suffering, rather than subjecting him to another operation.

Robert's advanced Alzheimer's disease adds further complications. A few ethicists cited by Robert Veatch (Text 9f) argue that because higher-brain functions represent what makes one a human person (as distinct from the biological fact of belonging to the species *Homo sapiens*), losing those, as can happen with Alzheimer's, by itself constitutes death. Robert cannot speak or reason, indicating that he has lost the functions controlled by the cerebral hemispheres; he no longer has awareness of himself as a person. Those conditions might allow Robert's family to argue against performing a heart operation on a man who has already died. On the other hand, if Robert has not suffered complete cessation of all higher and lower brain function, or if we maintain the respiration standard Rabbi Waldenberg champions as essential to Jewish ethics (Text 9e), Robert remains a living patient—possibly a *goses*, but certainly alive.

If Robert's family considers him a *goses*, his children must decide what it means to treat him as "a living person for every purpose in the world" (Text 4a). They could decide to authorize the bypass operation, which any living patient with a similar heart condition would receive. Thinkers like Rabbi Reisner who prefer to retain the category of *goses*, redefined as an imminently dying patient (Text 8a), would encourage that decision. Even though Robert might survive longer than three days, the classic definition of a *goses* (Text 4b), he should still receive all available medical care.

On the other hand, Robert's children might agree with ethicists like Sinclair (Text 8b) who propose that modern life-support machinery renders the category of *goses* obsolete. They might, as just mentioned, even believe that the machines sustaining their father's body amount to an impediment to his natural dying (Text 6), and should therefore be disconnected. Rabbi HaLevi (Text 7a) would agree that Robert's condition amounts to "artificial" life, which halakhah imposes no ethical duty to extend. Since the machines no longer serve any purpose in curing Robert's illness, they may be removed. Even more, Robert's children could choose to follow the minority of Jewish ethicists who agree with Sherwin (Text 8c) that Jewish tradition must be reinterpreted to permit euthanasia. That choice would allow them to end Robert's suffering immediately.

Finally, and however reluctantly, we must advise Eleanor against invoking her legal right to a physician-assisted death. Our study showed that our first obligation when ill is to seek care (Text 3c). Eleanor should ask for treatment to relieve her suffering as much as possible rather than seek to decide the moment of her death. Additionally, from earliest times, halakhah opposed suicide (Text 10a). Nothing in Eleanor's situation makes her an exception to this rule (Text 10b). Anyone who helped her end her life would violate the moral injunction not to cause the blind to stumble by allowing Eleanor to think she is doing the right thing (Texts 11a–b). Jews are forbidden to help wrongdoers (Text 12). Further, as the Reform movement's Task Force on Physician-Assisted Suicide pointed out, helping terminal patients end their own lives might open the door to further moral violations (Text 13). As much sympathy as we may feel for Eleanor's desire to avoid pain and suffering in her final illness, Judaism encourages her instead to adopt every measure that can ease her distress and allow her the best possible quality of life as her illness takes its course.

Perhaps more than in other challenging areas, the end of life requires us to recognize that both medical and metaphorical conversations will continue as we seek authentically Jewish responses to the rapidly changing realities we face.

Notes

Introduction

1. Mark Washofsky, "Reform Halakhic Texts."

1. Parents and Children

1. Golinkin, "Is It Permissible to Institutionalize Parents?"
2. Dorff, *Love Your Neighbor as Yourself*, 133.
3. Diamant, *Choosing A Jewish Life*, 30.
4. Tigay, *Etz Hayim*, 1025.
5. Nevins, "Between Parents and Children," in Cohen and Katz, *Observant Life*, 675.
6. Dratch, "Honoring Abusive Parents," 111–12.
7. Jacob, "Responsibility of Children to Their Parents," 209.
8. Nevins, "Between Parents and Children," in Cohen and Katz, *Observant Life*, 685.

2. Honesty

1. Penn State University, "Case Study #4: Other's Thoughts," Study for Success, Academic Integrity Case Studies, posted August 2017, http://tutorials.istudy.psu.edu/academicintegrity/academicintegrity9.html.
2. Leff, "Whistleblowing," 4–5.
3. "Copyright and the Internet," unsigned Central Conference of American Rabbis responsum no. 5761.1, accessed July 2018, https://www.ccarnet.org/ccar-responsa/nyp-no-5761-1/.

3. Social Media

1. Jonathan Sacks, "The Limits of Secularism," ABC Religion and Ethics, May 17, 2012, https://www.abc.net.au/religion/the-limits-of-secularism-and-the-search-for-meaning/10100542.
2. Kashmir Hill, "Lower Merion School District and Blake Robbins Reach a Settlement in Spycamgate," *Forbes*, October 11, 2010, https://www.forbes

.com/sites/kashmirhill/2010/10/11/lower-merion-school-district-and
-blake-robbins-reach-a-settlement-in-spycamgate/#3985919c2c60.

3. Plaut and Washofsky, *Teshuvot for the Nineties*, 90n19.

4. Gil Student, "A Torah Guide for the Digital Age: Ten Tenets of Social
Media," *Jewish Action: The Magazine of the Orthodox Union*, August 24, 2012,
https://jewishaction.com/religion/jewish-law/a-torah-guide-for-the
-digital-age-the-ten-tenets-of-social-media/.

5. Ilana Kurshan, "The Danger of Being Seen," D'Yo Ilu Yamey (blog), September 26, 2009, https://ktiva.blogspot.com/search?q=bava+batra+2a.

6. David Segal, "Mugged by a Mugshot Online," *New York Times*, October 5,
2013, https://www.nytimes.com/2013/10/06/business/mugged-by-a-mug
-shot-online.html.

7. Dorff, *Love Your Neighbor and Yourself*, 36.

8. Arnold Samlan, "Ten Commandments of Social Media," Jewish Techs,
accessed January 17, 2017, https://jewishtechs.com/rabbi-arnold-samlans
-10-commandments-social-media/.

9. Louise Matsakis, "The Wired Guide to Your Personal Data (and Who Is
Using It)," *Wired*, February 15, 2019, https://www.wired.com/story/wired
-guide-personal-data-collection/.

10. Charlie Warzel and Stuart A. Thompson, "How Your Phone Betrays
Democracy," *New York Times*, December 21, 2019, https://www.nytimes.com
/interactive/2019/12/21/opinion/location-data-democracy-protests.html
?searchResultPosition=11.

11. Jennifer Valentino-DeVries, "Tracking Phones, Google Is a Dragnet for
the Police," *New York Times*, April 13, 2019, https://www.nytimes.com
/interactive/2019/04/13/us/google-location-tracking-police.html.

12. Ryan Nakashima, "Google Tracks Your Movements, Like It or Not," AP News,
August 13, 2018, https://apnews.com/828aefab64d4411bac257a07c1af0ecb
/AP-Exclusive:-Google-tracks-your-movements,-like-it-or-not.

13. Lanier, *Ten Arguments*, 6.

4. Sex and Intimacy

1. Ruttenberg, "Jewish Sexual Ethics," 388.

2. Ruttenberg, "Jewish Sexual Ethics," 384.

3. Teutsch, *Guide to Jewish Practice*, 47.

4. Yoffie, "Encourage Conversion: Judaism's Teachings on Teen Sexuality,"
November 8, 2005, https://ericyoffie.com/conversion/.

5. Novak Winer, *Sacred Choices*, 28–29.

6. CCAR, "Mission Statement," 7.

7. Salkowitz, "Reform Jewish Sexual Values."

8. Plaskow, *Standing Again at Sinai*, 206.

9. In Eskenazi and Weiss, *Torah: A Women's Commentary*, 692.

10. Sharzer, "Transgender Jews and Halakhah," 7.

11. Sharzer, "Transgender Jews and Halakhah," 6.

12. Sharzer, "Transgender Jews and Halakhah," 6–7.

13. Waldenberg, *Responsa Tzitz Eliezer* 11:78.

14. Sharzer, "Transgender Jews and Halakhah," 30.

15. Sharzer, "Transgender Jews and Halakhah," 29.

16. Dorff, Nevins, and Reisner, "Homosexuality, Human Dignity and Halakhah," 19.

17. "A Word about Resolutions," Reconstructionist Rabbinical Association, https://therra.org/resolutions-statements-guidelines.php.

18. *Report of the Reconstructionist Commission on Homosexuality*, 37.

19. Litman, "'Bisexual' Identity," 158–65.

5. Medical Ethics at the Beginning of Life

1. Luke Ranker, "Shawnee County Judge: Topeka Sperm Donor William Marotta Not Legally Child's Father," *Topeka Capital-Journal*, November 28, 2016, http://cjonline.com/news/2016-11-28/shawnee-county-judge-topeka -sperm-donor-william-marotta-not-legally-child-s-father.

2. "Be fertile and increase," *JPS TANAKH*, 1985; "Be fruitful and multiply," *The Holy Scriptures*, JPS, 1917.

3. Dorff, *Matters of Life and Death*, 335.

4. Dorff, *Matters of Life and Death*, 41.

5. Jacob, *American Reform Responsa*, 404.

6. Panitz, "A Conservative Answer," Jewish Values Online, posted April 11, 2013, http://www.jewishvaluesonline.org/question.php?id=970&cprg= %2Fsearch.php%3Fsearchtxt%3Dchildless%26what%3DA.

7. Waldenberg, *Responsa Tzitz Eliezer* 9:51.

8. Broyde, "Establishment of Maternity and Paternity."

9. Golinkin, "Artificial Insemination for a Single Woman."

10. Grossman, "Choosing Parenthood," 38–39.

11. Spitz, "On the Use of Birth Surrogates," 538.

12. Gellman, "The Ethics of Surrogate Motherhood."

13. Freundel, *Contemporary Orthodox Judaism's Response to Modernity*, 207–8.

14. Jakobovits, *Jewish Medical Ethics*, 264–65.

15. Jacob, *American Reform Responsa*, 506.

16. Spitz, "On the Use of Birth Surrogates," 550.

17. Loike and Tendler, "Gestational Surrogacy," 132.

18. "Surrogacy in Israel," State of Israel Ministry of Health, accessed June 11, 2017, https://www.health.gov.il/English/Topics/fertility/Surrogacy/Pages/default.aspx.

19. Quoted in Grazi, *Overcoming Infertility*, 431.

20. Broyde, "Modern Reproductive Technologies and Jewish Law," 310.

21. Dorff and Zoloth, *Jews and Genes*, 241.

22. Waldenberg, *Responsa Tzitz Eliezer* 15:45.

23. Rosner, *Contemporary Biomedical Ethical Issues and Jewish Law*, 28.

24. Grazi, *Overcoming Infertility*, 424, 431–32.

25. Grazi, *Overcoming Infertility*, 434.

6. Abortion

1. Ruth Padawer, "Two-Minus-One Pregnancy," *New York Times*, https://www.nytimes.com/2011/08/14/magazine/the-two-minus-one-pregnancy.html.

2. Adapted from Eliyah Touger, *The Rambam's Mishneh Torah*, Chabad.org, accessed July 7, 2016, https://www.chabad.org/library/article_cdo/aid/1088917/jewish/Rotzeach-uShmirat-Nefesh-Chapter-One.htm.

3. Hersh Goldwurm, ed., Schottenstein Talmud, tractate *Arachin*.

4. Abortion, Resolution Adopted by the CCAR at the 86th Annual Convention of the Central Conference of American Rabbis, 1975, CCAR, https://www.ccarnet.org/ccar-resolutions/abortion-1975/.

5. Agudath Israel of America, National Public Policy Position Paper, Jewish Law website, edited by Ira Kasdan, accessed September 1, 2016, http://www.jlaw.com/LawPolicy/OU4.html.

6. Feldman, "Abortion: The Jewish View," in *Responsa of the Committee on Jewish Law and Standards 1986–1990* (New York: Rabbinical Assembly, 2001), 803–6.

7. Bleich, *Judaism and Healing*, 108–10.

8. Tirzah Meacham, "Abortion," *Encyclopedia of Jewish Women*, Jewish Women's Archive, http://jwa.org/encyclopedia/article/abortion.

9. Waldenberg, *Responsa Tzitz Eliezer*, 13:102.

10. Moshe Feinstein, *Responsa Iggrot Moshe*, vol. 11 of *Hoshen Mishpat*, responsum 69 (New York: self-published, 1963).

11. Irshai, *Fertility and Jewish Law*, 179.

12. Jacob, *Contemporary American Reform Responsa*, 23–27.

13. "Israel: Reproduction and Abortion: Law and Policy," Library of Congress, posted June 9, 2015, http://www.loc.gov/law/help/il-reproduction-and-abortion/israel.php#_ftnref85.

14. Schiff, *Abortion in Judaism*, 215.
15. Yael Hashiloni-Dolev, "Let's Abort Quietly" [in Hebrew], Ynet, October 31, 2009, https://www.ynet.co.il/articles/0,7340,L-3796232,00.html.
16. Alpert, "Sometimes the Law Is Cruel," 36–37.
17. Danya Ruttenberg, "Why Are Jews So Pro-Choice?," *Forward*, January 30, 2018, https://forward.com/opinion/393168/why-are-jews-so-pro-choice/.
18. Analia Bortz, correspondence with the author, August 2, 2020.
19. Bortz, correspondence with the author, August 2, 2020.
20. Bortz, correspondence with the author, August 2, 2020.
21. Daniel Gordis, *Does the World Need Jews?*, 159.

7. Medical Ethics at the End of Life

1. Rachel Aviv, "What Does It Mean to Die?," *New Yorker*, January 29, 2018, https://www.newyorker.com/magazine/2018/02/05/what-does-it-mean-to-die.
2. Dorff, "A Jewish Approach," 102.
3. Quoted in Zohar, *Alternatives in Jewish Bioethics*, 46.
4. Waldenberg, *Responsa Tzitz Eliezer*, "Ramat Rachel," 5:29.
5. Reisner, "A Halakhic Ethic of Care for the Terminally Ill," Responsum for the Committee on Jewish Law and Standards, Rabbinical Assembly, December 12, 1990, 8. https://www.rabbinicalassembly.org/sites/default/files/assets/public/halakhah/teshuvot/19861990/reisner_care.pdf.
6. Daniel B. Sinclair, *Tradition and the Biological Revolution*, 20–22.
7. The term also describes an animal with a fatal defect such as a pierced windpipe or gullet. Such an animal can never be kosher for consumption.
8. Eilberg, "On Halakhic Approaches," 1–2.
9. Sherwin, *Jewish Ethics for the Twenty-First Century*, 60–61.
10. National Conference of Commissioners on Uniform State Laws, Uniform Definition of Death Act, 1980, 7. Accessed December 4, 2019, http://www.lchc.ucsd.edu/cogn_150/Readings/death_act.pdf.
11. Rosner, *Biomedical Ethics and Jewish Law*, 289–90.
12. Waldenberg, *Responsa Tzitz Eliezer* 10:25.
13. Veatch, "Evolution of Death and Dying Controversies,"17.
14. Nikas, Bordlee, and Moreira, "Determination of Death," National Center for Biotechnology Information, https://www.ncbi.nlm.nih.gov/pmc/articles/PMC4889813/.
15. Veatch, "Evolution of Death and Dying Controversies."
16. Allyson Waller and Derrick Bryson Taylor, "They Thought She Was Dead. Then She Woke Up at a Funeral Home," *New York Times*, August 25, 2020,

https://www.nytimes.com/2020/08/25/us/michigan-woman-alive-funeral-home.html.

17. Daniel Sinclair, "What Jewish Law Says about Suicide and Assisted Dying," *The Conversation*, December 19, 2017, https://theconversation.com/what-jewish-law-says-about-suicide-and-assisted-dying-88687.

Bibliography

Adler, Rachel. *Engendering Judaism: An Inclusive Theology and Ethics.* Philadelphia: The Jewish Publication Society, 1998.

Alpert, Rebecca T. "Sometimes the Law Is Cruel: The Construction of a Jewish Antiabortion Position in the Writings of Immanuel Jakobovits." *Journal of Feminist Studies in Religion* 11, no. 2 (Fall 1995): 27–37.

Bleich, J. David. *Judaism and Healing: Halakhic Perspectives.* New York: Ktav, 1981.

Borowitz, Eugene. *Renewing the Covenant: A Theology for the Postmodern Jew.* Philadelphia: The Jewish Publication Society, 1996.

Broyde, Michael J. "The Establishment of Maternity and Paternity in Jewish and America Law." *National Jewish Law Review* 3 (1988): 117–22.

———. "Modern Reproductive Technologies and Jewish Law." In *Marriage, Sex, and Family in Judaism,* edited by Michael J. Broyde and Michael Asubel. New York: Rowman & Littlefield, 2005.

Cahana, Michael Z. "'Who Shall Live . . .': A Report from the CCAR Task Force on Assisted Suicide, June 11, 2003–11 Sivan 5763." *CCAR Journal: A Reform Jewish Quarterly* (Winter 2005): 54.

Central Conference of American Rabbis Ad Hoc Committee on Human Sexuality. "Mission Statement." *CCAR Journal* 48, no. 4 (Fall 2001): 7–8.

Cohen, Michael, and Michael Katz, eds. *The Observant Life: The Wisdom of Conservative Judaism for Contemporary Jews.* New York: Rabbinical Assembly, 2012.

Diamant, Anita. *Choosing a Jewish Life, Revised and Updated: A Handbook for People Converting to Judaism and for Their Family and Friends.* New York: Knopf Doubleday, 2007.

Dorff, Elliot N. "A Jewish Approach to End-Stage Medical Care." Committee on Jewish Law and Standards. Rabbinical Assembly. December 12, 1990. https://www.rabbinicalassembly.org/sites/default/files/assets/public/halakhah/teshuvot/19861990/dorff_care.pdf.

———. *Love Your Neighbor and Yourself: A Jewish Approach to Social Ethics.* Philadelphia: The Jewish Publication Society, 2002.

———. *Matters of Life and Death: A Jewish Approach to Modern Medical Ethics.* Philadelphia: The Jewish Publication Society, 1998.

Dorff, Elliot N., Daniel S. Nevins, and Avram I. Reisner. "Homosexuality, Human Dignity and Halakhah." A Combined Responsum for the Committee on Jewish Law and Standards. Rabbincal Assembly. December 6, 2006. https://www.rabbinicalassembly.org/sites/default/files/assets/public/halakhah/teshuvot/20052010/dorff_nevins_reisner_dignity.pdf.

Dorff, Elliot N., and Laurie Zoloth. *Jews and Genes: The Genetic Future in Contemporary Jewish Thought.* Philadelphia: The Jewish Publication Society, 2015.

Dratch, Mark. "Honoring Abusive Parents." *Hakirah: The Flatbush Journal of Jewish Law and Thought* 12 (2012).

Eilberg, Amy. "On Halakhic Approaches to Medical Care for the Terminally Ill: A Response." Responsum for the Committee on Jewish Law and Standards. Rabbincal Assembly. December 1990. https://www.rabbinicalassembly.org/sites/default/files/assets/public/halakhah/teshuvot/19861990/eilberg_care.pdf.

Eskenazi, Tamara C., and Andrea L. Weiss, eds. *The Torah: A Women's Commentary.* New York: Women of Reform Judaism, 2008.

Freundel, Barry. *Contemporary Orthodox Judaism's Response to Modernity.* Jersey City NJ: Ktav, 2004.

Gellman, Marc. "The Ethics of Surrogate Motherhood." *Sh'ma, A Journal of Jewish Responsibility* 17, no. 334 (May 15, 1987): 106.

Golinkin, David. "Artificial Insemination for a Single Woman." Responsa for Today. September 10, 2018. https://responsafortoday.com/en/artifical-insemination-for-a-single-woman/.

———. "Is It Permissible to Institutionalize Parents with Alzheimer's Disease?" *Responsa in a Moment* 10, no. 5 (February 2016). https://schechter.edu/?sfid=4789&_sf_s=alzheimer%27s&authors=rabbi-prof-david-golinkin.

Gordis, Daniel. *Does the World Need Jews?* New York: Scribner, 1997.

Grazi, R. V. *Overcoming Infertility: A Guide for Jewish Couples.* New Milford CT: Toby Press, 2005.

Grossman, Susan. "Choosing Parenthood: ART, Adoption and the Single Parent." Responsum for the Committee on Jewish Law and Standards. Rabbinical Assembly. May 11, 2020. https://www.rabbinicalassembly.org/sites/default/files/2020-07/Choosing%20Parenthood%20teshuvah%20Final%20July%202020.pdf.

Grushcow, Lisa J., ed. *The Sacred Encounter: Jewish Perspectives on Sexuality.* New York: CCAR Press, 2014.

Irshai, Ronit. *Fertility and Jewish Law: Feminist Perspectives on Orthodox Responsa.* Waltham MA: Brandeis University Press, 2012.

Jacob, Walter. *American Reform Responsa: Jewish Questions, Rabbinic Answers.* New York: Central Conference of American Rabbis, 1983.

———. *Contemporary American Reform Responsa.* New York: Hebrew Union College Press, 1987.

———. "Responsibility of Children to Their Parents." Responsum 53. *Yearbook of the Central Conference of American Rabbis* 92 (1982): 207–9.

Jakobovits, Immanuel. *Jewish Medical Ethics.* New York: Bloch, 1975.

Lanier, Jaron. *Ten Arguments for Deleting Your Social Media Accounts.* New York: Henry Holt, 2018.

Leff, Barry. "Whistleblowing: The Requirement to Report Employer Wrongdoing." Responsum for the Committee on Jewish Law and Standards. Rabbinical Assembly. https://www.rabbinicalassembly.org/sites/default/files/assets/public/halakhah/teshuvot/20052010/leff_IP.pdf.

Litman, Jane Rachel. "'Bisexual' Identity: A Guide for the Perplexed." In *The Sacred Encounter: Jewish Perspectives on Sexuality*, edited by Lisa J. Grushcow. New York: CCAR Press, 2014.

Loike, John, and Moshe Tendler. "Gestational Surrogacy." *Hakirah* 16 (October 29, 2013): 113–32.

Newman, Louis. "Woodchoppers and Respirators: The Problem of Interpretation in Contemporary Jewish Ethics." *Modern Judaism* 10, no. 1 (February 1990): 17–42.

Nikas, Nikolas T., Dorinda C. Bordlee, and Madeline Moreira. "Determination of Death and the Dead Donor Rule." *The Journal of Medicine and Philosophy* 41, no. 3 (June 2016): 237–56. https://www.ncbi.nlm.nih.gov/pmc/articles/PMC4889813/.

Novak Winer, Laura. *Sacred Choices: Adolescent Relationships and Sexual Ethics: High School Module.* New York: URJ Press, 2007.

Plaskow, Judith. *Standing Again at Sinai: Judaism from a Feminist Perspective.* New York: Harper & Row, 1990.

Plaut, W. Gunther, and Mark Washofsky, eds. *Teshuvot for the Nineties: Reform Judaism's Answers to Today's Dilemmas.* New York: Central Conference of American Rabbis, 1997.

The Report of the Reconstructionist Commission on Homosexuality. Wyncote PA: Federation of Reconstructionist Congregations and Havurot, Reconstructionist Rabbinical Association, 1993.

Rosner, Fred. *Biomedical Ethics and Jewish Law.* Hoboken NJ: Ktav, 2001.

———. *Contemporary Biomedical Ethical Issues and Jewish Law.* Jersey City NJ: Ktav, 2007.

Ruttenberg, Danya. "Jewish Sexual Ethics." In *The Oxford Handbook of Jewish Ethics and Morality*, edited by Elliot Dorff and Jonathan Crane. Oxford: Oxford University Press, 2013.

Salkowitz, Selig. "Reform Jewish Sexual Values." Central Conference of American Rabbis Ad Hoc Committee on Human Sexuality. CCAR *Journal* 48, no. 4 (Fall 2001): 9–13.

Schiff, Daniel. *Abortion in Judaism*. Cambridge: Cambridge University Press, 2002.

Sharzer, Leonard A. "Transgender Jews and Halakhah." Committee on Jewish Law and Standards. Rabbinical Assembly. June 7, 2017. https://www .rabbinicalassembly.org/sites/default/files/public/halakhah/teshuvot/2011 -2020/transgender-halakhah.pdf.

Sherwin, Byron. *Jewish Ethics for the Twenty-First Century: Living in the Image of God*. Library of Jewish Philosophy. Syracuse NY: Syracuse University Press, 2000.

Sinclair, Daniel B. *Tradition and the Biological Revolution: The Application of Jewish Law to the Treatment of the Critically Ill*. Edinburgh: Edinburgh University Press, 1989.

Spitz, Elie Kaplan. "On the Use of Birth Surrogates." Responsum for the Committee on Jewish Law and Standards. Rabbinical Assembly. June 4, 1997. https://www.rabbinicalassembly.org/sites/default/files/assets/public /halakhah/teshuvot/19912000/spitz_surrogate.pdf.

Teutsch, David. *Bioethics: Reinvigorating the Practice of Contemporary Jewish Ethics*. Wyncote PA: Reconstructionist Rabbinical College Press, 2005.

———. *A Guide to Jewish Practice*. Vol. 1, *Everyday Living*. Wyncote PA: Reconstructionist Rabbinical College Press, 2011.

Tigay, Jeffrey. *Etz Hayim: Torah and Commentary*. Philadelphia: The Jewish Publication Society, 2001.

Veatch, Robert M. "The Evolution of Death and Dying Controversies." *Hastings Center Report* 39, no. 3 (May–June 2009): 16–19.

Waldenberg, Eliezer Tzvi. *Responsa Tzitz Eliezer*. Jerusalem: self-published, 1957–78.

Washofsky, Mark. "Gossip between Husband and Wife." In *Teshuvot for the Nineties: Reform Judaism's Answers to Today's Dilemmas*. New York: Central Conference of American Rabbis, 1997.

———. "Reform Halakhic Texts." My Jewish Learning. Accessed November 2016. https://www.myjewishlearning.com/article/reform-halakhic-texts/.

Weiner, Jason. *Jewish Guide to Practical Medical Decision-Making*. Brooklyn NY: Urim Publications, 2017.

Zohar, Noam. *Alternatives in Jewish Bioethics*. SUNY Series in Jewish Philosophy. Albany: State University of New York Press, 1997.

In the JPS Essential Judaism Series

*Thinking about Good and Evil: Jewish Views
from Antiquity to Modernity*
Rabbi Wayne Allen

The Jewish Family Ethics Textbook
Rabbi Neal Scheindlin

*Thinking about the Prophets: A Philosopher
Reads the Bible*
Kenneth Seeskin

*Thinking about the Torah: A Philosopher Reads
the Bible*
Kenneth Seeskin

Thinking about God: Jewish Views
Rabbi Kari H. Tuling

*Justice for All: How the Jewish Bible
Revolutionized Ethics*
Jeremiah Unterman

To order or obtain more information on
these or other Jewish Publication Society
titles, visit jps.org.

Lightning Source UK Ltd.
Milton Keynes UK
UKHW011356290821
389562UK00010B/430